Too
Famous

Too Famous

The Rich, the Powerful, the Wishful, the Notorious, the Damned

Michael Wolff

Henry Holt and Company
New York

Henry Holt and Company
Publishers since 1866
120 Broadway
New York, New York 10271
www.henryholt.com

Some of these essays have appeared elsewhere, in slightly different form and different titles: "Oh, Rudy!," an Audible Original, October 15, 2020; "Trump at Home" in the *Hollywood Reporter*, June 10, 2016; "Jann" in *British GQ*, July 2015; "Hitch" in *British GQ*, April 2013; "Arianna" in *British GQ*, June 2011; "Judith" in *Vanity Fair*, March 2007; "Tina" in *New York*, July 23, 2001; "Ingrid" in *New York*, October 23, 2000; "Rupert in Love" in *British GQ*, online March 4, 2016; "Rupert Alone" in *British GQ*, December 2015; "The Death of Roger Ailes" in the *Hollywood Reporter*, online May 18, 2017; "The Rise of Fox 1" in *New York*, February 26, 2001; "The Rise of Fox 2" in *New York*, December 9, 2002; "The Rise of Fox 3" in *British GQ*, January 2012; "Bloomberg" in *British GQ*, online June 7, 2020; "Hillary" in *British GQ*, online July 2016; "Weiner" in *British GQ*, August 2011; "Cuomo 1" in *New York*, April 16, 2001; "Cuomo 2" in *New York*, July 11, 2003; "Gore" in *New York*, February 21, 2000; "The Future Prime Minister" in *Vanity Fair*, September 2004.

Library of Congress Cataloging-in-Publication Data

Names: Wolff, Michael, 1953– author.
Title: Too famous : the rich, the powerful, the wishful, the notorious, the
    damned / Michael Wolff.
Other titles: Columns. Selections
Description: First edition. | New York : Henry Holt and Company, 2021.
Identifiers: LCCN 2021019069 (print) | LCCN 2021019070 (ebook) | ISBN
    9781250147622 (hardcover) | ISBN 9781250147639 (ebook)
Subjects: LCSH: Celebrities in mass media. | Gossip in mass media. | Mass
    media—Political aspects. | Television broadcasting of news—Social aspects. |
    Fame. | Politicians—Biography. | Executives—Biography. | Journalists—
    Biography. | Publishers and publishing—Biography.
Classification: LCC PN4725 .W65 2021 (print) | LCC PN4725 (ebook) |
    DDC 973.93092/2—dc23
LC record available at https://lccn.loc.gov/2021019069
LC ebook record available at https://lccn.loc.gov/2021019070

Our books may be purchased in bulk for promotional, educational,
or business use. Please contact your local bookseller or the Macmillan
Corporate and Premium Sales Department at (800) 221-7945, extension
5442, or by e-mail at MacmillanSpecialMarkets@macmillan.com.

First Edition 2021

Designed by Meryl Sussman Levavi

Printed in the United States of America

1 3 5 7 9 10 8 6 4 2

For
Elizabeth, Susanna, Steven, Louise, and Jack
and
Sidney and Lillian

Contents

Murdoch

Fox News

Defeat

Boris

Monster

Too
Famous

Introduction

One night in the spring of 2016, with the presidential campaign heading in its loopy direction, Janice Min, the editor of the *Hollywood Reporter*, where I was writing a regular column, called excitedly to say that I'd be able to interview Donald Trump if I could get from New York to Los Angeles, where he was doing a campaign stop, by midafternoon the next day. I confess to thinking that this was quite a lot of effort for a candidate who, while breathtaking in his novelty and ludicrousness, and confounding in his success to date, seemed to have no more of a chance of being president than I did.

But, for the sport of it, I went. That next evening, sitting with the candidate in his Beverly Hills home, filled with overstuffed furniture not unlikely cast off from one of his hotel lobbies, I looked Donald Trump in the eye and asked him the essential question: "Why, exactly, are you doing this?" He replied, with a clarity that few candidates have about their own motives and ambitions: "To be the most famous man in the world."

I should have been more appalled. And yet it had an obvious logic. Most public people in my broad acquaintanceship with public people see notoriety and celebrity as key aspects of their identities. Whatever else they might have accomplished—work they had done, organizations they had built, money they had made—was enhanced by, or depended on, or was meaningless without their public profile and renown. Trump was merely throwing pretense away and eliminating the need to perform for any reason other than attention itself. He had arrived at a place that other equally as craven but not as shameless fellow attention seekers could only dream about.

The road here is a tragic one—for the culture at large and, as well, for so many of the people who take it. But it is also the central thoroughfare: you can't understand public life without understanding the motivation for ever-increasing and eternal notoriety, and the mechanisms by which it is achieved, and, as well, the price you pay for it.

In 1998, *New York* magazine hired me to write its weekly media column. Writing about media had, theretofore, mostly involved the court politics at newspapers and network news divisions, journalism ethics and practices ("media criticism"), and sometimes a guilty fascination with the wealth and power of media CEOs—the moguls.

But, by the late nineties, several developments had pushed the media story into a new dimension: the trial of O. J. Simpson in 1995—wherein the media gave up the pretense of its role as witness to the news and became the eager producer and stage manager of it; Bill Clinton and Monica Lewinsky in 1998, demolishing the line between public and private lives; and mass connectivity, which gave everybody a rooting interest in, and passionate opinion about, public actors, large and small.

News was personality. Personality was drama and entertainment—that is, conflict. Notoriety, that is publicity, became the leading currency of our time. The needs, hubris, and ruthlessness of people at the apex of attention, celebrity, and influence—and those striving to reach it—became the grease that kept the world spinning and news cycles rolling. The news was psychopathology. The media did not merely report on but created the people who made the news; likewise, self-promoters with ever-increasing skills and cunning gamed the media.

And then the world began to revolt against these modern monsters and the agents and enterprises who made them.

This new social and political force of personal aggrandizement and media power, the characters it has propelled, and the backlash it has inspired, while in many obvious ways deleterious for the commonweal, was propitious for me. As a journalist my interest wasn't so much subject-specific (e.g., politics, health care, prison reform, tech) as it was about how we live now. This vast, unquenchable thirst for attention among people I knew—or was able to get to know precisely because they wanted public attention and I could help confer it—has been, to say the least, a compelling window through which to see the world.

Icarus anyone?

In the shadow of this celebrity culture, there slowly grew a finer understanding of how this need and quest for attention changed not only the people seeking it and the institutions and technology providing it, but the body politic itself: we expect a show, heroes, villains, life and death. And here, too, we began to understand, there was a new social and business system fostering all this ego and conflict, full of the scoundrels, swindlers, and self-promoters you might find in a Trollope novel.

If you are lucky as a writer, you get to match your interests, sympathies, hankerings, and fears with the culture of your time. I have had more than just a passing or arm's-length relationship with many of the figures in this book. We were interested in the same thing—or, more to the point, I was interested in them, hence they were interested in me. Everybody knew that most likely, if not explicitly, I would write about them, and yet persisted in talking to me. (Still, many would come to carry a grudge about the fact that I ultimately did write about the things they said to me.)

In my experience, the worst thing you can say about a social climber—and almost everyone in this book is a determined social climber—is that they are a social climber. It has always confused me why the obvious—the emperor's nakedness—is not obvious to all, and why we all cannot acknowledge the underlying comedy.

But pretense is the requirement of fame. And, perhaps not surprisingly, the more famous you become, the thinner your skin gets.

Almost everybody herein has been burned, often badly, by the fame they have sought—opprobrium, humiliation, prosecution, jail, even death. But few, other than the dead, have not continued to pursue it. Hillary Clinton has been shamed and maligned at a level impossible for mere mortals to appreciate and yet has consistently returned for more. Why? Because the famous and would-be famous see themselves as warriors—and implicit in the fight is the possibility of humiliation and defeat? Or because they are self-destructive? Or merely because fame is just the world they live in—what else is there?

Several years ago, at one of the regular luncheons hosted by the British satirical magazine *Private Eye*, long dedicated to the pursuit of the overweening and famous (yet pleased to host lunch for them, too), I sat next to Jemima Khan, the socialite daughter of billionaire James Goldsmith, former wife of world-famous cricketer and present prime minister of Pakistan Imran Khan, and ex-girlfriend of Hugh Grant. She was convivially indiscreet about her relationship with Grant—"just a boy from Chiswick"—and dropped a detail that I have cherished since. To the list of hurdles and impediments and limitations of life, Grant, according to Khan, added a new one: "too famous." He had achieved not just fame, but way too much of it, such that it had the opposite effect and he had to be constantly vigilant about its blowback threats. Everything he did had to account for and be weighed against inevitable resentments, preconceptions, potential scandal, and social media schadenfreude, as well as constant selfies.

An irony is that fame is no longer a very exclusive position. At one time, real fame, like real wealth, was so rarefied that it existed as an exception to the rule, a novelty. But like the growth of the financial industry that made so many more people richer, the growth of the media industry has made so many more people famous.

Notoriety, rather than being exceptional, became an upper-middle-class aspiration, like the Ivy League. In upper-middle-class meritocratic culture, you need to keep competing. Greater and greater levels of public recognition—media recognition—became, along with more money and more real estate, part of that scorecard. Arguably, this gave an edge to those already tipping toward personality disorders. No surprise that fame began to get a bad name given the spreading dislikeability of the famous.

Then, social media expanded this algebraically. Anybody could compete for public attention, not just the upper middle class. Indeed, so many people are now famous, you might not even know they are famous.

Still, given the general demographics of fame, and the disproportionate focus of this book, the question arises as to the extent that fame might be largely a white man's privilege—or folly. And whether the very nature of fame is derived from the entitlement and dominance of the already privileged, and from its self-perpetuating mechanism, the system ever elevating people in its own image, ruthless, bloodthirsty, and charming. There is currently a zero-sum sense as the nobody outsiders, with revolutionary zeal, try to defenestrate the famous insiders. The nobodies surely want their taste of the fame pie. Good luck. Maybe the democratization of fame will change its nature. But one message that might be taken from the various notable women who are part of this rogues' gallery is that as much as they have broken through fame's ceiling they have, too, as clearly, been consumed by fame's fires.

There is surely nobody more obsessed with notoriety than media people themselves. It's the product they sell; it's the power they hold. And, in a trifecta, it's the status they can achieve. It is hardly an overstatement to say that the media is only interested in people who are famous or people it believes it can make famous. Nor is it going too far to generalize that the more successful you are in the media business, the more time you spend with famous people.

The inevitable backlash has certainly not derailed the quest for fame, but it has tended to draw a tighter and more accusatory circle around people who were already famous. Hence, Twitter mobs, aspects of #MeToo, cancel culture, and the righteous pursuit of prosecutors everywhere. Fame is dangerous—sometimes lethal.

And then there is Donald Trump, with the media in open and savage rebellion against its own Dr. Frankenstein creation. It is far from clear whether this taking up of arms will create a reset and new moral attention, or if Trump merely confirms the exceptional power of being able to command attention and of the shamelessness that is the necessary element of it.

This book collects pieces I've written as a columnist for *New York*, *Vanity Fair*, *British GQ*, and the *Hollywood Reporter*, and adds several new ones. The pieces were written over a twenty-year period, roughly spanning that moment when personal attention became one of the world's most valuable commodities and ending with Donald Trump, fame's most hyperbolic exponent.

Some of these pieces exist in the amber of a particular news moment, some as character portraits—as colorful now, I might hope, as when they were written—and some as possibly lasting observations about human nature and folly. The common ground here is that everyone in this book is a creature of, or creation of, the media. They don't exist as who we see them as, and who they want to be, without the media. They are actors, sometimes succeeding but often failing in their performances in the media's eyes.

The glossy magazines in which most of these pieces first appeared flourished by reflecting the celebrity culture—often glorifying celebrities, but at the same time keeping close watch on their weaknesses and vainglories (indeed, ever ready to chop the mightiest down). With a little critical interpretation, fame was a self-policing industry. But in a confusing development, these magazines are now shadows of their former selves. My old boss at *Vanity Fair*, Graydon Carter, quite the ultimate curator of celebrity culture, was replaced by an editor with a new sense of earnestness and correct purpose, who, even in the face of steadily declining readership, has seemed determined to deny the celebrity world from which *Vanity Fair* came.

This hardly means an end to celebrity culture so much as it does less expertise in understanding the true nature of the egomaniacs, narcissists, soulless attention seekers, and media moguls and middlemen of our time. Arguably, we allow broken personalities much more latitude now. If their politics conform to whatever the currently acceptable standard is, we count them as legitimate players. We don't have the lens or the language to see them as wanting something more than they should reasonably want and becoming something much different from you and me in their quest to get it and hold on to it.

Nobody is on this beat anymore, paying close attention to the corrosive and humbling vanities. Hence, we take the too-famous more seriously than we ought to, either embracing them or hating them.

I was once asked how I hoped people would see themselves after I had written about them. I said I hoped they would see themselves as uniquely flawed human beings.

I am fairly sure that has never happened.

Kakistocracy

President Jared

NOVEMBER 2020

There are some things even in the age of Trump that might still seem inconceivable—like *President* Jared. That's a sitcom setup. And yet who would not want to bet that the thirty-nine-year-old—already the beneficiary of a political opportunity as extreme and unwarranted as any in modern times—isn't planning his future? That the currents of the remade Republican Party, and the new oligarch-tilted world, won't lead, once again, somewhere unimaginable?

Since encountering the president's son-in-law on the campaign trail in 2016, I've watched him with fascination, maybe even sympathy—the young man in way over his head but determined to prove, often with some petulance, that he could stay in the game. But the Trump administration's game was clearly Jumanji and Jared Kushner seemed among the least ready to survive it.

We first met not long after he had been drafted into the Trump entourage as a point-person family member—a kind of Trump-brand monitor overseeing his wild-card father-in-law on behalf of the ultimate Trump-brand beneficiaries. The contrast between the candidate and his son-in-law was quite a sight gag. The hulking older man occupying all the space with his size and bluster and the quivering-filament younger man as though hoping to disappear. Kushner moved silently and ghostlike around the perimeter of his father-in-law, like sons-in-law everywhere perhaps avoiding the patriarchal force field. But attentive, too—an anxious butler. To my question to his father-in-law one evening, with Trump planted heavily on the couch in the living room of his Beverly Hills home, about why exactly he wanted to be president, Trump replied, as though it ought to be obvious, "To be the most famous man in the world." Pivoting to his son-in-law, hovering nearby, he snapped his fingers: "Jared, am I the most famous man in the world yet?"

"Yes, you are," said a prudent Kushner. "Virtually one hundred percent name recognition."

My sense then was that Kushner found himself between great suffering and great adventure—unsure which was greater.

A West Wing source described Kushner during the peak days of the Black Lives Matter protests after his father-in-law had angrily emerged from the White House bunker. Kushner had been trying to reassure the president that the protests were best handled locally and that the president should remain above it all. Kushner and his wife knew that in any situation involving perceived challenges to the president's authority, not to mention race, no response was better than any he might give. But the president was calling for troops and demanding he be able to do something, with almost everyone in the White House suddenly, madly, scurrying around to find something for him to do. Jared, Ivanka, and Hope Hicks, the presidential aide and their close ally, tried to propose do-something alternatives that did not involve troops, decrees, and news conferences. Ivanka had long been trying to get her father to go to church, specifically to St. John's, the simple and tasteful, particularly un-Trump-like, lemon-yellow, nineteenth-century Episcopal church, the "Church of the Presidents," a block from the White House. Although the president had no interest in this or any church, here was suddenly a do-something something to do. Except that the president wanted to be seen walking with his generals. Church okay, but with a show of force. With the president in high and choleric dudgeon, Ivanka and Hope Hicks soothed, dithered, fretted, implored. Jared, on the other hand, stood aside for the train wreck, accepting the inevitable, receding, closing down, as though paralyzed. "He can't breathe either," noted a White House wag, echoing the gasps of Black police victims. Here was Jared's frequent response to Trump events when they ran chaotically away from him, to see, hear, or speak no evil, in fact to nearly dematerialize.

Through one lens this might be a picture of a painful disconnect, even revulsion, some Trumpers have noted, for his father-in-law. His detachment or absence has been confusing even to people close to him, who describe it as sometimes coming close to a trance. Similarly, on the rare occasions that he would step out in public, blinking in the light, to defend a White House position or face a difficult development, he appeared more spacey and lost than the time before. His small circle, sensitive about the charge that he lacks backbone, or even free will, would struggle to explain his lack of presence—"he keeps his own counsel" is a favorite gloss. But through another lens this evidently benighted and passive figure, and often, it seems, quite a wounded one at that, became the picture—at least in Trumpworld—of an incredibly gifted bureaucratic infighter, one with extraordinary ambitions and an unlimited future.

For all his negative space, he was a survivor in a land where there were precious few. Here was the Zelig of executive branch management initiatives, again and again making himself the face of new commissions to limit or expand the administrative state and extend his own reach in it. He was the Trump administration's own deep state, with foreign leaders at their most effective when they were whispering to him. He was hated by Trump true loyalists who always believed they had finally relegated him and convinced the president to send him home. But there was hardly a meeting of consequence in the Trump White House that he wasn't in. The reelection campaign was his bailiwick, an almost personal project—and yet remote enough to avoid responsibility for it. Brad Parscale, the former Trump Organization freelance website designer who rose to campaign database minder and to campaign manager, was his personal apparatchik (until Jared dispatched him). Kushner has certainly been the least popular, most mocked and scorned person in the Trump White House, but, by wide consensus—however much through gritted teeth by however many—its second most powerful person.

In the earliest days of the administration, he and his wife, imagining a Trump Camelot, decided, in a sort of White House prenup, that she would be the future politician, the Trump of it all, and he the behind-the-scenes operator—a sort of Deng Xiaoping, without title, but with his hands on the levers of power. But Ivanka came to take the Trump administration's ever-careening fortunes very personally. Resentful, bitter, gun-shy, she argued that perhaps they ought to go home. Her husband, on the other hand, mostly hidden from the public—"maybe a little emotionally remote," described one supporter—was able to shoulder the slurs and outwait his enemies. With his willingness to accept the things he cannot change about his father-in-law, and the patience to change what he can, he came to feel his was quite a preternatural gift for executive power.

It has baffled him that more people have not recognized all that he has endured and risen above.

In an interview with me toward the end of his first year in the White House, Kushner specifically wanted it to be noted that while he had had advantages, he had also overcome large odds, even that overcoming odds was what distinguished him. A possible implication here, I thought, was that the Trump administration itself was something else in his life to overcome.

Kushner's father, Charles Kushner, a New Jersey real estate developer, by most reports as brutish and demanding a figure as Trump, was convicted of tax evasion and witness tampering and sent to federal prison. Carrying this family stain, Jared sought to remake himself in Manhattan. Out of Harvard, an internship at Goldman Sachs, and a summer at Paul, Weiss, the Democratic law firm, when he was at NYU Law School, Kushner concentrated on his social and business identity, marshaling bankers, PR people, and consultants, as well as hostesses to connect him to advantageous circles. His acquisition at age twenty-five of the *New York Observer* in 2006, the elite-class broadsheet, for $11 million—that is, nearly $11 million more than it was worth—was meant to give himself a personal platform. But its then editor, Peter Kaplan, a media-class favorite, ran "the kid" down across Manhattan (as did most of his many subsequent editors). Bitter about his own paper, and often replacing its editors, Kushner seemed even more determined to find his way to becoming a bold-faced figure in the city. This effort would come to include buying—here, too, at an inflated price—a piece of prime Fifth Avenue commercial real estate and, in 2009, marrying Donald Trump's daughter.

"He's very ambitious," said Rupert Murdoch, no stranger to ambition, but seemingly surprised by the young man's intensity, when I asked him about his budding relationship with the *Observer* owner in an interview in 2008, after Murdoch's then wife, Wendi, and Ivanka Trump became close friends, and with Kushner assiduously trying to court him. "Hold on to your address book," added Murdoch.

But in the White House, Kushner was suddenly back under a father's thumb and, again, threatened by disgrace—even prosecution. His reception in Washington was similar, though by a quantum leap more brutal, to what he had faced in New York. In 2018, Kushner and his wife even felt that their D.C. neighbors' disdain might drive them from their tony neighborhood. And it wasn't just liberals and snobs who taunted him and the various prosecutors who were pursuing him. It was the dedicated Trumpers who despised him most, making his end one of their key priorities.

Among the first and second waves of high Trump administration officials, from the Steve Bannon period through Chief of Staff John Kelly's departure in the beginning of 2019, a concerted wish and secret effort on the part of almost everyone was Jared's removal—in a sense their central, even historic, miscalculation was to think this possible. Once, early in the administration's first year, I sat talking to Bannon on a spring afternoon in the chief of staff's office. An obsequious Kushner poked his head in, trying to be included in the conversation. He lingered awkwardly, then, summoning himself, finally sat down. Bannon failed in any way to acknowledge that Kushner was in the room, until, like a sadistic schoolmaster, with the young man by then wholly absorbed in his own embarrassment and self-consciousness, he caught him unawares: "Isn't that so, Jared?" Bannon demanded. "Yes? No? Yes . . . No?" Kushner's mouth opened and then, long moments later, as though on a time delay, with nothing whatsoever coming out, finally closed. On another occasion, during a lengthy interview I had with Kushner in his office—mostly spent with Kushner trying to get me to tell him what others were saying about him—his hands shook through the entire conversation.

And yet, while Kushner might have entered the White House as one of its historically most callow and unprepossessing figures, a harmless social world arriviste, he yet became its ultimate power broker. No self-respecting bureaucrat was willing to take the chief of staff job because Kushner in essence held it (he and his wife were instrumental in marginalizing John Kelly, who tried to marginalize them; then they demanded obeisance from Kelly's successors, Mick Mulvaney and Mark Meadows, before approving them for the job). He weighed in on almost all high-level personnel decisions—often with a veto over them—and had a hand in dispatching not just those disloyal to his father-in-law but those insufficiently abject to him. The party leadership, in its efforts to move or mollify the unmanageable and often irrational president, would come to depend on Kushner's intercessions. The back-scratching relationships to key foreign governments lay in Kushner's hands. And Kushner's self-selected team controlled Trump, Inc.: the Trump campaign's vast voter data operation and the incomparable Trump fundraising apparatus.

I doubt anyone could have seen this coming, save perhaps for his own wife, who appears to live in a particular marital and political fantasy bubble, ever pointing out her husband's strength, sagaciousness, and acumen.

He became a designated President Jared, with the actual president far removed from details, plans, strategy, and cause and effect. (It's a worthy irony that when the press started to refer to Steve Bannon as President Bannon, it was Jared who helped stoke his father-in-law's fury about this slight and usurpation.)

Right-wing and left-wing media may have agreed on nothing so much as Kushner's absurdity, and yet he became the only figure in the Trump White House to have built something like an independent power center. While almost everyone around Trump waited for him to express his in-the-second desire or tried to anticipate what that might be, Kushner's approach, on the other hand, no matter how much he appeared to be the fragile reed to Trump's great wind, always seemed designed to outwait the sycophants and outwait even the president himself. With others heaping flattery on his father-in-law, he seemed to make a point of his restraint, understanding that the flattery Trump required undermined you with him at the same time, and that, while Trump demanded your constant presence, he preferred not to see you.

Part of Kushner's affect was as though to look beyond Trump. "We'll see," he'd say when confronted with disbelief or incredulity over what his father-in-law might have said or done. Or, "It's a long way from over." Or, "It's a work in progress." Deflecting rather than defending.

With such patience, or ambivalence, or long-suffering countenance, and as a signal that he somehow had never entirely drunk the Trumper's drink, he built his singular office, more powerful and effective than any other in the West Wing.

One New York billionaire with experience dealing with Trump in the White House described Jared's power this way: Communicating with Trump, overcoming his lack of comprehension and distraction, was the constant hurdle; it was almost never possible to get from point A to point B. But Jared forged a functioning system. You met first with Kushner and pitched your case (for incentives, say, or tax relief or investment programs), during which Kushner often advised a focus on one or two points maximum; then Jared filtered that conversation for his father-in-law, reducing it further; then there followed a meeting, hosted by Jared, in which the president would seem at least to appear minimally informed and attentive, with a self-effacing Jared smoothly in control of subject, of agenda, and of his father-in-law.

The wild swings of the Trump administration, threats issued and retracted, policies proposed and then buried or forgotten, allies cast out, derived not only from Trump's impulsiveness, insist members of the anti-Kushner faction, but from Jared's ubiquity and his advocacy of big-business billionaire views. The president listened to Jared touting his rich friends' ideas—invariably backed by his wife—not necessarily for very long but long enough, for a few hours or a few days, to create the administration's continuing whipsaw or pay-no-attention-to-what-you-just-thought-you-heard effect. The haywire pandemic response, from dismissal to concern, to annoyance to responsiveness, to center stage and finally to be-done-with-it, represented once more the seesaw between the president's own instincts to skirt past what didn't interest him and give the job to someone else, and Jared and Ivanka's desire for him to at least halfway meet the standards of what any other president would be expected to do (although for key weeks in January and February, Jared was apparently as unconcerned and uninterested in virus issues as his father-in-law).

Bannon by the summer of 2017 was widely declaring that every mistake of the new administration was founded on Jared and Ivanka's advice and efforts to court the liberals and that the administration would fail because of them. Tucker Carlson, as the summer of 2020 began, opened his show with a long direct-to-camera warning that blamed Kushner for undermining or muddling the president's true and popular (at least among Trumpers) instincts.

Some core Trumpers have believed that Ivanka and Jared actually ran quite a counter-regime. In this, Trump himself was expendable, and their future, based on the telling of their tale as soulful and practical resistance to right-wing forces, would be the story propelling their careers. "They only care about themselves" is what all their Trump circle enemies invariably say. In their future story, Trump will not be the pernicious force that created them but the force whom, to the extent possible, they restrained and managed. Early on, Kushner, a skillful leaker, established as a "senior aide" a long record of reproachful comments on the behavior and policies of the White House.

In the Kushner duo's telling, Trump, without the Trumpers' influence, would be happy in a world of social and business aspiration. A Jared and Ivanka social and business future in New York—and, indeed, a once-and-future Jared and Ivanka White House—would likely involve the world that Trump, before politics, in their sanitized telling of Trump's history, sought to occupy, a world of exceptional and accomplished rich people. (Of course, Trump was often shunned by this world, arguably helping to push him into populist arms.) Ivanka, on various occasions, brought up the famous evening when JFK and Jackie invited Pablo Casals to perform in the East Room of the White House for the pleasure of the great and good.

Shortly after the 2016 victory, one experienced government hand questioned Kushner closely about the incoming administration's choices for Treasury and for the president's other economic advisers.

"Billionaires!" replied Kushner. "That's the caliber of people we're going to have."

Here was an aspirational view. The background was Kushner's efforts in New York to find his way into circles of privilege and status. That was his personal career approach, buttering up older rich men like Rupert Murdoch, or the billionaire investor and Revlon chairman Ronald Perelman (whose private synagogue the Kushner couple availed themselves of on High Holidays), or Blackstone CEO Stephen Schwarzman. In Washington this would become not just part of a social-climbing lifestyle but, in practical terms, Kushner's governing ethos.

Kushner, who grew up a Democrat in a household where his family was not only a major party contributor but where his father had a close relationship with former New Jersey Democratic governor Jim McGreevey, reluctantly shifted his party registration to Republican. But the kind of Republican he seemed to become was precisely the kind his father-in-law (also formerly a Democrat) so forcefully bent the populist curve against (that is, when he wasn't heaping flattery on the bankers, hedge funders, developers, consultants, investors, and CEOs who were his son-in-law's friends). Arguably, the person in the administration most at temperamental and policy odds from Trump's hard rejection of global expertise, systems, relationships, and ritual and propriety was Kushner. His own father, trying to rationalize his son's party shift, told friends his son was a "Rockefeller Republican," that old-fashioned sobriquet meant to indicate a reasonable and moderate liberalism and wish for general improvements to the social and business status quo.

And yet, despite his lack of populist bona fides, Kushner surely represented an important aspect of the Trump governing ethos—a belief that governing should as naturally work for those doing the governing as for the governed.

Kushner may have been the greenest and most unbaked player ever to reach the highest levels of political power. But, as the world's elite logged their phone calls with him after the election, he enthusiastically told a wary Steve Bannon that he knew this world. He got it.

Family- and inner-circle-dominated regimes around the world—among them, the Russians, the Saudis, the UAE, the Qataris—sought out Kushner.

This moment arguably cemented the way the Trump administration would interact at the highest international levels—both with the outside world perceiving the family as the unit of influence and with the family knowing no other model but to happily accept this role. What Kushner and the Trumps understood was the pluses of a personal business bond: we profit together.

Part of the background here for Kushner was the tension with his own family, who largely saw Jared's sudden high profile as troubling for its own interests: real estate deals and financings hardly benefit from close scrutiny. Jared had to prove that his position in the White House wouldn't harm and might benefit the family. Kushner's official portfolio, including the entire Middle East, gave him responsibility for states and individuals who might now or in the future be helpful to the Kushner family business interests. This was an issue that Kushner's West Wing enemies tried to exploit but which was always, with irritation, rebuffed by the president. (For the administration's first two years, the Kushners were actively trying to refinance a looming debt payment on their premier Manhattan property,

666 Fifth Avenue. This was finally accomplished when the Toronto-based fund Brookfield Asset Management, with significant backing from Gulf State sovereign wealth funds, bought control of the property in August 2018.)

But another aspect of the governing ethos of mutual back-scratching related to Kushner's new awe for Henry Kissinger (once, himself, a noted Rockefeller Republican). This partly came from Kissinger's courtship of the younger man. Kushner, who, after the election, briefly championed the ninety-three-year-old Kissinger as secretary of state, took from their blooming relationship, and from a Kissinger-recommended reading list, a new respect for realpolitik. Nasty players could offer advantageous deals (personally and otherwise). Mohammed bin Salman (MBS), the Crown Prince of Saudi Arabia, with an addiction to video games as well as a much-rumored cocaine problem, whom Kushner befriended and sponsored at the White House, and who American intelligence agencies would come to believe ordered the death and dismembering in 2018 of the journalist and regime opponent Jamal Khashoggi, might nevertheless help bring peace in the Middle East—that is, it would be worth it, even necessary, for the realpolitik Kushner to overlook and even help smooth away the details of a grizzly murder.

True, at a private lunch in the summer of 2018, Kissinger, with Jared's other patron Rupert Murdoch sitting nearby, erupted in bitter condemnation of Trump foreign policy strategy, declaring it based solely on Trump's caprices and on which state or leader was flattering him most lavishly. But by this time, Kushner had already, in part by encouraging such flattery of his father-in-law, built a clubby, friends-of-Jared, back-channel network outside of the institutional structures of American foreign policy. (At one point, Kushner, in the many permutations of his Middle East peace plan, imagined a region-wide Marshall Plan–type investment fund that would be run by one of MBS's own bankers.)

Indeed, the administration whipsawed bizarrely between Trump's diplomatic belligerence and Kushner's behind-the-scenes mutual stroking transactions. Kim Jong-un went from mortal enemy to bosom buddy largely because of Jared's back-channel initiatives.

In the oligarch-dominated favor-bank world, Kushner turned out to be quite adept. Trump might aspire to be an oligarch-despot, or at least have

man crushes on them, but it was Kushner who kept his eye on and sorted the benefits of those relationships, politically, diplomatically, and personally. It was Kushner who was the cool head.

A scene in the dramedy of a Kushner presidency might have a murderous MBS in the White House snorting a prodigious amount of cocaine with an abstemious Kushner patiently waiting to get down to business.

Kushner, ever dismissed as a hopeless cipher, has never gotten his due as a dramatic figure. Hence, we may have missed an opportunity to understand, through Kushner's hothouse example, Trump's confusing power over people who actually do know better.

The two views of Kushner (other than him simply being an idiot) are that he must be perverse and masochistic and beyond even the Trump era's extended bounds of rapaciousness to have put up with minute-by-minute exposure to his father-in-law. Or that he was a model of the Machiavellian mandarin. "Politics is the art of the possible" is a cliché Kushner repeats often. His point, though, seemed not to be a broader one about the competing interests of the system but much more specifically about the impulsive-child nature of his father-in-law and, in the face of this, Kushner's own patience and perseverance.

In Kushner's close personal circle there is a matter-of-fact view that "Jared hates Trump." I cannot, however, find anyone to whom he has uttered those precise words. Rather, it is that he conveys a sense of burden, of heavy heart. He wants you to know he is a martyr—not that different from what is conveyed by many in close proximity to Trump, except that Jared's proximity is even closer, and the burden he carries, he wants you to know, is so much heavier.

Among Kushner's justifications for ignoring just about everyone's advice to forgo an official role in the Trump White House was that, in the White House, he could become a pillar for Israel, seeming to imply that left to his own devices his father-in-law might not be. In the White House, he became Trump's designated Jew and holder of the all-important Israel portfolio—directed by the president to bring peace to the Middle East. For Trump, this was a way to avoid direct responsibility for the problem and indeed for having to devote any attention to it. For Jared it was another significant extension of his power base. But, of course, the advantage turned against Kushner—as almost every advantage allowed by Donald Trump ultimately does turn against whoever holds it—with Trump demanding to know why American Jews failed to respond positively (that is, rapturously) to all he did for them. With Trump naturally blaming this both on the character of the Jews and on Israel—and on Jared.

People familiar with the interactions here, who have heard Kushner's summaries of his father-in-law's rants, borderline anti-Semitic in nature, acknowledge Kushner's frustration but cast it as something almost saga-like, with Kushner accepting his father-in-law as the natural force. To oppose it would be useless. There is no arguing, there is just waiting. And suffering.

But one of the rewards for this suffering is to have achieved more political power in the world than any Jew in history.

Outside of his wife, Kushner's closest personal and professional relationship is with his brother Josh. Together they have helped manage their family's fortune, invested in outside projects, and dealt with their father's mercurial temper. For more than five years, Charlie Kushner shunned Josh's longtime non-Jewish girlfriend, the former Victoria's Secret model Karlie Kloss, until finally, from the White House, Jared was able to negotiate a truce—and Kloss's conversion—on his brother's behalf. The couple married in the fall of 2018.

Josh Kushner, who runs his own investment fund and is a founder of a health insurance company (one largely dependent on the policies of Obamacare), is "a screaming liberal," in Jared's description. He has, since the 2016 campaign, been open, indeed scathing, about his contempt for Trump. He's the George Conway of the Kushner family. But when Kushner does discuss his future, in business or politics, or "not-for-profits," or "wherever," it always involves Josh. His brother, according to Kushner, is his Bobby Kennedy.

Josh's defense of his brother is that they are not far apart on most issues. While he expresses constant incredulity about Trump, and about his brother's ability to tolerate close quarters with his father-in-law, he allows that his brother has found himself in a circumstance without precedent—which is surely true. And, in semi-heroic terms, he sees his brother as having sacrificed his own reputation, even putting himself into potential personal legal peril, in order to manage the furies of his father-in-law.

This heroic sense goes further and involves a kind of logic of redemption and transformation. In this, there is a future in which the Kushners can show their true selves. The Trump presidency, if it has marked them in one sense, has also given them the wherewithal to help correct history. Jared Kushner, in his brother's view, has a fair-minded, rigorous, even-tempered, and nuanced governing heart, if he can only be allowed to express it.

And, to the extent possible, again in a near-heroic sense, he does. In the face of the furies, he promoted (gingerly) immigration reform and opposed his father-in-law's wall. Similarly, against almost all Trump logic, Kushner made the African American vote a key target of the reelection campaign, convincing his father-in-law that here was a way to victory.

It is an upside-down theme in Jared's rationalizations about the Trump presidency that a White House that fundamentally always headed in the opposite direction of Kushner's better nature could also be a stepping-stone to allow him ultimately to do positive things and express his better nature. When asked about his proudest accomplishment in the White House, Kushner invariably points to prison reform and the Middle East deals that he's cut.

As exceptional as Jared's rise is Don Jr.'s. Trump's oldest son has become the Trump family member to have best channeled the Trump message to the Trump base. Next to his father, Don Jr. is the biggest stadium draw. Various longtime Trump circle people have noted—with surprise—Don Jr.'s new political acumen. But this has not much moved his father. Open disdain for Don Jr. has long been part of Trump's running commentary. He is not the brightest bulb; Trump wishes he could take his name back; Don Jr. shoots guns, which, in spite of Trump's dedicated pursuit of Second Amendment cred, Trump finds low-class; and Trump, who didn't like his son's wife, now doesn't like his girlfriend, former Fox News host Kimberly Guilfoyle (not so helpfully, Guilfoyle insists Trump has tried to put the moves on her). The more Don Jr. seeks to support his father, the more his father pushes him away.

Jared, on the other hand, carefully maintains his distance. "Jared's a liberal," the president was always announcing. Of all the flattery that Trump demands, Jared's may be the most limited. Indeed, possibly even with a hint of derision, Jared called the president "Donald," jarring to almost all political insiders. "In public, Jim Baker never called George Bush 'George,' and they were best friends," notes one appalled Republican who frequently observed Kushner and Trump together. And, certainly, there was no dearth of people eager to fob off the administration's failures on Kushner—and letting the president know it was all Jared's fault. And yet Jared remained the chosen one.

In part, this was because Ivanka's circle is inviolable. And it surely helped in that ultimate Trump accolade that Jared looked the part. He is tall and wears a tie and white shirt. Even at Bedminster, with the slightest chance of public exposure, he suited up. His hair is always in place. And he doesn't, in Trump's words, "babble." But, perhaps most of all, Kushner speaks to Trump's insecurities. He went to Harvard (Trump also notes that Jared's father bought him into Harvard, but that seems like a positive virtue, in Trump's telling); the billionaires like him; he has his own fortune; and, well, he's Jewish, and Jews are smart and his sons are dumb.

But if not Jared, it might actually be Don Jr. to inherit Trumpdom! So once again, Jared's patience and perseverance are quite a selfless act.

And then Ivanka—Jared's ultimate calling card.

Many Trumpers, as well as party regulars, believe that Ivanka is a key unexploited asset, that the base regards her with great awe. Trumpers dislike her because they believe she is a liberal, but in some sense they dislike her even more because she was largely unwilling to do what her brother does. When the going gets tough, it was often noted, she was somewhere else. At the same time, she remains a powerful enigma. What does she want? What does she aspire to? How might she use her power and influence if she truly chose to use it? To help get the Trump base to elect the first Jewish president?

In the grim months leading up to the 2020 election, there was a sphinx-sense about Jared's real expectations.

"You're not going to win, you're going to lose," an influential Republican confronted Jared in the days before. "You're running against Google, Facebook, China, and everyone with a college education. And when you lose you're going to be punished for it."

"No," said Kushner. "We're going to win."

And yet Kushner was said to have a realistic command of the dire polling numbers. A view among some dedicated Trumpers was that Jared seemed equanimous about a loss. The first couple might have survived so far, but a second term could be seriously pushing their luck.

There's an obsession among some Trumpers over what Kushner might have put in place for himself and his family for after the Trump White House; the extent to which the relationships he has made with family governments and the soft trade-in-kind deals that may have been implied in his dealings with various cohorts will move the Kushners into the true oligarch leagues. Certainly, the duo seem made for a world in which the U.S. presidency is truly internationalized, with global powers and wealthy patrons actively and openly seeking to influence the selection—that's a horse that has now certainly left the stable. Trump's own efforts here could seem like amateur stuff, Trump the goofy would-be oligarch. Kushner, on the other hand, finally with some real money in the family, a billionaire x-times over if he has astutely monetized his White House years, could be the real thing.

Of course, the specter of the Kushners' ability to call on the invisible hand of power around the world, as well as to seem like plausible players to anyone, is tempered, in the rational mind and to the naked eye, by the couple's obvious and comic insubstantiality. But that so far has hardly limited their rise, outweighed not just by a natural Trumpian shamelessness, but by their own true lack of cynicism and certain conviction that they really are good people.

Oh, Rudy!

Prologue: Going Rogue

R udy Giuliani was on his own.

As the House of Representatives rushed to impeach Donald Trump before the 2019 Christmas holiday, Giuliani, whose actions were at the heart of the charges against the president, was telling friends he was at the apex of his career and, at seventy-five, looking forward to new chapters— even a high position in the next Trump term. Even his dreamed-of job, secretary of state.

In fact, Giuliani may have had no actual friends anymore, at least not of the supportive and uncritical kind. In some extraordinary act of personal rebellion he had abandoned all reason and caution in favor of public spectacle, sometimes a hallucinatory one. Even for people with a great tolerance for the exigencies of power and influence, Giuliani had demonstrated quite a never-before-seen level of shamelessness and political fuck-youism to turn himself into . . . no one was quite sure what.

The man who had helped hold the country together after 9/11 was now unraveling, arguably along with the country, in a one-man show played out in hundreds of television "hits," nearly all of them surreal performances.

Giuliani and his public meltdown framed some of the great political questions of the age: How had evidently unstable people come to have such success in institutional politics otherwise defined by cautious tedium and procedural requirements? How had the mean and nasty achieved such heights in a system that has valued—insisted on—likability and conventionality?

In contrast to Rudy, even Trump seemed to have some self-control.

No one, not even the president, who demanded kamikaze-type loyalty from his lawyers, had quite seen such self-destructive devotion. Theories, many involving an altered mental state, were plentiful. This simply wasn't Rudy. Or even for a mercurial Rudy this was freakishly off the charts, breaking new thresholds of hysteria and derangement.

There, too, was his own evident joy. Joy in being allowed to say anything, without restraint, or logic, or coherence. His mouth clogged with spit, and features bouncing in disconnected ways, eyes popping and lip spiking, he had the world's attention and he wasn't going to waste it on judiciousness, politesse, or ceremony.

Save only for the president of the United States himself, never before had a national political figure been so transparent and unselfconscious in demanding his due. Rudy was out there on his own, without cover.

He wasn't going gently anywhere seemed to be the point. He was grabbing on to Donald Trump for dear life even if that meant taking Donald Trump down with him.

But to be self-destructive was not necessarily to destroy yourself, as the world was learning, but just to call more attention to yourself. The political system had moved its focus from issues to temperament. Might someone self-immolating set fire to the world, too? And might a working majority cheer him on?

For Rudy's New York circle—a close, caring, and concerned one—the debate was about the nature of his "break." Was this a place that the volatile former mayor had always been heading to, or was it another terrible result of the Trump psychic storm?

1. Rudy and Roger

In early August 2016, Rudy Giuliani was on the phone with his client Roger Ailes.

A few weeks had passed since Ailes's abrupt ouster from Fox News, the network he had founded and led for twenty years. The man who had done so much to alter the rules of political temperament and disrupt American politics had been routed by as disruptive a change in workplace norms. His career-long objectification of women, a programming as well as a personal view, had, with a surprise lawsuit from former Fox News anchor Gretchen Carlson, suddenly garnered a new label: predatory behavior.

In the living room of his ranch house in Cresskill, New Jersey, the seventy-six-year-old, deserted equally by former allies and by the syco-phants in the television business and the Republican Party, nursed his iced tea and chatted with his lawyer and friend, who was calling in from his house in the Hamptons.

Both men were on their speakerphones. Ailes, plotting his memoir and comeback, had someone listening in and assumed his friend Giuliani was doing the same—these were public men, after all.

"They get you when they can. I don't have to tell you that. They saw weakness," said Giuliani whose job was less legal strategy than to rehash, on an almost daily basis, the bitter details of his friend's downfall. For something like the hundredth time, they went through the list of women whose careers, Giuliani agreed, Ailes had made only to have them stab him in the back. For both men, women represented quite a black hole of human nature.

They had known each other for more than thirty years. In 1989, in his first race for New York City mayor, Rudy had hired Ailes, the key media adviser to Nixon, Reagan, and Bush Sr., to run his campaign. For Ailes, Giuliani—the federal prosecutor in New York who had broken up the Mafia five families and brought the 1980s generation of Wall Street vultures to its knees—was "gold, real political money, candy, and," added Ailes, who prided himself on a long memory and a strict accounting of political virtues and drawbacks, "just a little crazier than might be alto-gether healthy—but still in the ballpark."

Rudy was now bucking up Ailes, but Ailes had spent the last eight years bucking up Rudy, out in the wilderness since his aborted run for presi-dent in 2008—and stuck, in Ailes's view, in a "hell-on-earth marriage." So when Ailes hit bottom he called Rudy, not for legal advice—that would come from Rudy's partners at the two-thousand-lawyer firm Greenberg Traurig—but for what they shared and understood. They had both lived zero-sum lives. They prospered at their enemies' expense. And, conversely, their enemies prospered at their expense. Hence, because this was a game of opportunity and advantage, often coming in unlikely ways, it wasn't necessarily over, no matter how over it might seem.

As much as Ailes's vertiginous fall was their subject, so, too, was the freaky rise of their mutual friend Trump.

Both men claimed credit for Trump. Ailes because he put Trump on the air and advised him on his television career, and Giuliani because as mayor of New York he'd helped Trump's real estate deals. Still, for both men, Trump was less an equal than a court jester type, a good-time guy with an entourage of girls and sports figures. You could laugh at Trump. Aides remember Trump appearing at city hall and Giuliani then telling stories about how ridiculous he was. And yet there was a bond—a famous guys bond. They were all veterans of the New York media wars. By sheer endurance, alligator skins, and walls and moats of personal defense mechanisms, they had survived the contempt of elite New York and somehow, in some extraordinary jujitsu, come to thrive because of it.

That among them it was Trump who was waging the most splendid fight for the ultimate prize merely confirmed the fickleness of fate. Could there be a better sign of politics' strange fortunes and why you ought never to give up?

"Donald doesn't listen. He's incapable of listening," Ailes was saying, still peevish about his recent conversation with the candidate.

"Donald is in his own world," Giuliani agreed. "He doesn't want to leave his comfort zone."

"That's a helluva way to run a campaign."

"He needs some better thinking. He's ready. He understands. He gets it."

"Yeah, well, he's seventeen points down."

"Granted."

Here was the real reason for Giuliani's call: he wanted Ailes to come with him out to Bedminster, Trump's golf club in New Jersey, to help him get Trump ready for his first debate with Hillary Clinton.

"He wants you," said Giuliani. "He needs you."

"He doesn't listen."

"He'll listen to you. Do you want me to have him call you?"

"I can call him. But yes, have him call me."

"He'll call you."

But these were ritual maneuvers. Both men, over the hill, each variously humiliated in the public life they craved and deprived of the influence they needed in order to breathe, had somehow found themselves in the inner circle—the epicenter of the inner circle, in a way the only members of it—of their party's nominee for president.

Of course their chauffeurs would take them out to Bedminster that weekend. This was their game. They were still in it.

"He needs to listen," said Ailes.

"He will, he gets it, he does," said Giuliani.

Unbeknownst to both men, Trump, in a spur-of-the-moment inspiration, had the day before invited Steve Bannon, the Breitbart News chief and associate of the far-right political contributors Bob Mercer and his daughter, Rebekah, out to the Bedminster conclave. Likewise, Bannon did not expect to walk in on Sunday morning and find Ailes and Giuliani relaxing in one of the private dining rooms, waiting for Trump to finish his round of golf—which neither Ailes nor Giuliani, both vastly overweight and with rickety legs, could play that day.

As they waited, Ailes and Giuliani were happily telling war stories, recalling their first campaign together. In his phone call the day before with Trump, Bannon had spelled out, and had thought Trump appreciated, that with ten weeks to go the campaign was in a catastrophic state. Even the Republican National Committee was ready to give up on it. The campaign was on life support with no time to waste. But here was Trump's brain trust, Ailes and Giuliani, both men barely able to walk, Rudy with a lunchtime drink, reminiscing about 1989.

"This was the world that time forgot. It was Damon Runyon," said Bannon describing the scene not long afterward.

Shortly, they were joined by Paul Manafort, the titular head of the campaign. Manafort, sixty-seven, a lobbyist for foreign companies and governments, had not worked a political campaign in decades, but Trump had hired him for his country club bona fides and because he was willing to work for free.

"Trump likes guys his own age. This is a whole new dimension to being past your prime. And what I suddenly realized is that I was auditioning for them. They were running this show. Or they thought they were running this show! Suffice to say there was no debate prep that day. This was just putting back clubhouse franks. And talking about campaigns of yore and evil women," recounted Bannon.

Ailes saw it slightly differently. No one was actually running for president, in his view. This wasn't actually a political campaign. Ailes, no matter the disruptions he had wrought, still saw politics in relatively conventional terms. To be president "you at least have to know how to read," said Ailes, laughing, implying that his friend Trump didn't. The way Ailes saw it was that he and Rudy could do something together with Trump. They weren't ready to be put out to pasture. They should be able to have a better last act than they were looking at. The Trump Channel was what Ailes was thinking. Trump would not be president—and thank god, in Ailes's view—but there was opportunity here. He and Rudy had something by the tail. But, meanwhile, they were pretending to wage a presidential campaign. "It's a teaser," said Ailes.

Trump and Giuliani tried to convince Ailes to replace an incompetent Manafort and run the campaign. Ailes turned it down. In fact, because Trump was always offering jobs, often the same job, to many people, it was never possible to tell if you had actually been offered the job unless you took it—taking the job may be how you actually got the job. Rudy was annoyed at Ailes for not stepping up. In politics, proximity is everything. Staying close to Trump was the key here to taking advantage of whatever they could take advantage of. Since neither of them could walk very well, a mordant Ailes thought it might be difficult to stay close. In recounting this, Ailes said Rudy had said that he, too, had been offered the job but had deferred to Ailes. But Ailes didn't believe this because, obviously, Rudy would have taken it if it had been offered.

Bannon took it, surprising both Ailes and Giuliani. Both men assumed this meant Bannon wanted in on their Trump Channel plan. They were wary but thought that the more youthful Bannon—even at sixty-two—coming from Breitbart with the digital thing, might be a good addition.

Formally taking over the campaign a few days after the Bedminster meeting, Bannon saw one of his immediate jobs as distracting Trump from his over-the-hill inclinations and sidelining Trump's over-the-hill gang. Himself an unsteady figure with swollen legs, Bannon was scathing in his critique of Trump's guys—lost, out of it, broken, senile.

He made immediate common cause with Jared Kushner, the president's son-in-law. Giuliani had been hectoring Kushner, trying to introduce him to various clients of his firm, and calling with advice about what the younger man should be doing to help his father-in-law. The reserved

Kushner was puzzled by the babbling Giuliani. Bannon and Kushner were united in keeping Giuliani at arm's length from the campaign.

And, yet, Bannon found himself impressed by Giuliani's sheer will. That he could ignore all the obvious reasons why he might not be a likely top campaign operative and adviser—ideological reasons, physical reasons, conflict-of-interest reasons, personal-life reasons, mental health reasons—was, for Bannon, as heroic as it was fantastic.

"I understood his need. It was overwhelming," said Bannon.

"Rudy certainly had his eye on the prize, whatever the prize was. But, in addition, it was just extremely urgent," said Ailes, "that Rudy find a reason to get out of the house."

2. Judi

The debate over the relative levels of privacy a politician might expect for his private life takes on an altogether different dimension when it is the politician, as much as the media, who casually lets it all hang out, demons, mania, and love affairs alike. What happens when, instead of displaying at least a pretense of careful self-control, reasonable judgment, avuncular predictability, sensible prioritizing, and prudent language, the politician reveals himself to be a hot mess?

By the summer of 2016, Giuliani's marriage, in Ailes's description, was "a crime scene—homicide detectives taking statements, medical examiners putting on gloves."

Up until Donald Trump, no successful national politician in modern media times had been so open in his disregard of the public protocols of marriage as Giuliani. As mayor, he cheated on his then wife—his second wife—Donna Hanover, carrying on a longtime affair with a twenty-eight-year-old junior staffer, Cristyne Lategano, who was suddenly promoted to top staffer. Despite official denials, Giuliani made little effort to hide the affair, her promotion, or, then, the breakup of the affair and the unceremonious shunting of Lategano to a lesser city government job. In the throes of his next public affair, with Judi Nathan, a pharmaceutical sales representative whom he met in his favorite cigar bar, he informed his wife—still Hanover—of the formal end of their marriage in a news conference (in fairness, Giuliani's side believed Hanover was about to hold a news conference and publicly break up with him). In 2014, Trump assured an aide that his own very public sexual exploits and marital breakdowns could be handled if he ran for president, "like Rudy's—he proved it. No one cares."

The difference here, between Trump and Giuliani—and this is a distinction that perhaps should go to the credit of the former mayor—is that Trump's marital and sexual issues seemed cold and transactional, while Giuliani's were emotional and operatic. "He bleeds, really," said Ailes.

Trump did not appear to have real relationships, whereas Giuliani had genuinely real, albeit terrible, relationships. Giuliani was a primitive man in modern times, ever peevish about the new rules for the upwardly mobile American man and his nuclear family. Giuliani grew up in an unreconstructed Italian American home and neighborhood. His father was a low-level mob enforcer, whose regular work included breaking legs, arms, and kneecaps—a part of Rudy's biography he sometimes tried to hide; other times he seemed merely to scoff at the idea that this might be relevant to anything at all. His first wife, Regina Peruggi, was his second cousin, which, after he met Hanover, became the reason for an official church annulment, with Rudy pleading, in the face of Peruggi's stunned disbelief, that he didn't know she was his *actual* second cousin. When one of his press aides, Ken Frydman, got married—on the steps of city hall, with Giuliani presiding—the mayor took the young man aside to counsel him about how best to accommodate other women in his life.

And yet, he had left the old neighborhood with a desire to make it in yuppie Manhattan, proud that Hanover was a television journalist and that they were referred to as a power couple. He, however, was happiest out after dinner with his circle of political, police, or neighborhood chums—and the women who joined them. Lategano was almost always by his side and was shortly accorded the status of the second most powerful player in city government—"the co-mayor" was her not affectionate sobriquet—with every staffer suddenly having to please her as well as him. "Everybody was publicly living inside Rudy's fucked-up private life," remembers an aide.

But where the profane and aggressive Lategano failed to force a divorce, the even more profane and aggressive Nathan succeeded, resulting in the marriage-ending news conference that would go down as perhaps the loopiest and most unnerving in New York mayoral history. Was the mayor having a breakdown? Guiliani's tight circle was united in its incredulity about Judi.

"She was stupid. She was greedy. She was charmless. She was petty. She was bad tempered. She was possessive. She was needy. She was imperious. She was quarrelsome. She was a nag, a ball breaker and a bitch on steroids," said Ailes, in summation of his friend's situation, and with some awe.

Two things changed Rudy at this point in his life: 9/11 and Nathan.

For eight years, his constant level of mania, from steady agitation to fever and derangement, held the city's amused or concerned attention. But suddenly, with the unimaginable attack, the city's hysteria came into line with his. In a perceptual reversal, he appeared preternaturally calm and in control. His always hyped-up, carping, adrenaline voice became eerily precise, paced, and often even gentle. His transformation and his civil usefulness—on television every second, holding the furies back—became as great a story as the attack itself. Like Churchill, another hysteric, Rudy was the calm in the storm.

At one funeral after another, he represented the city's collective grief.

Instead of being married to a spent mayor, Judi Nathan found herself married to a worldwide celebrity. She now helped effect a further transformation in Rudy, alarming to his circle. As a prosecutor and as mayor, Rudy seemed satisfied with a civil servant lifestyle. Money was a long way from a top priority. He had never had it and, without material or social aspirations, there wasn't much to suggest he would know what to do with it. But now, he told friends, it was a small window between leaving city hall in 2002 and beginning his widely anticipated campaign in 2006 for the 2008 presidential race—he needed to seize the opportunity.

There began a peripatetic international life of six-figure speaking fees, rainmaking for the security firm he started and the law practice that signed him as a figurehead partner, and of putting favors and goodwill in the bank for his coming presidential campaign. It was Rudy and Judi on the road, an arduous, friction-filled life, making it all the more necessary to make ever-more money to lessen the heavy lifting and the exhaustion with private planes and luxury hotel suites.

Civil servant Rudy disappeared into a new, demanding, international-brand, prima donna Rudy. Judi, too, was indulging extravagant tastes and imperial demeanor while waiting for her coming role as first lady.

If Judi is blamed for ruining civil servant Rudy, his circle equally blamed her for ruining his presidential possibilities. A leader in the early polls, the campaign, with Judi as a controlling presence, upbraiding candidate and staff alike, hardly made it to the first primaries.

"Rudy was tired, spent, fat, and unlikable," said Ailes, whom Rudy was on the phone with nearly every day of the race.

It was a profound personal defeat, and an existential one. Judi would later describe her husband as "catatonic" and take credit for nursing him back to a functional existence. Other Giuliani friends, including Ailes, would note that this was the moment that Rudy, the hail fellow drinker, became Rudy the drunk.

Hence, his wilderness years, the fifth stage of his career—after prosecutor, mayor, celebrity, and presidential candidate—began.

3. "What Do We Do with Rudy?"

For all practical purposes, Rudy Giuliani as significant player and individual power center was over—"The decline and fall of the holy Rudy Empire," in the words of one former aide. He was sixty-four years old without a clear or viable political path in front of him. As 9/11 receded, as the Obama administration defused the terrorism-fear state, Rudy seemed ever more a specific sort of memory and complicated symbol. He represented something that many people clearly wanted to forget.

He drank more. And put on weight.

He stewed about Michael Bloomberg, whose political career he rightly claimed he was wholly responsible for, anointing Bloomberg as his stand-in after 9/11 when he was term-limited from another race. His bitter resentment became a reliable part of his nightly drinking routine.

Money, or more money, became a certain kind of solace. It was also what was needed to soothe Judi's disappointment, or wrath, about, inconceivably, not finding herself first lady. And, indeed, he remained a prodigious moneymaker, but it was never enough, only single-digit millions a year—$7.9 million in 2016, $9.5 million in 2017, $6.8 million in 2018, for instance, according to the couple's divorce papers. Virtual poverty in the world of oligarchs and billionaires that he now traveled in. To make the sums he was making, to leverage his brand, he more and more found himself on the margins of respectability. Dubious guys in dubious capitals were buying respectability through him. That's where his value was highest.

His brand turned inside out. Rudy the righteous prosecutor, the scourge of corruption, had become the backroom fixer, the seller of influence, the front man for bad characters.

"Rudy's Hole-in-the-Wall Gang," quipped Bannon about Giuliani's associates.

Judi regularly reminded him of his failed lot and of his low-class fellow travelers. She wasn't the only one. Much of Rudy's New York circle dined out on tales of his desperate avarice as well as his frightful marriage.

By 2015, Rudy watched with increasing incredulity the campaign of his friend—he would shy away from this designation, saying, more precisely, "Well, I've known him for a long time"—Donald Trump. Notably, Trump, even though he was leading in almost every poll for the Republican nomination, really had only two personal relationships in politics. There was New Jersey governor Chris Christie, a valuable ally through Trump's Atlantic City casino phase, and Rudy, his helpful ally in New York City real estate. Christie, too, was running in the Republican race for president, so to the extent that Trump needed political advice, and mostly he believed he did not need political advice, he now called Rudy.

The rise of Trump as the New York figure taking the Republican Party by storm cast a cloud over the Giuliani household. For Judi, it was an easy point of new derision in their bitter verbal wars. Judi regarded Trump as stupid and vulgar, and here Trump was doing what Rudy had promised her he would do.

By the spring of 2016, Rudy was trying to rationalize his relationship with Trump. Rudy having regarded Trump as a lesser member of his own entourage—Rudy was the celebrity, and Trump the friend and host of celebrities—now was having to consider joining the Trump retinue. Curiously, Trump, in an instance of compassion and warmth unfamiliar to anyone in the Trump circle, had, several years before, reached out to Rudy's estranged son, a hopeful pro golfer. Rudy, who had once seen this as evidence of Trump trying to suck up to him, now saw this as a debt he owed Trump, and another reason to now support him.

In April, as the primaries finished and as it appeared that no other Republican could overtake Trump, Rudy endorsed him.

Trump, in return, suggested that in a Trump administration Rudy might lead a "radical Islam commission." Rudy, fantasizing about higher cabinet rank, took this as a slight.

Still, Rudy's appetite was whetted.

"Rudy convinced himself that Trump was a singular opportunity, however implausible this might seem. He saw himself as somehow the real thing to Trump's fanciful thing. And, not incidentally, he bought some peace by telling Judi that if Trump won he had promised to make Rudy secretary of state," said an amused Ailes. "Trump got Rudy out of the house."

If Judi Giuliani had contempt for Trump, Trump couldn't abide her and, helpful to Rudy, virtually banned her from his presence. Hence, campaign Rudy was stag Rudy, always his preferred condition.

Curiously, in a campaign of odd figures—Corey Lewandowski, the feral campaign manager; Paul Manafort, the corrupt lobbyist who replaced Lewandowski; Tom Barrack, the real estate mogul with his many shadowy partners in the Middle East and the candidate's main confidant; Michael Cohen, the designated Trump bagman; Steve Bannon, the self-appointed populist hero who replaced Manafort—Rudy, old, angry, sleeping in meetings, drinking too much, and, perhaps most peculiarly, a moderate Republican among the virulent new right wing, seemed like one of the oddest, raising red flags even for the other Trump people who themselves should have raised red flags.

This oddness culminated at the 2016 Convention, at which Rudy delivered what was, even in the context of a peculiarly aggressive convention, a screeching, frenzied, eye-popping, demented-seeming performance.

"THE VAST MAJORITY OF AMERICANS TODAY DO NOT FEEL SAFE! THEY FEAR FOR THEIR CHILDREN. THEY FEAR FOR THEM-SELVES. THEY FEAR FOR OUR POLICE OFFICERS, WHO—ARE—BEING TARGETED, WITH—A TARGET ON THEIR BACK!" . . . he seemed to be spitting or frothing . . . "IT'S TIME TO MAKE AMERICA SAFE AGAIN! IT'S TIME TO MAKE AMERICA ONE AGAIN! ONE AMERICA! WHAT HAPPENED TO . . . THERE'S NO BLACK

AMERICA, THERE'S NO WHITE AMERICA, THERE IS JUST AMER-
ICA? WHAT HAPPENED TO IT?" He was screaming now, his hands
outstretched and quavering. "WHERE DID IT GO? HOW HAS IT
FLOWN AWAY? I KNOW WE CAN CHANGE IT BECAUSE I DID IT
BY CHANGING NEW YORK CITY FROM THE CRIME CAPITAL OF
AMERICA TO THE SAFEST LARGE CITY IN THE UNITED STATES.
WHAT I DID FOR NEW YORK DONALD TRUMP WILL DO FOR
AMERICA.... IN THE LAST SEVEN MONTHS THERE HAVE BEEN
FIVE MAJOR ISLAMIC TERRORIST ATTACKS ON US AND OUR
ALLIES. WE MUST NOT BE AFRAID TO DEFINE OUR ENEMY. IT IS
ISLAMIC EXTREMIST TERRORISM! ... WE MUST COMMIT OUR-
SELVES TO UNCONDITIONAL VICTORY AGAINST THEM!"

Even the audience seemed hesitant before launching into its expected
chant of "Ru-dy! Ru-dy!"

Trump called Ailes during the speech. "Is he okay?" Trump complained
that the speech was more about Giuliani than about Trump. "What does
he think he's doing, running for president?"

After Bannon's arrival in mid-August and with Kushner's taking on a
larger role in the campaign, Rudy was relegated, in Bannon's description,
to "crazy uncle" status.

"Hey, Rudy, losing a step," Trump teased Rudy when he came out on
the campaign plane—indefatigable in his efforts to be on the plane—as his
head reliably fell to his chest shortly after takeoff.

Then, on October 7, 2016, with four weeks until the election, the *Washington Post* released the *Access Hollywood* "grab them by the pussy" tape.
The campaign, already in meltdown, given the dismal polls, went into free
fall. Every senior adviser, with the exception of Bannon, urged Trump to
reassess the campaign's viability. The RNC forcibly argued for Trump to
abandon the campaign. Virtually all the primary surrogates canceled their
scheduled rally and television appearances.

But not Rudy.

In one of those ultimate political daredevil acts, he took bookings on
all the major—and news-making—Sunday morning political talk shows.

The revelation of the tape seemed to move in him some Catholic
notions of depravity and sin—or, from the old neighborhood, a husband's

sense of anger, shame, and fortitude. And a bitterness that his, and Trump's, enemies were being given a pass on the human condition.

"You know, you confess your sins and you make a firm resolution not to commit that sin again and the priest gives you absolution and then hopefully you're a changed person," he said. "I mean, we believe that people in this country can change."

He seemed to speak from some deep and personal experience.

Sputter, sputter . . . he began with NBC's Chuck Todd, "the reality is that in both cases"—that is, Trump and Hillary Clinton—"both people have things in their personal lives that maybe if they could redo it they would do it differently . . . and the reality is that this is a situation in which neither side should throw stones because both sides have sinned . . ."

There was awe, among the campaign staff, that Rudy would so boldly put himself out there—and bewilderment. Why would he? However many disappointments he might have weathered in the past number of years, he still commanded great respect and maintained extraordinary national, even bipartisan, stature. Now, though, he was the spokesperson for one of the most tawdry, ludicrous, and inexplicable episodes in modern politics, one that, by any reasonable logic, was about to end a presidential campaign in historic humiliation.

The reason, concluded the Trump staff, including Bannon who was urging forbearance in the face of the scandal, was that Rudy was crazy. It was an explanation that extended from the logic that Trump is Trump (shrug), to the same logic now explaining Rudy, that Rudy is Rudy. In this there was arguably a new political formulation, that individual pathology, rather than being carefully disguised, was to be embraced as yet another wild card in a wholly unpredictable game. Rudy was willing to risk his own humiliation and reputation out of a desperate desire to be at the center of the action. So be it.

"It's a helluva long bet," said Ailes after Rudy's performance during *Access Hollywood* week, laughing.

"He's definitely a kamikaze guy," said Bannon, "but he's our kamikaze guy."

"Rudy," an amused Ailes analyzed, "has turned himself into very good television." Added Ailes, "Drinking sometimes helps."

Trump was in fact less than happy with his only defender—he wasn't defending him enough; he was making weak excuses. Why was Rudy "such a girl"?

Then, on November 8, 2016, astounding to all, including the candidate, the unimaginable happened.

With its founding premise that it would lose the election never seriously challenged, the Trump campaign team was wholly unprepared to become a government-in-waiting. The candidate, both superstitious and lazy—and, for once, realistic—had repeatedly dismissed the idea that they ought to make even rudimentary what-if preparations. Hence, starting on November 9, every consideration and decision related to taking control of the world's most powerful government, largest bureaucracy, and biggest national budget had to begin from the beginning, absent clear policies, ready personnel, and executive leadership. And yet even here, amid the most chaotic transition in modern politics, one question kept constantly rising to the top: "What do we do with Rudy?"

Even the president-elect, congenitally ungrateful, did not question the fact that he owed Rudy a great deal, whatever his faults—and yet could not clearly imagine what Rudy might reasonably do.

"What the fuck," said Bannon, "it's Rudy."

Giuliani had become quite a weird, and to some extent unwanted, mascot of the campaign. If he had distinguished himself during the grab-them-by-the-pussy crisis, this had also confirmed to virtually everyone that he was without restraint and, in fact, sense.

Still, he was owed.

He wanted to be the secretary of state. His credential to do this was in essence a list of his conflicts of interest—all the relationships and experiences he had amassed in almost fifteen years of moneygrubbing around the globe.

The president-elect floated it, but without enthusiasm. He thought Rudy was too tired—and too fat. In Trump's world, where looking the part was an important criterion, fat Rudy, the president-elect kept pointing out, "doesn't look the part." Almost everyone to whom he floated the idea agreed. Not just about his looks, but about his temperament, his conflicts, his management experience, his wife, and his drinking.

Almost everybody in the still-inchoate senior-staff circle wanted Rudy to be kept out of a significant place in the administration.

Bannon put it out that Rudy was in the early stages of dementia. Trump said he thought that might be true.

Still, he was owed.

Rudy was offered, and dismissed out of hand, Homeland Security or director of National Intelligence. He did not want to be "9/11 Rudy."

Trump was looking to put a friend at the Justice Department, and Bannon was sent to offer Rudy the attorney general spot. A disappointed and realistic Giuliani demurred, "I'm too old to practice law."

Curiously, and quite incomprehensibly, Trump, casting about, briefly considered Rudy as his first nominee to the Supreme Court—a selection that, with the death of Antonin Scalia and the Republican Senate's stalling of the nomination of Obama choice Merrick Garland, would have to be made in the first weeks of the new administration.

"Yes, perfect," said Bannon, "a pro-choice nominee. Let's go home."

In early January, two weeks before the transition team working out of Trump Tower in New York was set to pack up and move to Washington and into the White House, Bannon sat down with Ailes. The discussion involved, among other things, what to do with Rudy.

"I'll tell you what they could do with him. Just have Donald take him on the plane with him now and again. Special adviser. Special envoy. Rudy's good. He'll fix his speeches and tie his shoes. Once people see him on the plane as the special adviser, he'll be all right," said Ailes.

4. Mini-Me

There was no job for Rudy.

The White House chief of staff, Reince Priebus, regarded this as at least one bullet the new administration had dodged.

Rudy entered another wilderness period—without clear goals or direction or, it reasonably seemed, any meaningful future possibilities.

He was seventy-two years old, heading past 275 pounds, infirm on his feet, and in a crumbling marriage. Still, he and a few faithful friends continued to insist, he was Rudy.

People who have so much adversity and success may believe more optimistically than most, or more stoically, that the worm always turns. In the first months of the Trump administration Rudy more than ever saw himself as naturally belonging in it.

True, almost all of the Trump policies—whether Trump himself believed them or not—were nearly the opposite of Rudy's more or less moderate New York Republican views. Immigration, abortion, tariffs, the environment, regulation. But, in this regard, the policy side, Rudy could hardly have been less interested. He told people he was frustrated to be stuck on the sidelines because everything Trump was doing, *he* had done before. He was defining correctly that the Trump era was much less about policy than it was about temperament. And here he rightly claimed to be one of the signature models of a politician as diva, insulter-in-chief, media hog, in-your-face guy, my-way-or-the-highway sort. In his eight years as mayor between 1994 and 2002, he helped transform the city, and at the same time he transformed the office of mayor from an executive and governing function to a daily personal drama, a reality show format featuring the moods, whims, impulses, adventures, verbal and legal altercations, and off-the-cuff ruminations of The Mayor. And now, with more than a little dudgeon, he saw his shtick alive in the White House.

"I'm not saying he's stealing my thing," he told Ailes in one of their many calls in the first months of the Trump administration, as he continued to try to find a key that would unlock an office for himself (notably, Trump had given Rudy's son Andrew, not faring too well as a hopeful professional golfer, an office and title, "public liaison assistant"). "But he's learned from me."

In fact, this view of himself as a Trump Mini-Me was an uncharacteristically self-deprecating view of his time in office. Rudy as drama queen had, at least for periods of his two terms, been balanced by a strong administrative hand and an energetic governing philosophy.

Rudy was in your face, vituperative, and mean-spirited, but he managed to turn that into something of a rallying cry and forward movement against an ungovernable city.

Here was the culmination of at least a two-decade slide into maximum urban dysfunction: highest recorded crime rate, high point of the crack epidemic, record homelessness, surging gang activity, record youth and underclass unemployment, along with a gilded, obscenely conspicuous Wall Street.

Rudy took the movie role of protector and cleanup guy. His predecessor, David Dinkins, had seemed, in the face of breakdown, oddly calm if not impervious. Rudy's natural levels of hysteria much more clearly matched the moment.

For reasons yet unsettled, shortly after Giuliani took office, New York's crime rate, as well as that of other major American cities, began to precipitously, and, as the trend continued, miraculously, fall. Giuliani claimed credit—and got credit—for one of the greatest turnarounds in urban history. What's more, the early-nineties recession gave way to a historic economic expansion, a boon for Wall Street, media, fashion, and real estate. Poverty certainly did not go away, but it became less visible in a newly glittering city. Rudy's city.

Success unleashed the inner Rudy, which, at any rate, had never been hidden. It was an ever-more-uninhibited, larger-than-life, attention-seeking, unyielding Rudy. It was anti-political in the sense that he seemed to go out of his way not to be politic. In this, David Dinkins, mild and tempered, and Giuliani's later opponent Ruth Messinger, a longtime city bureaucrat and reformer, became archetypes of politicians whose very reasonableness and process-orientation prevented them from doing anything. Rudy was the bull in the china shop and, in some wary but affectionate sense, the nutty dictator who got things done. You could see it, or anyway see his red face and popping eyes.

The system itself, being so sclerotic, inbred, and unyielding, needed an explosive element in its midst. Chaos and psychodrama presented a clear competitive advantage: people paid attention. Your message gets across, even if it has no meaning. You become the center of attention. You are the message.

Choose your battles, that wisest of political advice, became for Rudy a new philosophy of never overlooking a reason to battle, no matter how tangential or pointless—losing battles or winning battles, take them all. The certainty of battle, the joy of engagement, the size of the headlines was the point; the outcome was irrelevant. In 1995, during a celebration at Lincoln Center for the fiftieth anniversary of the United Nations, Rudy had Yasser Arafat thrown off the premises. That was an early "nut" moment, recalled a close aide from that time.

The courtroom was often his battlefield. Rudy used courtrooms not as most lawyers use them, to stay out of them, but as they are used in television dramas—as plot device, as deus ex machina, and as stage for a star turn. The fact that he so regularly lost in court was fine because there was nothing really at stake. Did it matter to him if the Brooklyn Museum was not in fact evicted from its city-owned building, as he sought, after showing a work of art that Rudy decided was insulting and blasphemous?

In 1997, *New York* magazine, a media outlet that had long courted Rudy as he had assiduously courted it—like so much media in the city, carrying on a love-hate fest with the combative prosecutor and showboat mayor—placed a promotional ad on the side of New York city buses. The ad, for which the magazine paid the Metropolitan Transit Authority $85,000, boasted that *New York* magazine was "possibly the only good thing in New York Rudy hasn't taken credit for."

Rudy ordered the ads taken down. A federal judge ordered them kept up. A passionate fight through the courts was launched, dominating headlines for weeks. This called far more attention to the small ad buy than it would otherwise have gotten, and painted Rudy as an enemy of free speech, a particularly thin-skinned sort, one using city resources and, to say the least, a frivolous warrior for, at best, limited rewards.

And yet it was worth it—sort of. It was the "principle," the mayor insisted, meaning, by some stretch of the circumstances, and without specifying what the principle exactly was, that he was a man who would do anything to defend his principles, even look foolish—even declaring, as the newscaster Sam Donaldson put it, and Giuliani did not disagree, "nuclear war" over a "cute spoof."

It was this seizing the moment, whatever the moment might be, that helped make Giuliani a national figure, seldom the case for a New York mayor, and suddenly talked about—well before 9/11—as a future presidential contender.

But not long into the second term the slippage started to be apparent.

Wayne Barrett, a relentless reporter of a certain old-school New York type, took on Rudy as his whale, trying, to Giuliani's fury, to unravel both the contradictions in his character and the dubious elements of his background. (Barrett also wrote a book about Trump—long before his presidency might even have been imagined.)

Jack Newfield, another dogged New York reporter obsessed with Giuliani, believed that Rudy was not just nuts but clinically "insane," proclaiming that this was not a political issue but a mental health case.

And then his marriage blew up publicly. And, publicly, his children turned on him. And then he got prostate cancer. "Keeping up with him" during this time, wrote Barrett, "was a psychedelic experience." In 2000, he was, with uncharacteristic ambivalence, gearing up for a Senate race against Hillary Clinton who, trying to rehabilitate herself after her husband's disgrace and her humiliation, was remaking herself as a New York resident and liberal political hope, much to Giuliani's scorn. Vowing to take her on, he suddenly turned tail. The prostate cancer spooked him. He reverted to a figure of self-pity. Instead of going to a fundraiser in Rochester, he announced he was going to a Yankees game. "It was like he didn't care anymore," recalled an aide. His health gone, his marriage gone, his life was a sad sloppy mess bursting at the seams.

And then, just weeks before the election of his successor and his own retirement, came 9/11—and he was remade as a twenty-first-century political hero.

"You might think he's the comeback kid. But that's losing your way and finding your way back. That's not Rudy. He's not changing, he's not learning. He's just Rudy," said Ailes.

5. Eyes on the Prize

While much of the political world, Democrats and Republicans alike, was confused and alarmed by Trump's first months in office, Rudy was commending him.

"He's gotten the attention of the world," Rudy told an increasingly skeptical Ailes.

However much Rudy had been in fact rejected by Trump and his team, and even publicly humiliated by the new president and his circle, he nevertheless continued to regard the Trump White House as his personal opportunity, one to be seized in whatever way possible.

"Rudy was unshakable," said a bemused Ailes a few weeks before his death, in May 2017, from a fall in his Palm Beach home. (Rudy, along with Trump and other figures in the White House, passed on showing up at Ailes's funeral.)

He was, yet self-appointed, a Trump whisperer, courtier, and emissary without portfolio. He joined a circle of perhaps a dozen or so whom Trump called on a reliable, and for some a daily, basis. While these calls had much more to do for Trump with companionship and reassurance than political strategy, being on the receiving end certainly made you think you had high standing in the new government. And, indeed, regularly talking to the president gave you a sort of carte blanche to call other members of the new government as though you were his messenger and representative.

Rudy extended this carte blanche around the world.

Among old Rudy hands and senior staff in the first phase of the Trump White House, there was continued conjecture about whether Rudy's effort here was to enrich himself or insinuate himself. In part, Rudy hands saw the money Rudy was generating from his close association with the president as a consolation prize. If he was not going to get public status, then he deserved private reward. But in a way both goals, money and power, were part of the same whole. Rudy's globe-trotting deals were a helpful subject for Trump, indeed a better entry to the world's issues than the weighty and ponderous presentations from the State Department and intelligence community.

In the White House, Trump's off-the-books conversations with Rudy became a distracting thread. "He was talking to Rudy" became a category of policy direction, or misdirection.

Rudy was a Trump ambassador for reverse hire—a messenger for unsavory despots to the new president—in whatever capital that was offering top dollar, including Ankara and his new friend Turkish president Recep Tayyip Erdoğan. It was certainly unusual, if not unprecedented, for someone representing foreign interests—ones conducting pivotal negotiations with the United States—to be at the same time in so many various direct and indirect ways acting for the president.

In one instance, Giuliani tried to spring from a U.S. jail an Iranian Turkish gold trader, Reza Zarrab, who appeared to have had a pivotal role in moving $10 billion worth of gold and cash through a Turkish bank to Iran, contravening U.S. sanctions. Erdoğan wanted him out of prison not least of all because he could implicate officials of the Turkish bank and government. Giuliani took this campaign directly into the Oval Office where, in the spring of 2017, according to the *New York Times*, he faced off with then secretary of state Rex Tillerson, who argued that the release was improper and inappropriate. The president, pointedly not siding with his secretary of state, told the two men—one a high official in his administration, the other having no official role at all—to work it out for themselves. In another instance, pursuing a longtime Erdoğan campaign, Giuliani lobbied the president to eject the Turkish cleric and Erdoğan enemy Fethullah Gülen, a permanent U.S. resident, from the country and return him to Turkey for prosecution (and, not unlikely, a death sentence).

Rudy may not have made the grade to secretary of state, but Trump was always seeking his true comfort level: Rudy, despite whatever interests he was pursuing, and by whatever back channels, for whatever reasons, spoke Trump's language. To an uncommon degree, Rudy, a paid representative of foreign governments and related entities, was also among the president's key intelligence sources and an effective operative of the U.S. government. He may not have gained the status he sought, but he was holding tight to the proximity he had earned. And he had accomplished one other thing: he was out of the house almost constantly, free of Judi.

In the summer of 2017, at a gathering at their Southampton house— one of the many houses he had acquired since leaving the mayor's office— "his right leg gave way on the first day of his vacation on Long Island," according to the *New York Post*.

Or, reported Bannon, "Rudy got thrown out of the house—literally," a cause of great gossip and satisfaction in the West Wing.

An already unsteady Giuliani could now hardly get around on his own, quickly putting on more weight as he recuperated.

* * *

On May 9, 2017, in a move agreed upon by no one, and managed only by himself, the president fired James Comey. The director of the FBI had been under the president's skin. Trump's ire had been fueled by reports from Giuliani, who had styled himself as an inside source at the Justice Department (even though he had not worked there for more than thirty years), about Comey's disloyalty.

On May 17, Robert Mueller, former FBI director and a longtime veteran of the Justice Department—overlapping with Giuliani's career at the DOJ—was appointed special prosecutor.

Within the West Wing there was little agreement on how to handle the legal and political crisis of facing a special prosecutor. Many among the senior staff, wary of finding themselves involved in potential cover-up activities, wanted to distance themselves from the investigation. The more you took an interest, the more your own exposure and the more your personal legal bills rose. Bannon argued for a Chinese wall, with a team of outside lawyers, high-powered Washington litigators, brought in to take over all special prosecutor–related matters, hence keeping the senior staff's hands clean and keeping Trump as far away as possible from the mess. Bannon sought to professionalize the response, noting the importance of keeping the president's cronies, Giuliani foremost among them, out of the process.

But one major law firm after another turned down the business. By the summer, a team of three lawyers, John Dowd, Ty Cobb, and Jay Sekulow, were installed as the president's team. None had the backing of a major firm, and Dowd and Cobb were already in quasi-retired late-career mode.

Giuliani, again rebuffed, again determined to soldier through the rebuff, became, even greater than before, a West Wing irritant and provocateur. The effort to keep the president at a personal remove from the investigation and from the White House defense was undermined not just by the president's own worst instincts but by Giuliani's calls with advice, gossip, and suggestions of anti-Trump conspiracies—after all, he knew the DOJ; and, he said darkly, he knew Robert Mueller. The very system and institutions that had taught him and propelled his career now became the enemy that with his special knowledge and talents he could undermine.

The president's daughter and son-in-law were, to Bannon, the chief culprits in fueling the president's worst instincts, but they were followed closely by Giuliani. Reince Priebus, chief of staff, regarded Giuliani as a West Wing Whac-A-Mole. Every time he thought he had blocked Giuliani's influence—it would be hard to exaggerate the ever-increasing scorn Trump's West Wing had for Giuliani—he found him back again.

At the same time that a Keystone Cops legal defense of the president was coming together, the West Wing itself was blowing up. On July 21, the eleven-day farce of Anthony Scaramucci began. He was hired by the president's daughter and son-in-law as White House communications director, superseding all other senior staff and reporting to the president. Scaramucci's tenure ended almost immediately in an on-the-record rant about other staffers. Simultaneously, Scaramucci's appointment led to the exit of Priebus and press secretary Sean Spicer, with Bannon's fate in high limbo.

The only saving grace seemed to be that Rudy, too, by early August, was out of commission—in bed after his fall.

But for Rudy, with the exit of Bannon in mid-August—just as Giuliani was undergoing knee surgery—one more roadblock that had kept him from the president had fallen, and, with undaunted determination, he spent much of his time in his sickbed in August and September trying to get Trump's attention.

To say that the defense of the president was not going well would be a risible understatement. The president's raging insistence on his innocence, or on what he saw as the perfectly reasonable justifications for his actions, together with his demands that the investigation be closed down and Mueller fired, had led Dowd and Cobb to the only way possible to steady their client's tantrums—that is, to assure him that he had nothing to worry about. He was innocent and all would be well, and, hence, practically speaking, he needed no defense. If later the White House would become a black box, offering up nothing, now it was utterly transparent, with carloads of documents daily departing from the West Wing to the Special Counsel's Office.

Bannon, now outside the White House, sounded the alarm against the almost blind dump of White House papers, and argued for a new legal team.

Rudy added to this—directly into the president's ear—darker admonishments. He knew who Mueller was talking to. Rudy's obsession with the Steele dossier—that collection of reports from Russia that put Trump in the presidential suite at Moscow's Ritz-Carlton Hotel watching hookers give a golden shower to the bed where Obama once slept, which had leaked shortly before Trump's inauguration—was as great as the president's.

This was a political war and not a legal war, Rudy kept repeating. The president didn't need lawyers, or he needed a lawyer who could fight for him outside of the legal process. Someone who could go mano a mano with Mueller. To the president, Rudy, barely ambulatory himself—on the way to senility, in Bannon's description—brought reports of Mueller's physical and mental weakness. Stand up to him and he would fold, Rudy assured the president. He knew his man Mueller. And Rudy knew his man Trump, and what he wanted to hear—confrontation, balls out, hit 'em again.

All of this, his catering to Trump's worst impulses, Rudy's own physical and mental weaknesses, his constant, off-the-books communications, his conspiracy pandering, made him the one person the more cautious and responsible elements of the White House—especially the White House counsel Don McGahn and the new chief of staff, retired general John Kelly—tried to keep out.

A search for a new legal team began in the fall of 2017 extending into the new year. Again, the White House went down the list of prestige law firms and litigators. But executive committees at blue-chip firms quickly slammed the door (they were afraid of a revolt by junior staffers, Trump not paying his bills, and Trump firing them ignominiously). Trump, anyway, did not want a faceless firm. Trump wanted a star; he wanted lawyers who could defend him on television. He tried to get Alan Dershowitz, the celebrity defender, retired Harvard professor, and TV gadfly; then he almost hired the husband-and-wife TV lawyer team Joe diGenova and Victoria Toensing, but they turned out to have a conflict. Other lawyers came through the Oval Office, but they wanted assurances from the prospective client that *they* would be running legal strategy and not him—they didn't get it. In the end, there was, comfortable for the president, only Giuliani—who, helping matters, would work for free.

It is a measure of how important this was to Giuliani that, when his firm Greenberg Traurig ruled against taking the president as a client, he walked away from the firm and his multimillion-dollar draw. In Giuliani's not incorrect view this back door into the Trump White House was opening directly into the Oval Office.

On April 19, 2018, Giuliani formally took on his pro bono client Donald Trump. Trump told people Giuliani was crying on the phone for the job; Giuliani told friends Trump begged him to take it.

6. The President's Lawyer

It is a certain pinnacle for a lawyer, a bid for professional immortality, to represent the president of the United States. It is the ultimate professional responsibility and demonstration of craft—navigating complex and often arcane civil, criminal, and constitutional issues, managing litigation strategy, and facing off against the best lawyers of the day. And, even in the most contentious situations, it affords you the ability to rise, at least modestly, above partisanship. Nixon's lawyers became the honest brokers between the president and the good of the nation.

In fact, it had been almost thirty years since Giuliani had seriously practiced law. Even in his position at Greenberg Traurig, he had few, if any, actual lawyering and certainly no litigation responsibilities. At the firm, Rudy was the "door opener," and Marc Mukasey—the son of his old friend Michael Mukasey, a federal judge and George W. Bush's last attorney general—was the actual lawyer.

That was the original proposal to the president. Rudy would be Rudy and Mukasey would supply the legal work. But, with Greenberg Traurig cutting him off, it was suddenly just Rudy, a lawyer without any practical legal wherewithal or support.

This detail did not bother Trump. The kind of lawyer Trump wanted was pure attack dog. Through his long, contentious, and litigious career, Trump had learned that those attacks happen most effectively and efficiently outside of court. Their purpose was to intimidate, confuse, and exhaust the other side. The legal system fought one way, Trump another.

In fact, Giuliani as a prosecutor had often used similar tactics, prosecuting the mob and insider traders as much through the press as in a courtroom.

Here, against the special prosecutor, it was to be an asymmetrical war. Robert Mueller, famously straitlaced and by the book, was ever endeavoring to reinforce the legitimacy of the investigation with a scrupulous, fair-minded, and confidential approach, far removed from the headlines. The Trump side, after months of cooperation—for him, fruitless cooperation, Trump had decided—was now seeking to delegitimize Mueller's investigation by public attacks on its purpose, bias, process, and competence.

Hardly anybody thought Rudy was up to it. Beyond his atrophied legal skills, the seventy-four-year-old, given his weight and his knee injury, could barely rise from a chair or get out of a car. There was the belief among many that, at best, his intellectual prowess had sorely dimmed. He was, as he told Bannon, and as most believed, too old to go back to practicing law. What's more—not to put too fine a point on it—he was often drunk.

"Oh my god," said Bannon, after the president hired Giuliani. "Oh my fucking god."

Donald McGahn, the White House counsel, used his signature putdown of White House behavior, adopted from Taylor Swift, about Giuliani, "This is why we can't have nice things" ("because you break them").

Chief of Staff John Kelly told people, echoing John Dean's assessment of Watergate, that Rudy Giuliani was a "cancer on the presidency."

Even within the closest Trump circle, including his daughter and son-in-law, there was, as much as any other Trumpian twist had produced, incredulity.

Almost simultaneously with his new appointment as the president's lawyer, his marriage formally broke up. This was accompanied by a new affair—with a hospital administrator, fifty-three-year-old Maria Ryan. In standard Giuliani style these were tabloid domestic developments. Little effort to hide but, yet, repeated denials, then a half admission—he was "in effect separated," he said, when this new relationship began—and a public rebuke from his wife. "My husband's denial of the affair with the married Mrs. Ryan is as false as his claim that we were separated when he took up with her."

The president, on his part, seemed undisturbed, telling one friend: "Judi was bringing him down. Not a good person. Didn't like me."

Giuliani moved his base of operations—largely a one-man operation—to the Trump International Hotel in Washington, becoming a reliable presence in the sprawling lobby lounge, a decorative feature almost, Rudy on his cell phone. His defense of the president was conducted almost entirely on television, most of it in the Fox News studios, eight minutes from the Trump International.

Over a generation, Fox, led by Giuliani and Trump's friend Ailes, had reshaped American politics and most dramatically the Republican Party.

But now, post-Ailes, it had become wholly a Trump outlet. The Trump channel that Ailes, Giuliani, and Trump had once imagined had, in effect, come into existence. (Trump often groused that he was not getting any cut of its success.) Its three evening anchors had direct access to Trump and he to them. Sean Hannity, the nine p.m. anchor, many in the White House believed, was among Trump's most important advisers. Now Fox became the main tool in Giuliani's singular campaign to disrupt, annoy, spook, confuse, bully, hector, and steamroll the Mueller team and Mueller himself.

No matter how harebrained and contrary to reason and out of the ordinary legal norms Giuliani's views might be, he could air them unchallenged on Fox. Having said it on one network, even if that network was Fox, it became somehow, however peculiar his view, an official position other networks had to give reasonable airtime to.

Giuliani's pitch, not by any stretch a legal argument, was a kind of parallel universe defense. There were no limitations, Giuliani argued, on what the president could do in the course of carrying out his duties.

Giuliani, curiously, was the exact opposite of a relativist seize-any-argument defense attorney. He was, or at least had been, a literal, zero-tolerance, law-and-order man, making his new contortions sound all the more feverish and baffling.

Of the many odd turns and plot digressions in the Trump presidency, one that particularly flabbergasted even the most jaded in the administration was Giuliani's television performance in the weeks after he took over the president's defense. The sense that so many around the president had so often experienced, that the Trump train was hitting the wall—the inevitable, spectacular crack-up finally arrived at—was in full force once again. White House staffers stood around and watched Rudy function entirely on his own, part of no one else's strategy, accountable to no one except the president, whose own idea of strategy conformed to nobody else's. In what seemed like an unglued spiral of digression, free association, conspiracy mongering, weird moments in which he appeared to be speaking to himself, he often, also, seemed to casually sacrifice the president's interests. Theoretically hired to defend the president in an investigation of his connection to Russian interests, Giuliani ranged far and wide over the Trump landscape. He would win the Nobel Peace Prize for his work in North

Korea. Hillary Clinton was the real villain. "I'm sorry, Hillary," he said addressing her directly from the Fox TV show *Hannity*. "I know you're very disappointed you didn't win, but you're a criminal." Stormy Daniels? No way the president had an affair with her. And even if he had, what of it? He had paid her out of personal funds!

Bannon, for one, believed that all of Giuliani's television appearances were in an alcoholic haze, upbraiding Hannity for letting a drunken Giuliani on the air.

The president, too, seemed alarmed. "He looks like a mental patient," declared Trump after one Giuliani television appearance.

It was a curious aspect of Giuliani's work as the president's "personal lawyer," a title that he took on as a kind of passport of entitlement, influence, and even omniscience—he, more than anyone, was privy to the president's thinking—that he really did no legal work. Most of the actual interactions with Mueller and his team were conducted through the White House counsel's office or through Jay Sekulow, also a "personal" attorney, or through several other lower-profile attorneys doing specific work related to defending the president in the investigation. But little of the actual dealings with the Special Counsel's Office—document requests, discussions about procedural matters, negotiations related to testimony of aides, the extended back-and-forth related to the president's own possible appearance before the committee, and the White House's shifting position on executive privilege—were handled by Giuliani.

And yet he was the public author—often improvising it from TV hit to TV hit—of the president's defense.

Mostly, no one in the president's inner circle even spoke to Giuliani. John Kelly, at pains to regulate Giuliani's conversations with the president, went out of his way to stay far away from conversations with Giuliani. This was both because it was unclear what Giuliani and Trump might, together, be plotting, and ill-advised to find yourself party to that, and because Giuliani was trying to involve himself in an ever-widening portfolio of White House concerns.

Giuliani, to everyone's mounting horror as his weird television performances continued, became the ultimate free agent in the White House. Not only did he have Trump's ear but no one knew what they were saying to each other.

John Kelly, Don McGahn, the president's daughter and son-in-law, and Senate majority leader Mitch McConnell all suggested to the president that he ought to seriously rein in Giuliani if not put minders around him. And what they really meant was that he should be fired immediately.

And yet, by early summer, after Giuliani's television blitz, and following the late-winter and spring belief that Mueller was a juggernaut, polls began to suddenly show new doubts about the investigation and the special prosecutor. For one thing, the investigation had already gone on for a year with apparently no end in sight, and for another it was conducting its business with a secrecy that both lent it a dark, deep state air and, as well, prevented it from making its case. But also, and perhaps not least of all, the juggernaut was suddenly confronted by a strange heat-seeking missile zigzagging toward it. America's mayor, speaking faster than anyone could understand, nearly screaming with righteousness, if not coherence, clouding the arguments with innuendo, conspiracies, and irrelevancies, and advancing, with eye-bulging intensity, legal theories that not only tickled the president but proposed giving him something like unlimited power, became a one-man disruption of norms and assumptions. He was a personal Reichstag fire. The fact that the special prosecutor, his office sworn to do its business confidentially, would not confront or even raise a public eyebrow at Giuliani's incessant balderdash gave the balderdash stand-alone currency.

Here was an asymmetric attack forcefully asserting with bewildering if not unhinged antics a parallel legal reality. Mueller and company did not seem to have the vaguest idea how to answer it.

Did Rudy know what he was doing? Or was he merely a drunk who managed to clear the room because nobody wanted to confront him?

Likely, as Bannon insisted to wide amusement within the Trump circle, Rudy was in the "mumble tank." But, at the same time, Rudy had always been, throughout his career, a great gossip. And the Justice Department, where Rudy, even after thirty years, still had sources, was among the juiciest gossip networks. Knowing what the Justice Department would do, knowing its thinking, knowing how its various personalities might tilt, was an ultimate currency in federal litigation circles. This was as good as, even better perhaps than, actual legal abilities.

What Rudy had fastened onto was a view that Robert Mueller didn't really have the taste for this fight. "He's gotten to be an old man," Rudy reported to various people, including the president, who, in turn, repeated this (older men seemed to take particular pleasure in identifying those who seemed like even older men). Giuliani heard about internal efforts within the special prosecutor's team to go after the president in novel and disruptive ways—including the possibility of indicting the president—and that this was all shot down by Mueller. Mueller, Rudy understood, was out-and-out afraid of Trump, afraid that Trump would take some destructive action, afraid that Trump was a crazy man who might be provoked in terrible and unpredictable ways. Rudy had a private rant, which he shared widely, likely in the hope that it wouldn't be too private, that Trump would fuck everybody, that he would take everybody down, that he was ready to fire Mueller, close it down, burn it all, let them try to impeach him. Let them try to rip him out of the White House. Giuliani and Trump, coming from diametrically different legal perspectives—Trump ever trying to get away with it, Giuliani the career prosecutor—shared a view about litigation: aggression nearly always paid off.

7. The Freelancer

Representing the president was only Rudy's part-time job. His other job was the pursuit of highly profitable business relationships in largely dodgy corners of the world that benefited from, or in some cases depended on, his relationship with the president.

To be clear: the president's personal lawyer was soliciting questionable people and entities abroad, both private and state-connected, who had business before the U.S. government and was doing this by highlighting his influence with the president if not directly promising to use it.

The question is only: Why would you pursue something so obviously troubling by any conventional standards, and, even in the realm of the highest speciousness, how could you possibly justify it—or hope to get away with it?

And, to boot, everyone was aware that this was going on.

Giuliani took the dare-to-challenge-me position that he was neither a lobbyist nor a business agent, but a lawyer representing clients on narrow legal issues or merely offering free advice to friends and acquaintances.

This was, to all, audacity of a kind permissible only because the president, apparently as aware as anyone of what Giuliani was up to, seemed to accept and tolerate it. But the highest reaches of the executive branch during the 2018 period—Chief of Staff John Kelly, Secretary of State Rex Tillerson, National Security Adviser John Bolton, Secretary of Defense James Mattis, White House Counsel Don McGahn—were all confounded, appalled, and personally worried that any interaction with Giuliani might tie them to god knows what private agenda, or, worse, an off-the-books plan, a trade-in-kind arrangement, that combined Giuliani's unsavory interests with the president's unsavory interests.

As the Trump administration was threatened on a daily basis by a criminal investigation involving the dealings of the president and his campaign with foreign interests, the man representing the president in that investigation was engaged in an array of discussions and arrangements with similar foreign interests. The convergence here of so many points of self-interest, indefensible practices, and high-risk behavior was so bold and extreme that it seemed to all, except Giuliani and the president, a countdown to destruction. But, given the boldness, disregard, and determination with which Rudy conducted his foreign escapades, ever in plain sight, no one seemed quite to have the language, or recourse, or any official higher legal or moral backing to call him out. His behavior was so flagrant that, if he wasn't already hoisted by it, it could only mean there was a new standard of behavior.

He was an adviser to Qatar on cybersecurity (Giuliani himself rarely used a computer and had only rudimentary digital knowledge and even awareness). Qatar, in a tense relationship with the UAE and Saudi Arabia, was engaged in a long push-pull over support from the United States. By late 2018, Giuliani was lobbying the president to name a personal ally as the U.S. ambassador to Qatar. He continued his longtime business relationship with Turkey and with people close to its autocrat president, positioning himself in the ongoing negotiations between Turkey and the United States. He added clients in Venezuela, Romania, and Ukraine—each with direct or indirect state interests.

And during this period Giuliani was "hired" by the two comic-book-like characters, Lev Parnas, a Ukrainian-born émigré, and Igor Fruman, a Belarusian. Beginning in the 2016 campaign, Parnas and Fruman—without clear professional bona fides, except their connection to Dmytro Firtash, a Ukrainian gas tycoon facing bribery charges in the United States, and accusations by the feds of having ties to Russian organized crime—had worked to insinuate themselves into the Trump orbit. Without prior Republican Party interests, one of them delivered a $50,000 donation to Trump and the RNC directly after the *Access Hollywood* episode. They billed themselves as Rudy "friends," "associates," and "partners." The duo, pursued by creditors, and with various failed business ventures in their wake, dined with the president, befriended his son Don Jr., splurged at Trump hotels in New York and Washington, got invitations to Mar-a-Lago, and arranged contributions totaling $630,000 to a Trump super PAC and to other Republican candidates (a federal indictment would subsequently claim this was all part of a scheme to use foreign money to "buy potential influence with candidates, campaigns, and the candidates' governments").

Again, there was nothing hidden here. Giuliani seemed to revel in his role as fixer, macher, the president's intimate, and ultimate cynical operator—and to understand that, having become the face of the president's Mueller defense, he had wide latitude to imply whatever he wanted about the breadth of the influence and portfolio he had with his client. "When you talk to me, you're talking to him," Giuliani had taken to saying, in tough-guy style. For many in the White House, the unanswered question, given the many dealmakers and hustlers always at work in Washington, given that this behavior had vastly expanded in Trump's Washington, given the president and his family's open efforts at personal benefit, was: What was too much? Many thought too much was Rudy Giuliani.

And then it got even more extreme.

By early 2019, virtually all of the upper echelon of Trump aides aghast at Giuliani's behavior, and putting some brakes on it, had washed out of government: Tillerson, Kelly, Mattis, McGahn, Sessions, and, within a few months, Bolton. In each case, they were replaced by factotums who understood that their chief function, in many cases only function, was to accommodate the president. This included Mike Pompeo at State, Mick Mulvaney, the acting chief of staff, Pat Cipollone, who had replaced McGahn in the White House counsel's office, and Bill Barr, the new attorney general, who all understood that Rudy had come to occupy a unique place in the Trump ecosystem that they needed to accept.

In mid-April 2019, Robert Mueller completed his investigation and delivered his report to the attorney general. Mueller carefully sought to avoid a direct confrontation, just as Giuliani had assured the president he would. The report's equivocal, convoluted, meandering, and finely rationalized conclusions, however damning, gave Barr the wherewithal to declare an effective exoneration. Next only to Trump, Giuliani, the harebrained, quixotic, crazy-man defender of the president, was the winner.

He was certainly not about to go home. Nor did a satisfied Trump seem inclined to let him.

8. Ukraine

Days after Trump escaped charges of collusion with a foreign government to aid his election efforts, he was back trying to collude with Ukraine, a foreign government particularly susceptible to an advantageous transaction, to aid his reelection efforts—using Giuliani as his primary go-between.

In fact, it is not at all clear who was driving this effort most or who would benefit most. Giuliani seemed to have two agendas that dovetailed nicely in the Ukraine. He wanted to maintain and build on his usefulness and closeness to the president and he wanted to use the influence he had with the president to aid his own interests. The president, for his part, was uniquely susceptible to any encouragement to avoid, sidestep, or subvert accepted procedures and best practices and seemed ever willing to seize an advantage no matter how small or irregular. Both men wanted what they wanted and seemed, given both their temperaments and their recent successes, to be incapable of listening to advice, moral, practical, cautionary, or otherwise.

The president's desires would become the subject of an extensive congressional probe and the reason for his impeachment. But they were simple on their face: he wanted the Ukrainians to help him diss Joe Biden, who he feared would be the strongest candidate against him in the 2020 race. To get this help, he was willing to use the weight of the White House, both carrots and sticks, dangling Oval Office visits and withholding aid—*hondling* as he had for most of his life, for any benefit he could get. This was, as most congressional Republicans would conclude with something of a shrug, Trumpian. As inappropriate as it might be, it was, they seemed to agree, no more than what might be expected from a man who was both uninterested in and incapable of learning the customs, rules, and good manners of governing. Whatever came out of Trump's mouth, whatever else he might seem to be saying, was, just as likely, meaningless gas. Don't hold him responsible.

Many Republicans even began to see Trump as Giuliani's dupe or puppet—it wasn't Trump's mess, it was Giuliani's.

Hardly anyone was clear on just what Giuliani was doing and why—except, obviously, managing and maximizing his conflicts of interest, and, while the getting was good, grabbing what he could, settling the scores that needed to be settled, and showing that he was the go-to man he wanted to be seen to be.

To untangle one thread:

In 2008, Giuliani was introduced to a Ukrainian prizefighter named Vitali Klitschko. Trump insiders believe the introduction probably came through Paul Manafort, the former political consultant and then lobbyist, who would become Trump's campaign manager in 2016 and whose business relationships in Ukraine would send him to jail in 2017.

Klitschko, allied with a variety of Russia-partial business and political interests in Ukraine, hired Giuliani to help him run for mayor of Kyiv. He lost the race but Klitschko remained in contact with Giuliani, providing him with further Ukrainian business and political introductions. In 2014, Klitschko won the mayor's race and was additionally appointed to the far more powerful position as the head of Kyiv's city-state administration, giving him nearly unchecked authority over a two-billion-dollar-a-year budget and making him a significant power center in the country. The appointment was made by then Ukraine president Petro O. Poroshenko. Formally the minister of foreign affairs and then the minister of trade and economic development in 2012, Poroshenko was a close Giuliani and Manafort contact. Both Klitschko and Poroshenko represented, to say the least, a nexus of what the *New York Times* called "the murky and lucrative world of Ukrainian municipal politics."

The Ukraine comedian Volodymyr Zelensky would regularly lampoon Klitschko on his popular television show as a moron, a boxer without a coherent thought, and as part of Ukraine's hopelessly corrupt governing class.

Then, in 2019, that same comedian was himself elected president, casting out Poroshenko, and, theoretically, Klitschko with him. Zelensky was also set to terminate Klitschko's appointment as Kyiv's financial administrator with control over building, transportation, and the funds for most other city operations. But Klitschko, in a bid to hold on to his job, went to New York to meet with Giuliani.

The new Zelensky government called a news conference to publicly brand Klitschko as corrupt and to accuse Klitschko of offering the Zelensky government bribes to keep him in office.

Klitschko then posted pictures of Giuliani and him together on Facebook, with an official-sounding statement about cooperation between the United States and Ukraine. On August 2, 2019, two days after the Zelensky government's public condemnation of Klitschko, Giuliani, accompanied by Lev Parnas, in a meeting that would become central to the impeachment case against the president, met in Madrid with a senior Zelensky official, Andriy Yermak. During this meeting, Giuliani connected President Zelensky's efforts to arrange an Oval Office meeting with President Trump with Zelensky's willingness to investigate Joe Biden and his son and the conspiracy theory about Ukraine's efforts to hurt Trump's 2016 campaign. And Giuliani brought up Klitschko, offering a personal assurance as to his honesty and rectitude.

Giuliani insisted later that he was speaking wholly in a personal capacity. Yermak, on his part, insisted that there was no effort here to influence him.

On September 4, the Zelensky government voted to fire Klitschko.

On September 6, Giuliani in a tweet challenged the government's actions and attested that "the former champion is very much admired and respected in the U.S."

Five months later, Klitschko was still in control of Kyiv's $2 billion purse.

And another string:

Lev Parnas and Igor Fruman, without experience in the energy business, had, in 2018, set up a company to sell U.S. natural gas in the Ukraine—with Giuliani as their consultant (or "associate" or "partner" or "friend," depending on whom they were talking to). The deal, however, needed more accommodating leadership at the Ukrainian state oil and gas giant

Naftogaz. But such a corporate shift was apparently being frustrated by the U.S. ambassador Marie Yovanovitch, who was directing the U.S. efforts against Ukraine's endemic corruption. Yovanovitch was also pushing to oust Ukraine's top prosecutor Yuriy Lutsenko, the key figure helping Rudy in his efforts, on Trump's behalf, to get the Ukrainians to investigate Biden's son Hunter for his work on the board of Burisma, a Ukraine oil company. At the same time, according to the *Washington Post*, Rudy was negotiating with Lutsenko for a large fee to represent the prosecutor's office in its efforts to recover what the prosecutor claimed were misappropriated funds. Getting rid of Yovanovitch, who was recalled by the U.S. State Department in April and fired in May, was good for the president, who wanted Ukraine to help him smear the Bidens, and good for Rudy, who wanted both to please the president and to prevail in his efforts to support the people who were supporting him in Ukraine. It was just business. And politics. And Rudy. And Trump. It was built into expectations. Shocked. Shocked.

9. Legacy

Ken Frydman was a young journalist who went to work for Rudy in 1993 as press secretary in his second mayoral campaign—and who would be married by Giuliani on the steps of city hall. Frydman's career in media and city government has been almost entirely spent in the thriving metropolis that he, and many others, would argue Giuliani was instrumental in making. For a generation, through his and the Bloomberg administration, Giuliani's right-of-center coalition helped transform New York into a crime-free magnet for the ambitious and the enterprising—the finance, media, art, culture, and entrepreneurial capital. The true capital of the world. Many people would argue about the fairness with which this success was spread; many could argue about how often Giuliani's mercurial impulses seemed to have threatened this success. But the remade New York could not be separated from Giuliani's drive, dominance, and, no doubt, luck. Few politicians get such a legacy.

When Giuliani took Trump on as his client in early 2018, Frydman sat down and wrote a column for the *Daily News* marveling that Rudy's hard-ball tactics, his "guts and conviction," might actually help save the unmanageable president. Less than a year and a half later, after observing the extraordinary spectacle of Giuliani's bizarre, say-anything, television defense of the president, and taking it as a personal affront, Frydman wrote a new column questioning Giuliani's integrity and mental state, and accusing him of a grim and bitter cynicism. "What do I care?" said Giuliani responding to a question about how he might be undermining his legacy in New York City. "I'll be dead."

For periods of 2018 and 2019, even Trump seemed to be the contrast gainer insofar as reasonableness, orderliness, and probity were concerned when compared to Giuliani. There literally might not be anyone from Giuliani's city hall and New York political circles who did not now regard Rudy as a Martian being. All in the White House, sometimes including the president, found him ridiculous, noisome, and dangerous. The foreign policy principals, the intelligence agency chiefs, and the DOJ leadership regarded him with anger and contempt. Among the main themes of the testimony before the House of Representatives during the impeachment of the president was Giuliani's constant, baffling, anomalous, and threatening presence at almost every stage of the White House's Ukrainian intrigue. A one-man hand grenade, in the description of former national security adviser John Bolton. The Republican Party and the congressional leadership seemed, with great relief, to take the opportunity in the defense of the president to cast Giuliani as both a rogue player and an irrelevant one—whatever Rudy did was on Rudy, and it wasn't important anyway. Nobody wanted to claim him. Instead of being the smoking gun that tied the president to the mess, Rudy's presence at the center of the story somehow explained it all away as just something reasonable men should not take seriously. It was just Rudy—finger circling at the temple.

And it didn't seem to bother him.

He had become a pariah to those who had once respected him and, as well, to virtually every significant player in the administration and in the highest Republican circles. And some believed he was increasingly losing the support of his singular backer—the president. But Rudy, perhaps understanding Trump better, believed that usefulness was all that counted for the president—and who had been more useful?

10. The Ailes Diagnosis

Roger Ailes, after a lifetime in close association with so many of the pivotal political figures of the last fifty years, judged many of them, in their vast hunger for attention and appreciation, to be crazy. (As a not incidental corollary, Ailes's boss Rupert Murdoch, taking stock of Ailes's own need for attention and appreciation, judged him to be crazy.) Defining an order of hubris, Ailes theorized that the craziness of politicians often ran in direct proportion to their political success, until it spiked into self-destruction. One of the useful things about the establishment and the system—which otherwise Ailes had deeply ambivalent feelings about—is that it kept a lid on the natural messiness of most politician's lives and inclinations. "Seventy-five percent are manic depressives," diagnosed Ailes. "They gravitate toward public life not just because it satisfies their craving for attention and because it ameliorates their loneliness, but because living in public exerts a certain control on them. Out from under a constant watchful eye they would show themselves to be uniquely susceptible to every human weakness—slough, greed, envy."

Ailes's theory reasonably prompted the question about what would happen if the watchful public eye ceased to take much critical notice anymore, saw so much that it became inured, began to adopt the same values as the media eye: it was all passing spectacle; the more attention it commanded, the more attention it was worthy of.

For thirty years Rudy Giuliani had tested the tolerance of the public eye. He seemed to bargain with it. Determination, work ethic, energy, balanced with what sometimes seemed like an overwhelming and helpless desire to act out, scream "fuck you," and to shit all over the dreams he had worked so hard to realize. And, indeed, in that balance, the public eye was tolerant—but not that tolerant. Seeing him clearly in the years after 9/11, it effectively retired the angry, sloppy, moneygrubbing, drunken former mayor, well before he wanted to be retired.

But then the public eye, confused by the hallucinogenic Trump spectacle, a daily perceptual imperialism on the part of the preposterous president, seemed no longer to believe what it was seeing, or to conclude that its own sense of ritual and propriety was irrelevant in the real world. All was now allowed. Rudy, dedicated only to his own survival and centrality, seemed clearly to understand that Trump's idea of loyalty was suicide-mission-level stuff. To serve Trump, your performance had to be even more extreme than even he might have dreamed of. But at the same time, it also seemed that Rudy was taking permission to be a Rudy who was more Rudy than even he had ever dared to be.

Epilogue: Southern District

Rudy hands in New York wondered among themselves to what extent he might be able to grasp what he had become. And not just the crazy one-man show. But that he was now, after the impeachment, no longer at the center of the Trump show—did he get that? Likely he was not one of the many who gained some self-knowledge by being discarded by Trump. Did he even know that he had been discarded? Was he aware how obvious this was—no longer on television, now struggling to be heard as a podcaster? Did he know, did he have any inkling, that he had come—in a way that had nothing to do with Trump and everything to do with his own pathos— once again to the end of the road?

As the impeachment proceeding in the House of Representatives came to its inevitable conclusion at the end of 2019, one former close Giuliani associate went to the annual Christmas party for the Southern District of New York. The associate had been an SDNY prosecutor under Giuliani. Now, and for many years, on the sidelines of Giuliani's wayfaring, he nevertheless found himself at the center of attention with SDNY alumni and current prosecutors all eager to fathom how Rudy had come to this point, some even darkly hinting that a career that had begun in the Southern District would end there as well. "They think he's a lunatic. What should I say to these people?" he asked another Rudy hand who, likewise, was struggling to understand what had happened to the mayor.

"I just say he's left the jurisdiction," said the other Rudy hand—the jurisdiction here being that of logic and reason. "It's like *Raging Bull*. He used to be middleweight champion of the world, but at the end Jake LaMotta's locked in his prison cell with his potbelly, banging his head against the wall."

The Strange Life of Steve Bannon

SEPTEMBER 2020

C an you be both a believer and a cynic?

The first time, at least in my recollection, that I met Steve Bannon—the architect of the 2016 Trump victory and self-appointed channel to the Leviathan monster of white rage—was in the Orlando Airport in February or March 2016, Trump still a risible notion.

I was on my way to give a speech to what group I don't remember, pulling my wheelie bag across the terminal concourse. At perhaps forty feet, a large, shambly, red-faced man with an expressive face and lit-up eyes was stopped in his tracks, staring at me with surprise, and then suddenly hailing me with enthusiasm, even pleasure. *We must obviously know each other, somehow, from somewhere,* I thought, while also drawing an alarming blank. There followed brief chitchat, kind words from him about some recent columns that I'd written, and mutual marveling at our chance meeting at such an unlikely crossroads. I assumed the missing pieces would come to me and I would shortly be able to put a name and prior acquaintance to a face. In fact, nothing came. Then, some weeks later, I happened to see a picture of the man who was running Breitbart News, the right-wing news site generating regular controversy and fabulous amounts of user traffic.

Him!

This, however, shed little light on why Bannon, the Breitbart CEO, would be embracing me, without a bone of right-wing sympathy in my body. (I subsequently learned it had something to do with the generally good relationship I had with the Fox News chief Roger Ailes and compliments he had paid me.) But, six months later, when, in a surprising and zany move, Bannon was appointed to run the failing Trump campaign, I thought, *Well, if he thinks we're buddies, why not?* In short order, we were exchanging e-mails and he was inviting me to Trump Tower.

Four years later, just as I was planning to meet Bannon for a Sunday cruise on the mega-yacht owned by his Chinese billionaire patron Miles Kwok, where he had been spending the COVID quarantine, he was arrested for defrauding contributors to a fundraising effort to privately erect a border wall.

I may not be the person who came to know Bannon best during this Trump period of history, for which he, as much as anyone, was responsible— I'm not sure *anyone* knows him much beyond their specific, compartmentalized use to him. But Bannon is a man who can't stop talking, and we logged hundreds of hours of conversation together in Trump Tower, the White House, the frat-style accommodations he occupied on Capitol Hill, the luxury suites he favored when he was in New York, during a trip to Europe we took together, and over dinners at my house in Greenwich Village.

The topics were fairly consistent: 1) The ludicrousness and insanity of Donald Trump and his family; 2) Trump's self-inflicted wounds and his destructiveness to the right-wing nationalistic cause; 3) Bannon's efforts to save Trump from himself and to save the cause at large; 4) the relative savvy or pathetic blundering of a wide range of powerful figures in politics and media; 5) his constantly picaresque overview of the absurdities, corruption, and inevitable collapse of modern political life; 6) China and the coming Armageddon; 7) the media and how to play it; 8) his autodidacticism on a series of evolving subjects (Lincoln; the popes and the coming collapse and bankruptcy of the Catholic Church; the cycles of history); 9) his personal philosophy.

Some of this was borderline nutty, but he rendered almost all of these topics at some high level of gossip and hilarity. The motor of his own voice, at maximum revolutions per second, and the turns of his own language— punctuations, exclamations, an uncanny confection of slacker and military usage, an originality of insults and near-perfect comic timing—held your absolute attention. If you are interested in performance, in character, in reverse-spinning in the world of spin, this was all irresistible. At the same time, all of this shed very little light on the central question and had the further effect of making you forget to ask it, of how someone like Steve Bannon, without clear skills, purpose, or provenance, had come to be at the center of American political life.

That, too, of course, is the basic question that needs to be answered about Donald Trump. But part of that answer is that Trump had been peculiarly facilitated by the rogues and promoters who found him to be their unique vehicle—perhaps none so much as Steve Bannon.

The Southern District of New York, that powerful entity of political righteousness and vendetta, and (maybe) instrument of deep state conspiracy, may now, with its indictment of Bannon and three other men for their fundraising scheme, be directly perusing this question. Theirs is probably not a bad approach: follow the money.

A central sell of the Trump candidacy was that Trump was already a rich man—the richest man to ever run for president—and hence money was of no concern to him. Naturally, the head of his campaign, and then the senior-most adviser in the White House, Steve Bannon, a former banker and entrepreneur, had considerable personal wealth, too (more than $40 million by some accounts).

Of course, for Trump, the exact opposite was true—money was among his primary, if not desperate, concerns. And, likewise, Bannon's professed lack of interest in a monied lifestyle probably had less to do with his populist beliefs than with his lack of ability to finance it.

A curious point in Bannon's personal professional history is that he was said to have ended up with valuable points in the mega-hit sitcom *Seinfeld*. This unlikely matchup—the white nationalist with the quintessential Jewish New York comedy—was meant to be the result of Bannon's work as producer, banker, and consultant in Hollywood. Bannon, the banker, theoretically received points for his part in the sale of Castle Rock Entertainment, the original *Seinfeld* production company. But I can't find anyone who was involved with Castle Rock who knows anything about this or who knows Bannon himself. When I've gingerly inquired about the specifics here, Bannon has explained his participation in terms of other entities who get paid, paying him down the line. Yes, possible, perhaps.

But I've seen the lifestyle. Before he took up his job at the White House, Bannon lived in a small row house on Capitol Hill, a property that he shared with Breitbart News—widely called the Breitbart Embassy. This was mostly the Breitbart office with a bedroom for Bannon. When he went to the White House, Bannon moved out of the Breitbart offices and into his own place, a one-bedroom apartment above a McDonald's in Arlington, Virginia, a graduate-student-style lodging (lots of books, no bookshelves).

During much of the 1990s, Bannon tried to find his way into mainstream movie production with only limited success. But, after 9/11 and with the increasing polarization in the country over the Iraq War, Bannon started to successfully produce low-budget conservative-oriented documentaries. Right-wing content had started to form a parallel media market—one separate from mainstream distribution. This was mostly centered around books, videos, and, increasingly, websites (the Drudge Report was the first big breakout; and, of course, Fox News was the ultimate demonstration of a vertical conservative audience). The books and videos were largely sold through direct-marketing channels, solicitations in conservative publications, and conservative mailing lists, which increasingly come to be facilitated by online targeting strategies. Conservatives turned out to be a uniquely responsive marketing niche. (Newsmax, a conservative news outlet, has done a robust side business in selling vitamins and nutritional supplements.) In other words, instead of marketing broadly to a book-buying or video-buying consumer base, you limited your marketing to people who identified themselves with right-wing causes and who have previously bought right-wing products.

This tracked as an efficient direct-to-consumer business channel, as, at the same time, it boosted conservative causes, hence increasing the conservative market. Indeed, the conservative movement was, in many ways, a direct-marketing movement. The rise of the Tea Party after the 2008 financial crisis was a function of direct marketing and, as well, helped expand the direct-marketing platform for conservative products—the list grew. Social media turbocharged the reach of direct-to-consumer conservative media. Bannon, already in the conservative product business, understood that Breitbart represented a perfect sort of vertical integration—media promoted more media; build a like-minded audience and sell more like-minded products to it. Breitbart was, Bannon told people, the next Fox News.

At the same time, nobody was really a businessman here. Or they didn't know if they were properly more businessmen or believers.

Andrew Breitbart, the Breitbart site's founder, was gifted with certain perceptions about the digital-media market and the conservative base and suddenly found himself running a high-growth business. But he wasn't much of a businessman. This was an opening for Bannon, who was nobody's idea of a disciplined, bean-counting business guy, either, but was a lot more so than Andrew Breitbart. So Bannon brought in new investment money and took over as the titular chairman—and became CEO after Andrew Breitbart's death in 2012.

Here was another aspect of the conservative business model. It is not just about business. The investment is also in belief. Robert Mercer, an oddball, far-right businessman billionaire, and his daughter Rebekah, had thrown in with Bannon in mutual Tea Party spirit—and funded his move into Breitbart.

Bannon was enjoying two financial streams. He had a direct-marketing business, selling products like *Clinton Cash* (books and videos) and building the Breitbart list—and renting it to other people. At the same time, he was taking money from the Mercers in the hope of building a right-wing movement.

For Bannon, this was a lucrative paycheck-to-paycheck situation, but there wasn't really any actual equity there (Breitbart, deficit-funded by the Mercers, wasn't strictly a profit-making business). Bannon, ever looking for a killing, hadn't found it. On the other hand, he was now becoming an ideological face, a political name in his own right.

This was confusing for Bannon; he'd never particularly imagined himself becoming a politician. Politics was his entrepreneurial platform. Sure, he was a believer, but more so he saw himself as a potential mogul.

Like any good mogul, he recognized that media was a bit of flimflam. He was amused by, and sometimes contemptuous of, people who took Breitbart News altogether seriously. For him, Breitbart, at least beyond the Mercers' ideological interests, was a purely commercial media enterprise—you spent as little as possible to attract as much traffic as possible. Within your budget, you did what was necessary to capture views, however hyperbolic and over-the-top and pandering you had to be. It was tabloid journalism. (No tabloid owner actually believes his tabloids.)

At the same time, of course, he needed to cater to the Mercers, stoking their belief in the coming right-wing revolution. Part of this effort was convincing them to support Donald Trump—conveniently, Trump, as tabloid character, consistently moved the Breitbart needle. Trump was the natural merger of right-wing ideology and right-wing marketing.

In promoting Trump, Bannon had teamed with David Bossie, another ideologue-slash-direct-marketing specialist. Bossie, occupying his own Capitol Hill business-residence row house, had spearheaded the Citizens United lawsuit that overturned campaign contribution limits. Bossie was an example of a particular Washington business model: identify a hot issue and solicit contributions to promote it and hire yourself as the director of the not-for-profit organization collecting the money.

Trump was a fantastic right-wing media product, not least of all because he was already hugely famous. Right-wing people were often not quite ready for prime time (like Bannon himself or Jeff Sessions, whom Bannon was promoting before Trump came along).

Bannon was still seeing his play as an integration of Breitbart and Trump enthusiasm into some media opportunity. Fox chief Roger Ailes was his model.

But then over the course of a few days, Bannon was transformed from hopeful entrepreneur to a central political player.

In August 2016, he read an article in the *New York Times* about the collapsing Trump campaign; he called the Mercers, worried that a landslide Trump defeat might damage Breitbart. The Mercers, political innocents but with a vast checkbook, immediately flew out to the Hamptons to meet Trump at a fundraiser to be held at the home of Woody Johnson, the Johnson & Johnson heir and New York Jets owner (whom Trump would subsequently appoint his ambassador to the Court of St. James's). Virtually no one showed up for the fundraiser, a humiliating moment for Trump, who, with the promise of a new influx of cash from the Mercers and desperate not to spend his own money, promptly agreed to make Bannon the head of his campaign.

This was not just without political or professional logic—tapping someone lacking any sort of campaign experience—but, more to the point, an effective admission from Trump that all was likely lost.

When, shortly thereafter, I took Bannon up on his invitation to come see him at Trump Tower, he outlined his pie-in-the-sky strategy. The path to victory would run through working-class white men in Florida,

Wisconsin, Michigan, and Pennsylvania—that's where the campaign would devote the bulk of its time and resources.

Later, Bannon would say that he had identified hidden Trump support from the online traffic patterns in these states (that Trump was a tested and exceptional target-market candidate)—but really, this was Hail Mary stuff.

* * *

And yet they won, quite a perplexing situation for Bannon. He was being handed the opportunity of a lifetime, except for having to work for Donald Trump and being paid only $179,000 a year (it's hard to be subsidized by rich patrons when you're in the White House).

I began to see Bannon regularly at this point. Here's what you couldn't miss about him: a truly profound disorganization for someone in a key administrative post. He couldn't schedule or delegate; he had an almost autistic level of unresponsiveness; when counted on, he invariably wouldn't show up.

What's more, he was utterly contemptuous of Trump and his family. Almost everyone in the White House would come to share this contempt, but Bannon's starts on day one.

To the extent that Trump, in the White House, was still acting like he was running the Trump Organization, Bannon was still acting like he was running Breitbart. He was trying to turn direct-marketing buzzword issues into policy, most reliably around immigration, which, in direct-marketing terms, always produced a high response rate.

It's a representative point that Bannon believed in the wall and he believed that Trump did not. Of course, Bannon didn't really believe in the wall, either—not its efficacy or practicality. But Bannon at least believed in the metaphor of the wall—it was an inspirational point: something can be done, globalism can be stymied, at least in one's imagination. Trump, on the other hand, was resentful when the subject even came up (he was particularly full of blame toward whoever had suggested to him that Mexico would pay for the wall, which it obviously would not).

Everything went quickly south for Bannon. He loathed Trump—even more so, he hated his entitled, know-nothing, obsequious-to-Trump, preening-to-everyone-else family. His legs were swelling, his skin molting, his rage building. Meanwhile, he was narrating, for almost anyone who would listen, tales of the imbecility, incompetence, grift, and coming catastrophe of the Trump administration.

He exited the White House almost a year to the day after he joined it. Partly because of his conversations with me, and my report of them, he was shunned by the White House and by the Mercers, hence losing his Breitbart platform to which he had hoped to return.

From this point on, I started to argue with him about the necessity to his own future of breaking with Trump—of publicly describing Trump's mendacity, stupidity, and corruption, about which, I knew, he could offer vivid chapter and verse. I argued that there would be a cascade of insider books and that his might be the first and most damning. I wasn't the only one making this case to him.

He didn't disagree—the facts of his true feelings were not at issue. But he demurred, saying he would know when the time was right.

He was, and you could see his mind at work, trying to triangulate a set of factors:

1) His own commitment to the populist-nationalist-White cause that, in part, he had conjured as much as a marketing scheme as a political program;
2) The extent to which his future depended on good standing with the far-right base;
3) The extent to which his relationship with the Far Right depended on his continued loyalty to Donald Trump;
4) The steps he could take to keep himself as a populist player but lessen his dependence on Trump;
5) His need to make a living.

He was having this discussion, or at least parts of this discussion, with a range of media, financial, and political people. This class of people— effectively the Establishment—was dealing with a similar set of issues: the current of rage in the nation (and the world); the power that an unstable and unfit man had derived from it; the extent to which this was giving him more power and a greater sense of impunity; and the dangers of crossing a crazy man. Bannon brought real experience to the table—and became sought-after for it.

The hardest truth might be that for Bannon his natural environment was far from the populist-nationalist-White cause. Rather, he was at home with hard-hearted, wealthy, world-beating players, whom his new notoriety now gave him easy access to. Power, its intricacies and insights, was different, and more interesting to him, than politics. To the extent that many of these powerful people were more liberal than conservative—in early 2018, he spent an enjoyable afternoon with former Clinton Treasury secretary and former Harvard president Larry Summers in Cambridge—he was perfectly comfortable.

More and more, he seemed to be consciously distancing himself from the Breitbart-centric populist-nationalist-White cause. He was now putting the emphasis on China: China was the culprit in destroying the manufacturing base that in turn fueled white working-class rage. On the China issue, he was conveniently able to bond with Miles Kwok, the billionaire Chinese dissident and fugitive now living in the United States, who became his new patron.

Still, and you sensed the difficult tug here, he couldn't entirely give up on the White right. After all, it was the one thing he knew how to reliably monetize. Indeed, he gave considerable thought to going back into the media business, looking at buying diminished "legacy" brands, including *Newsweek*, and turning them into a new phase of right-wing media.

And, in order to keep the White right in his back pocket, he believed he needed to keep up the pretense, however distasteful, of loyalty to Donald Trump.

He put a stake in the ground during the 2018 midterm race. Everyone else in Trumpworld was, he proclaimed, a hopeless incompetent—notably the entire campaign team—but Bannon, in an act of self-sacrifice, if not martyrdom, went on the road virtually nonstop for three months in an effort to single-handedly save the House of Representatives for the Republicans.

Sometimes it might appear that his natural pull was, most of all, to being on the road. He was a temperamentally rootless guy. He had no regular sleeping schedule or eating schedule; no evident personal life; and, indeed, no real home of his own (sometimes he was back in the Breitbart Embassy, which he now shared with an expanded Bannon, Inc., or as often in a suite in the Regency Hotel in New York—checked in under the name Alec Guinness).

At the same time, a clear goal was to get out from under Donald Trump— and, possibly, out from under the low-class American right wing. Speaking no foreign languages—and, arguably, quite a prototypical ugly Ameri- can—he nevertheless reconstituted himself as a guru to the European right. There was a method here, however quixotic: populism is a worldwide move- ment, one that Bannon might lead, and one that Donald Trump was only an incremental part of. Bannon would be the world figure.

Was he happy? I spent a fair amount of time trying to gauge this. There was certainly no break in his nonstop conversation, all focused on external events and issues, to indicate that he was not happy, that he was anything other than the public man, road warrior, constant campaigner, and inde- fatigable promoter that he seemed to be.

And yet, he was awfully alone. What is it like to spend your day plot- ting, conspiring, maneuvering, without interruption or respite, until you have to begin again the next morning?

Bannon saw himself in the character Bill Murray plays in *Groundhog Day*—explicitly so: "Bill Murray played me." This went well beyond just cinematic projection.

In his telling, there was a longtime group of Hollywood figures— among them, Murray, Harold Ramis, Andie McDowell, Debra Winger, and Sam Shepard—who had been engaged in a circle of belief inspired by "a super-esoteric discipline." These were the teachings of the Greek- Armenian mystic George Gurdjieff. According to Bannon, Murray and *Groundhog Day* director Ramis knew that he knew Gurdjieff "backward and forward." Gurdjieff's teachings led to the 1915 novel *Strange Life of Ivan Osokin* by P. D. Ouspensky, a Russian philosopher and journal- ist, postulating a unified field theory of "fourth dimension" conscious- ness, complementing Nietzsche's theory of eternal recurrence. That is, explained Bannon, every day of your life . . . is the exact same day, "all the lies you tell, all the misrepresentations, all the crap you serve up." You are stuck in your own predicament until you accumulate enough self-knowledge to move on and to reach something of an ultimate state of "not bullshitting yourself."

In many ways, Bannon could seem like a person both professing quite an extraordinary level of bullshit, and yet, as dramatically, not believing any of it at all. Or he could yet seem to be a person caught between bullshit and counter-bullshit.

* * *

One notable New York financial figure of my acquaintance, with whom Bannon had become very friendly—man-crush stuff for both men—began after the midterm election to express worry about his new friend. Bannon seemed to be an increasingly marginal figure, at best a gadfly player, and, having solicited funds from the financier, was apparently facing money troubles, too.

This financier urged Bannon to make the break from Trump—all Trump's allies were diminished by him, therefore the only option was to become his enemy.

You hardly had to convince Bannon of that obvious truth.

But at around this time—during the government shutdown over the 2019 New Year, with Trump ultimately capitulating on Congress's refusal to allocate money for the wall—Bannon's own wall enterprise began.

This was meant both as an embrace of Trump—or Trumpian ideals—and an affront to him. He couldn't get his own wall built, so Bannon would do it for him.

Bannon would *raise the money* to do it for him.

The wall had been the single greatest money hook of the 2016 campaign. It was Trumpism reduced to its essence. The wall was the money shot. It was gold.

Bannon is a second-stage entrepreneur. He doesn't start things—he's too distracted for that. He can't do only one thing; he needs to have many irons in the fire. Hence, he takes over projects that someone else, with more attention than Bannon can spare, has already launched. Almost all of his business efforts involve somebody else starting something—as happened with Breitbart—and Bannon coming in with a sense of personal authority and some basic financial know-how.

The wall project was started by Brian Kolfage, a profoundly wounded Iraq veteran who had turned his wounds and his politics into social media fodder. He was the kind of young, right-wing internet guy—internet troll—whom Bannon in the past had both disdained and put to profitable use. At any rate, by the time Kolfage's wall project came to Bannon's attention, it was already generating vast contributions—a direct-marketing bonanza.

As Bannon got more involved, he began to see this as a mega-project and a game-changing one. Not only was it a hot-button issue—the hottest button—but it did the thing the true right wing was more and more convinced that Trump couldn't do or wouldn't do—get the wall built.

This was big. Real estate had to be bought, zoning approved, land cleared, materials purchased, construction arranged and overseen. The funding here would need to be vast—unlimited, almost.

Bannon took command—and ownership—of the project. In effect, he bought it from Kolfage. The indictment of Bannon, Kolfage, and two other men, Andrew Badolato and Timothy Shea, both of whom Bannon had been involved with in the past, seemed to indicate that Bannon and his partners bought the not-for-profit wall project from Kolfage with a promise of continuing payments from the charity to Kolfage (who appears to have spent his gains on a variety of high-end leisure and luxury items). Bannon seemed, too, to have taken fees for his services from the charity. And, on this point, they appeared to run afoul of federal prosecutors (there is a fine line in not-for-profits between reasonably paying staff and bilking contributors).

The Southern District was framing the fundamental Bannon question: Are his right-wing politics mostly a hustle and a scam? Or, as Bannon would pose it, was the Southern District, which has long been known to be investigating Donald Trump, pursuing Bannon as part of its case against Trump's presidency, its right-wing beliefs, and its unholy cast of supporters?

Or, just as possibly, was the conspiracy-minded Trump administration conspiring against him?

Or was the real target here Miles Kwok?

Bannon's interests and hustles went in so many directions that it wasn't necessarily clear what was at issue.

During the impeachment of the president, Bannon had launched a daily streaming talk show in the president's defense. This then rolled into a coronavirus early warning system—more of the Chinese plot stuff (if

Trump was dismissive of the virus, the sixty-seven-year-old Bannon was deeply concerned about it—and about getting it). But, most of all, against the background of his broadcasts, his wall building (and fundraising), and his continued anti-China campaign and partnership with Kwok, Bannon was agitating to take over the failing (once again) Trump campaign.

Bannon and Corey Lewandowski, Trump's early 2016 campaign manager, had formed an alliance to take control of the campaign from Jared Kushner and his lieutenant Brad Parscale. It would be an unlikely development. There was still lots of bad blood between Trump and Bannon; it would almost certainly require a public demotion of Kushner, if not exile; and it would necessitate Trump doing the one thing he probably was incapable of doing—eating a little crow. Still, the campaign was surely sinking. There were many high-level emissaries to the president carrying the same message: Bannon and Lewandowski might be the only hope.

Now . . . in addition to his absolute contempt for the president's honesty and intelligence, Bannon has sworn to me on countless occasions that there could be no circumstance in which he would ever return to working for Donald Trump. If you are a player, however, and there is still (no matter how much you have tried to get something else going) only this single game in town . . .

One theory is that Bannon's indictment was a Kushner move urged on Bill Barr, the attorney general, because it would foreclose the possibility that his father-in-law could bring Bannon back (and shove Kushner out). But the other theory, canceling out this first theory, is that Barr tried to fire Geoffrey Berman, the U.S. attorney in the Southern District, weeks before Bannon's indictment, in a White House effort to protect Bannon—a man who knew too much. This effort presumably failed when Berman made the price of his resignation the elevation of his deputy into the top spot, who then continued the pursuit of Bannon.

If this second theory is correct, then the question might well be about Bannon's willingness and wherewithal to flip on Trump. This would be with some amount of irony because Bannon was always handicapping the likelihood of so many others flipping on Trump. Bannon also handicapped the likelihood of Trump pardoning this or that cohort and potential informer. Now, of course, Bannon, too, was likely lining up for a pardon.

So was it worth it? That's a question for Bannon as well as almost everyone else who has passed through the Trump White House.

Almost everybody came into the Trump administration in the spirit of a why-not opportunity—crazy, but who knows? Everybody made a deal with the devil and was aware of it.

It was never just politics . . . that's the underlying Trump fact of life. Few would make the mistake to think otherwise. Indeed, there's an aspect of Trump's general contempt for Washington that people there take politics, with its small-time sense of civic duty and institutional respect, seriously—or they pretend to. He doesn't for a minute actually think they really do. Certainly he doesn't; and he demands that no one around him does, either.

I don't know if Bannon is more cynical than Trump—though certainly he sees Trump as the ultimate joke, whereas Trump at least takes *himself* seriously. Bannon came into Trumpworld as partly a would-be savvy media guy, partly a reluctant cult leader, partly an insomniac who read a lot of books that had left him with an earnest and perhaps messianic sense of the world's fate, and partly as a man at the age when, having never quite succeeded, he had one last shot. Against that background, he understood that Trump was crazy but a major audience draw, and the far-right wing was nutty but delivered a significantly higher-than-average response rate. And, too, that the workingman in America *had* gotten a bum deal—and maybe Bannon could strike a positive blow (whatever that might be) on the workingman's behalf from a luxury hotel suite.

The question remains: Can you be a believer—in some consistent ideas, in your ability to implement them, and with the conviction that they should be implemented—while at the same time seeing the world as a colossal cosmic joke? A screwball marketing machine that turned Donald Trump—whom Bannon had once seen as his personal knee-slapper—into the destroyer of worlds.

The politics of this time will not yet allow us to see Steve Bannon as a tragic figure, but I think we will get there.

Trump at Home

June 2016

The long day is ending for Donald Trump with a pint of vanilla Häagen-Dazs ice cream. We're settling in for a late-night chat at his Beverly Hills house, a 5,395-square-foot colonial mansion directly across from the Beverly Hills Hotel. He's here for the final presidential primary, a California coronation of sorts, after rallies in Orange County (where violence broke out and seven people were arrested). He is, as he has been for much of our conversation—and perhaps much of the last year—marveling at his own campaign. "You looked outside before, you see what's going on," he boasts about the police surrounding his house, and the Secret Service detail cramming his garage and snaking around the pool at the center of the front drive. And he's just returned from a big-donor fundraiser in Brentwood for the Republican Party at the home of Tom Barrack, the investor and former Miramax co-owner. "There had to be over a thousand policemen. They had a neighborhood roped off, four or five blocks away from this beautiful house. Machine guns all over the place."

One thing to understand about Trump is that, rather unexpectedly, he's neither angry nor combative. He may be the most threatening and frightening and menacing presidential candidate in modern life, and yet in person he's almost soothing. His extreme self-satisfaction rubs off. He's a New Yorker who actually might be more at home in California (in fact, he says he usually comes to his home here on North Canon Drive only once a year). Life is sunny. Trump is an optimist—at least about himself. He's in easy and relaxed form campaigning here in these final days before the June

7 California primary, even with Hillary Clinton's biggest backers and a city that is about half Latino surrounding him.

Earlier in the day, I'd met with Trump at a taping of ABC's *Jimmy Kimmel Live!* at the El Capitan Theatre on Hollywood Boulevard, where he was the single guest for the evening (musicians The Weeknd and Belly canceled upon learning of his appearance). "Have you ever seen anything like this?" he asked. He meant this, the Trump phenomenon. Circumventing any chance that I might dampen the sentiment, he quickly answered his own question: "No one ever has."

His son-in-law, *New York Observer* owner Jared Kushner, married to his daughter Ivanka and also a real estate scion—but clearly a more modest and tempered fellow, a wisp next to his beefsteak father-in-law—offered that they may have reached 100 percent name recognition. In other words, Trump could be the most famous man in the world right now. "I may be," says Trump, almost philosophically, and referencing the many people who have told him they've never seen anything like this. "Bill O'Reilly said in his lifetime this is the greatest phenomenon he's ever seen."

That notion is what's at the center of this improbable campaign, its own brilliant success. It's its main subject—the one you can't argue with. You can argue about issues, but you can't argue with success. Hence, to Trump, you're really foolish to argue with the Trump campaign. "I've spent $50 million of my own money to go through the primaries. Other people spent $230 million and they came in last. You know what I'm saying?" And this provides him the reason to talk endlessly and repetitively about the phenomenon of the campaign. That phenomenon is, of course, Trump himself, about whom Trump spends a lot of time talking in the third person.

You can try, but it's hard to resist this admiration for himself. The certainty of it, the enthusiasm for it, and the lack of not just doubt but of any negativity. It's all upbeat and positive. The dark, scary, virulent heart of American politics is having the best time anyone has ever had.

If onstage he calls people names, more privately he has only good, embracing things to say about almost everybody. (For most public people, it is the opposite.) He loves everybody. Genuinely seems to love everybody—at least everybody who's rich and successful (he doesn't really talk about anyone who isn't). Expressing love for everybody, for most of us, would clearly seem to be an act. But with Trump, it's the name-calling and bluster that might be the act.

I offer that there are quite a number of people in New York, some we know in common, who are puzzled that the generous, eager-to-be-liked and liking-everyone-in-return Donald has morphed into a snarling and reactionary public enemy, at least a liberal enemy. This, I suggest, might be a source of the continuing dialectic—or, to some, wishful thinking—that he does not necessarily believe what he says.

I might detect the most mild sort of annoyance here. Trump says it's that he just never talked about his beliefs in the past—after all, he wasn't a politician. "Who thought this was going to happen?" But his larger point seems to be that such a topic—what he says—is a silly thing to focus on. The point is not about politics, or policies, but about how people, about how *many* people, have responded to him. It's too big to ignore the bigness. "You heard Jimmy announce tonight that I have the most votes in the history of the Republican Party," he says by way of explanation for the larger issues at hand—i.e., him.

In a way, what this evening's *Kimmel* show was about was treating Trump's positions as though they are, well, Trump's positions, qualitatively different than other politicians' positions. In fact, you might logically see the *Kimmel* show as a devastating attack on Trump's views and claims. Kimmel flat out doesn't believe him. That recording of the PR person alleged to be Trump sounding like a PR person? Trump: "It didn't sound like me." Kimmel: "No. Sounded like you." (An exchange repeated similarly several times, with no rancor from either Trump or Kimmel.) "And oh," says Kimmel, "remember when you liked Hillary?" Trump: "I just *said* I like her. I say I like everybody." And there was Kimmel, at every opportunity, happily mocking Trump, the overexposed media whore.

The effect is not only *not* damaging, it's fun-loving, comic, even joyous. Kimmel is tickled to have such a good sport to poke fun at, and Trump is tickled that Kimmel is tickled. Everybody's in on it. There are no phonies here. Or everybody here is honest about being a phony. Nobody is taking anyone very seriously—forget what might be at stake in a presidential election. If Trump is the subject of the conversation, then Trump is happy. If Kimmel has Trump as a guest, he's happy. Everybody's happy. (Trump has a staffer take a picture of another picture of Trump when he was previously on the *Kimmel* show that's now hanging on the studio wall.)

It is this media frisson that, with countless other professional and amateur analyzers, I'm trying to plumb. Surely a big part of the answer lies in the nature of Trump's performance, an unselfconsciousness so extreme that he has passed through hurdles of humiliation that would have destroyed nearly all others to emerge as though free of a private self. Trump is only fully alive in public. But another aspect is that, differentiating himself from every other candidate, he has a long, intimate relationship with nearly every significant player in the media and, indeed, lavishes copious praise on almost all of them. He may know few people in Washington, and care about them less, but he knows his moguls and where they rank on the modern suck-up-to list.

On Murdoch: "Rupert is a tremendous guy. I think Rupert [who for several years lived in the Trump building on Fifty-Ninth and Park Avenue in Manhattan] is one of the people I really respect and like. And I think Rupert respects what I've done." But what about Murdoch's grumpy Trump tweets? "When I got into the world of politics, that was a different realm for me and maybe he felt differently. But I think he respects what I've done and he's a tremendous guy and I think we have a very good relationship."

On Redstone: "Sumner, well, he's had a good run. Good run. Terrible it comes to this—" that is, his dementia "—but a good run. He'd give me anything. Loved me."

On Leslie Moonves: "Great guy. The greatest. We're on the same page. We think alike."

These are the bulls of his real party.

The party whips, to strain this metaphor, are the news heads: Roger Ailes at Fox News, Jeff Zucker at CNN (who previously at NBC bought *The Apprentice* and launched Trump as a national TV star), and Andy Lack, now the head of NBC News. Despite his tweets about the "dishonest media," Trump is lavish in his praise of all of them. I ask him to rate them. "That's an unfair question," he says, making a rare grab for politesse. "I know Jeff very well. I know Roger very well. And, less well, but I think Andy has done a very good job."

Among his frequent media and now political confidants is WME co-CEO Ari Emanuel—whose brother, Rahm, the mayor of Chicago, was once Obama's chief of staff—who Trump says has offered to take charge of the Trump celebratory convention film. Emanuel and Trump, while at seeming odds politically, might in fact be even better united in a kind of hypersalesmanship. "He's a very good friend of mine," says Trump. "He calls me a lot. I call him a lot and we talk. He's very political. Even though he's not political, he's political. He gets it. You're shocked to hear that, right? [About the movie.] But yeah, I might do something with Ari. Does he represent you?"

Trump will turn seventy on June 14, but he shows no sign of fatigue even as our conversation drifts toward eleven p.m. He's been at this since either four a.m. or six a.m. (he offers different times at different moments). "Today, I'm up at six in the morning, I'm meeting some of the biggest people in the world. I then had to give a speech to a big group, then I had to give a speech at twelve to [Dole Food mogul] David Murdock, [real estate magnate] Donald Bren, tremendous guys. Then I had to drive to Anaheim and give a speech in front of thousands of people. Then I came back and did more meetings, then I did a fundraiser tonight, then I did *Kimmel*. And now you. You're not a two-minute-interview guy."

He hands me a water bottle from the refrigerator (it contains only water and about a dozen pints of ice cream), and we walk through the dark house decorated with hotel-like furniture (a four-star rather than a five-star hotel lobby). He reclines, still in his standard boxy suit, tie slightly loosened, with his Häagen-Dazs on an overstuffed couch in the living room (he asks me not to put my water bottle on the fabric-covered ottoman).

If there's any pattern to his conversation, it's that he's vague on all subjects outside himself, his campaign, and the media. Everything else is mere distraction. But I press him about Peter Thiel, the Silicon Valley billionaire who, earlier in the day, has admitted to funding the $140 million Hulk Hogan lawsuit against Gawker. Thiel also is his most prominent Silicon Valley backer and will go to the convention in July as a pledged delegate. But Trump needs reminding who he is, and then concludes he must be a friend of his son-in-law Jared. ("Wow, I love him! So he funded it for Hulk Hogan? You'd think Hulk Hogan would have enough money, but he probably doesn't.") Indeed, Trump doesn't appear to be interested in Silicon Valley, except to roll off his numbers on each social media platform.

("On Facebook, I have close to eight million people. On Twitter, I have eight-point-five million. On Instagram, I have over a million people. I'm inching on twenty million people. I have friends, somebody that's a great writer, where they write a book and call me up and say, 'Can you do me a favor, can you tweet it?'" "Can you," I interject, "tweet my book, please?" "I will!")

Finishing his pint, he reflects again on the remarkableness of the campaign, asking his traveling staffers Corey Lewandowski and press secretary Hope Hicks, as well as his son-in-law, to confirm again how remarkable it is. Lewandowski recites the latest polls (as of press time, they show Trump inching to within a few percentage points of Clinton in a head-to-head matchup), and Trump, with something beyond confidence, seems to declare de facto victory.

I broach his problems with women and Hispanics and the common wisdom that he'll have to do at least as well with these groups as Mitt Romney did in 2012. The "pivot" is the word more politico pros are using to refer to his expected turn to the center. "Unless," I offer, "you think you can remake the electoral math." He says he absolutely can. So no pivot. "It'll be different math than they've ever seen." He is, he says, bigger than anything anyone has ever seen. "I have a much bigger base than Romney. Romney was a stiff!" And he'll be bigger with the people he's bigger with, but also he'll be bigger with women and Hispanics and Blacks, too. He believes that, no matter what positions he holds or slurs he has made, he is irresistible.

I ask if he sees himself as having similarities with leaders of the growing anti-immigrant (some would say outright racist) European nativist movements, like Marine Le Pen in France and Matteo Salvini in Italy, whom the *Wall Street Journal* reported Trump had met with and endorsed in Philadelphia. ("Matteo, I wish you become the next Italian premier soon," Salvini says Trump said.) In fact, he insists he didn't meet Salvini. "I didn't want to meet him." And, in sum, he doesn't particularly see similarities—or at least isn't interested in them—between those movements and the anti-immigrant nationalism he is promoting in this country.

"And Brexit? Your position?" I ask.

"Huh?"

"Brexit."

"Hmm."

"The Brits leaving the EU," I prompt, realizing that his lack of familiarity with one of the most pressing issues in Europe, and the vote in the U.K. that is just weeks away, is for him no concern or liability at all.

"Oh yeah, I think they should leave."

It is hard not to feel that Trump understands himself, and that we're all in on this kind of spectacular joke. His shamelessness is just so . . . shameless. So how much, I ask—quite thinking he will get the nuance here—is the Trump brand based on exaggeration? He responds, with perfect literalness, none at all. I try again. He must understand. How could he not? "You've talked about negotiation, which is about compromise and about establishing positions that you can walk back from. How much about being a successful person involves . . . well, bullshitting? How much of success is playing games?"

If he does understand, he's definitely not taking this bait. I try again: "How much are you a salesman?"

Salesman, in the Trump worldview, is hardly a bad word, and he is quite willing to accept it, although, curiously, he doesn't want to be thought of that way when it comes to real estate. But as a politician, he's okay as a salesman.

In this, he sees himself—and becomes almost eloquent in talking about himself—as a sort of performer and voter whisperer. He is, he takes obvious pride in saying, the only politician who doesn't regularly use a teleprompter. With a prompter, he says, you can't work the crowd. You can't feel it. "You got to look at them in the eye. Have you ever seen me speak in front of a large group of people? Have you ever watched?" He reflects on the lack of self-consciousness that's necessary to make spontaneous utterances before a crowd. He cites a well-known actor (whose name he asks me not to use, "I don't want to hurt anybody"), who had wanted to run for office but, without a script, was a blithering idiot. Trump was never fed lines on *The Apprentice*, he says. It was all him: "You have to have a natural ability."

I ask if he'll use a teleprompter for his acceptance speech at the convention and, almost sorrowfully, he says he probably will. I find myself urging him not to, precisely for the theater of it all. The spontaneity. Who would want to miss that? Let Trump be Trump.

"Very interesting. What he's saying is very interesting," he notes to Lewandowski.

He's punted on Hillary as a topic since we started our conversation, as though to talk about her was not to talk about him. If in public he needs to treat her as his cause, in private he doesn't want her taking up his time. But I sneak it back.

"Did you ever vote for Bill?" I ask, thinking that both men have as much in common as they have that separates them.

"Let's see . . . did I ever? Eh, I don't want to say who I voted for."

Indeed. These two '80s guys were undoubtedly once quite in sync.

The Antichrist Trump, the Trump of bizarre, outré, impractical, and reactionary policies that most reasonable people yet believe will lead to an astounding defeat in November, is really hard to summon from Trump in person (perhaps there is a large and secret population that sees him as rather cuddly). He deflects that dark-heart person, or, even, dissembles about what that person might have said (as much, he dissembles for conservatives about what the more liberal Trump might have said), and is impatient that anyone might want to focus on that version of Trump. It does then feel that the policies, such as they are, and the slurs are not him. They are just a means to the end—to the *phenomenon*. To the center of attention. The biggest thing that has ever happened in politics. In America. The biggest thing is the theme. It's what he always wants to come back to. Bigness is unavoidable and inevitable. Bigness always wins.

Before Trump trundles off to bed—actually, before that, never too tired, he plans to watch himself on *Kimmel*—I ask that de rigueur presidential question, which does not seem yet to have been asked of him. "What books are you reading?"

He knows he's caught (it's a question that all politicians are prepped on, but who among his not-bookish coterie would have prepped him even with the standard GOP politician answer: *the Bible*?). But he goes for it.

"I'm reading the Ed Klein book on Hillary Clinton"—a particular hatchet job, which at the very least has certainly been digested for him. "And I'm reading the book on Richard Nixon that was, well, I'll get you the exact information on it. I'm reading a book that I've read before, it's one of my favorite books, *All Quiet on the Western Front*, which is one of the greatest books of all time." And one I suspect he's suddenly remembering from high school. But what the hell.

Donald Trump simply believes he is a unique individual, one whose singular conviction that he is special makes him appealing. And pay no attention to everything else.

Media
People

Tucker

I think it is possible, and maybe likely, that at any given time in Washington there are a handful of sources that supply most of the off-the-record commentary and spread most of the high-level gossip. Woodward and Bernstein appropriated the high-ranking FBI official Mark Felt as Deep Throat, their super-secret Watergate source, at the same time he was widely known to be talking to everybody else, too.

In Trump's Washington, Tucker Carlson is a primary super-secret source. I know this because I know what he has told me and I can track his exquisite, too-good-not-to-be-true gossip through unsourced reports and as it often emerges into accepted wisdom. Too many times to count, after someone's confidence I've asked, "Did that come from Tucker?" And, equally, after I've shared a juicy detail, I've been caught out myself: "So . . . you've been speaking to Tucker."

This indicates Carlson's centrality in Trump's Washington—Trump and his family can't seem to stop talking to him—and the true divided nature of Trump supporters. Carlson may be a key Trump voice in the Fox News prime-time lineup, with a trackable influence on Trump's opinions and actions, but he is as clear-eyed, as subversive, and as deeply incredulous about Trump and his family as anyone I know.

It is also a character note about Carlson's particular journey as a conservative and as a television personality.

Not long after I wrote about Carlson in 2002 for *New York* magazine as a rising talking head, I suggested to Caroline Miller, then *New York*'s editor, that Tucker come to work at the magazine as a regular columnist.

He was an alternative voice, an insightful reporter, and had growing name recognition. In short order, he joined me in the front of the magazine. But soon enough, it became clear that this was a small disaster. His writing was sharp and waspish. But producing it on an enforced and demanding schedule was a painful and unsatisfying experience for him—and a vexation for the people trying to put out a weekly magazine.

The episode helped to cement his basic career view: television was easier. Daily television is intense in its own way but, in the end, it is in the moment. There is no rewriting. "You just have to show up," Carlson happily told me.

But this became the rap on him in his television career—just showing up. He told too many people how easy his job was. He was perceived among the liberals at CNN—and, after CNN, at MSNBC—as not earnest enough, not taking the news of the day seriously enough, and as perhaps not respectful enough of the work of his more exalted liberal colleagues. He was regarded (and his signature bow tie didn't help) as not just a conservative but as a certain sort of lazy, gentleman's-C, country club conservative, a graduate of Trinity College in Hartford, the last stop for boarding school bros short on grades and SAT scores.

The television news ground was shifting, too. The presumed need to have a contrary voice was now seen as lamely transparent—so don't bother—and, as well, taking a slot that could otherwise be occupied by a personality and a view more effectively targeted to the increasingly one-sided market. Why offer viewers something they don't want?

In an on-air dustup in 2004, Jon Stewart, for reasons that seem less apparent now, was thought to have humiliated Carlson for being "partisan" and, not incidentally, calling him a dick.

And then there was a rape allegation, a bizarre bit of mistaken identity or outright extortion, ultimately disavowed by the accuser but leaving a vague odor around Tucker, and, for him, a deep resentment.

His promising career as the liberal's conservative was going south. And, in due course, in the fate common to most on-air talent, he found himself off the air.

He started the *Daily Caller*, which, competing with hardcore Breitbart News in the ever-more-precise digital target market, moved his laid-back, libertarian-ish conservativism into the new weaponized right-wing commercial battleground.

Fox News chief Roger Ailes, who found Tucker personally entertaining and notably intelligent among television's conservative talking heads (Ailes had few illusions about most television conservatives), rescued him in 2008 from life without a TV platform (according to Ailes, he was actually thinking of buying the *Daily Caller*, but Steve Bannon, who would become the head of Breitbart, convinced him not to, so as a consolation Ailes hired Carlson).

At the same time Ailes continued to regard Carlson as a conservative liberals love, when, in the Fox formula, you not only had to be a conservative whom conservatives loved, but one whom liberals hated. Carlson largely warmed the bench as a fill-in host and as a weekend anchor, having to commute to New York from Washington. It was a grueling schedule and a backwater job. But as a father of four, and one with complicated tax troubles, he hung on.

I ran into Carlson as the 2016 Democratic Convention in Philadelphia was breaking up. We were both on our way to New York and shared the train ride together. A month before, Ailes had been fired from Fox over wide sexual harassment claims; the Murdoch family, father and sons, had taken over direct management of Fox News, and it was yet unclear where they would take the network. The political world seemed to offer only Hillary Clinton, for whom Carlson had nothing but disgust, as the inevitable president, not least of all—and here I can perfectly recall Tucker's disbelieving laugh, a cackle of the greatest incredulity—because her opponent was the unthinkable Donald Trump. Carlson, closely tied in to the Palm Beach circuit, was filled with extraordinary and derisive details about the Republican candidate.

Carlson is a Washington swamp creature, a social presence and information conduit at high levels of the Republican bureaucracy (he holds quite a mental file of Republican résumés, sharing the bullet points as he walks through a Republican crowd). His father, who got custody of Tucker and his brother when they were young (after their mother abandoned the family for a bohemian life), and to whom Carlson is exceptionally close, is a swamp creature, too, having held a set of high-profile Republican patronage jobs (including an ambassadorship and heading the Corporation for Public Broadcasting)—and, in Tucker's telling, generally enjoying the life of an adept bureaucratic operator.

The Carlson family's Republican Party is a picture-perfect one. It's blond, it's Episcopalian, it's country club. It is also, in every fiber of its being—except the need to be employed somewhere in the Republican bureaucracy and to be insiders in an insider town—anti-Trump.

Carlson's classy Republican pedigree and anti-Trump sensibility appealed to Rupert Murdoch and his son Lachlan, both aghast at Trump's election and with vague intentions of making a kinder, gentler Fox News post-Ailes. Carlson was not only a better conservative, but Murdoch was thrilled by his gossip. Shortly after Trump's election, the Murdochs promoted Carlson to his own, pre-prime-time show at seven p.m.

The ground at Fox News, which had begun its seismic shift with Ailes's ouster, continued to shift dramatically with the departure of Megyn Kelly, a key anchor. Carlson was given her eight p.m. prime-time spot. Not long after, Bill O'Reilly, Fox's ratings king, was also ousted in a harassment scandal. Suddenly the main Fox anchors were no longer Kelly and O'Reilly, but—in quite an unprecedented prime-time overthrow—Tucker Carlson and Sean Hannity.

It is a particular position in television news: the television-news personality who is most plugged into the Washington gossip flow. The vaunted example of this was NBC's Tim Russert, the Democrat-turned-talking-head, who not only reported back to his GE bosses on the political dirt and drift, but often acted as its ambassador on political matters that affected the company. At Fox, this role had long been occupied by Ailes himself.

Now, Carlson, the Washington creature, with (through the *Daily Caller*) deep contact to the new right wing—and, through Palm Beach, entrée to Trumpworld—became a politically inverted Russert. If you wanted access to the Trump White House, an up-to-the-minute picture of its dysfunction, and its weird family drama, and, as well, insight into the fragile Trump psyche, you could hardly do better than a conversation with Tucker Carlson.

As with the best gossip, its sheer vividness overwhelmed what agenda it might otherwise serve. Carlson seemed helplessly to speak against his best interests.

As Carlson's private commentary eviscerated almost every aspect of the Trump White House, he was seizing the moment—his last opportunity to dig himself out of his personal financial hole, and his last to succeed in television—to become one of the representative figures of Trumpism.

However much the Murdochs might have idealized a better Fox News, the Trump velocity, and profits, overwhelmed all better intentions. Where Ailes had always been the last word at Fox, the one person who had to be listened to and had to be pleased—offering a certain sort of political independence, if you will—now it was Trump himself effectively calling the shots.

Tucker sought to thread a peculiar needle. He became a leading Trump voice mentioning Trump as little as possible. Here, on the air, was the aging preppy giving no quarter—not to fads, fancies, feminists, or pantywaists. He was mad as hell at modernity, hypocrisy, the encroachments on individual liberty, and the right to obnoxiousness everywhere. His racial consciousness was articulated possibly with less pretense than even Trump's: a browner nation was different than a less brown one—and he was rooting for the less brown one.

In real life, he was this, but not. He was his own dramatic counterpoint.

In one reality, he was the most affable, convivial, companionable guy in town. Mr. Schmooze. Mr. Handshake. Big laugh. Major smile for the ladies (especially the older ladies). So clubbable. He had lunch on most days in Washington, as did his father, at the Metropolitan Club, around the corner from the White House. There he's greeted by staff and members alike. He's in his element. He's a man of ritual and propriety. And then the pretense falls. Washington is his burg, a ludicrous one. He's the stage manager in *Our Town*, but ruder and funnier, crueler, seeing into everyone's dark heart.

In another reality, on air, he is Trumpian, dystopian, mounting a nightly MAGA defense (one afternoon at the Metropolitan Club, a waiter became unhinged, publicly cursing Carlson out). But immediately off the air his critique of Trump is full of disgust and repugnance. (What's more, his critique of the other Fox News Trump sycophants is bitter and lacerating.)

He is, along with Steve Bannon—whom he doesn't like at all—one of the most damning witnesses to Donald Trump's presidency. Liberals have nothing at all on Trump and his administration compared to the people who have been closest to it. And Carlson is on the phone with the president and members of his family on an almost constant basis. (While it is Hannity who is on the phone with Trump nearly every day, often many times a day, it is Carlson whom Trump calls to complain about Hannity.)

Carlson has succeeded in an age of political identification, but it's not simple to identify his politics. In some sense, his deep conviction about the absurdity and psychopathology of Trump and his family is part of a fatalism, a true end-of-the-world view, that may be the bedrock emotion of much of modern conservatism (giving rise to Donald Trump). Carlson began as a good-natured laissez-faire conservative but, as for many, the world has led him to an end-times moment.

The public voice is appalled, stupefied, incredulous, seeing the end of White America—a nation overrun by liberal sanctimony and hypocrisy. At the same time, the private voice is absolutely up-to-the-minute on the most horrifying details of people at the highest reaches of public life—not least of all, the Trump family and its gothic dysfunctions. It's confiding the most graphic tales of systemic idiocy and abuse, knowing more, knowing who, knowing what, and confiding it with a sense of impunity that seems to come from the belief that the world will end before he is exposed as the Trump world's Deep Throat.

He is in the existential void, seeing the Trump apocalypse in front of him, and, as well, doubting the Murdochs' commitment to Fox News, and, what's more, doubting the entire organization's ability to function beyond Donald Trump. He sees his career in a way that on-air talent should always, but never does—as wholly existing in the moment. His private conversation is often about how long he can last on air, and what comes after the inevitable end of being on air.

His show is now the highest-rated cable news show. In that capacity, he has surely stoked the Trump base, while—with rising talk of Carlson as a post-Trump presidential candidate—in his other life as confidential source, he has done everything possible to undermine the preposterous president.

There is, possibly, a political logic in that.

Ronan

A basic part of Ronan Farrow and his family's attacks on Woody Allen, Ronan's likely father, involve Allen's power in the media and what the Farrow family characterizes as the fearsome publicity operation Allen has assembled to protect himself and beat back criticism. In fact, the eighty-four-year-old Allen's media team is mostly a relic from the 1970s. Virtually all digital and social media currents have passed it by. The *New York Times*, once Allen's cultural champion, has rolled several generations forward and his defenders and admirers have long retired. Allen now largely ignores the media or hides from it, rather than courts it. Forced to interact with it, he will likely say something unguarded that gets him into trouble.

But this is a significant part of how Farrow sees himself: up against other people's overwhelming media power, insidious and conspiratorial. He's David facing the Goliath media and its legion of sexual predators. The Farrow family is a victim of the media's injustice.

His book about the Weinstein case, *Catch and Kill*, is much less about Harvey Weinstein's sex crimes than it is about the unfairness and deceit and downright corruption of the media overlords working full-time against Farrow. That's his real story, how he has overcome other people's media power.

At the same time, Ronan Farrow is an ultimate creature of the media—the opposite of an outsider to it. We would surely not know of Ronan Farrow save for the media light he was born under.

After Farrow set himself up as the bête noire and avenging angel to his former employer NBC News, there was considerable finger-pointing within the news division as to who hired him anyway and why. Most fingers were pointed at Noah Oppenheim, the NBC News president and sometime screenwriter and Hollywood wannabe who thought the news network could use some glamour status. Although there were, too, fingers pointed at Phil Griffin, MSNBC's chief, himself a noted starfucker.

The certain fact is that the twenty-five-year-old Farrow, without television experience of any sort, was given his own show, a daytime celebrity- and entertainment-oriented format, because he was Mia Farrow and Woody Allen's son and often in a swirl of media attention because of it.

In fact, at this point, he was best known for his mother's public suggestion in an interview in *Vanity Fair* that he might not be Woody Allen's child, but the son of Frank Sinatra (this would be easy to prove either way, but the Farrows have not pursued that further clarification, at least not publicly).

And yet, even as a born-and-bred media family, Ronan and various other members of his family believe that other media people have more media power than they do. It's zero sum.

Allen, their whalelike foe, is one of the most famous men of his age—commanding more than half a century's worth of steady media time. In addition to being her longtime lover, Allen was Mia Farrow's primary employer in the media, depriving her of a career after their breakup. It is Allen's entitlement as a person of such stature and power that might seem to have allowed him—Allen famously saying, "the heart wants what it wants"—to forswear all sense of propriety and reputational concern in 1992 and take up with Mia Farrow's twenty-two-year-old daughter, Soon-Yi Previn, whom Farrow and composer André Previn adopted from Korea when she was seven. Fighting back against Allen's betrayal, Farrow leveled charges of sex abuse against him involving their then seven-year-old adopted daughter, Dylan, precipitating what might be one of history's great domestic meltdown media circuses. It was, in the Farrow camp's telling, the power of Allen's lawyers and PR operation—and friends in the media—that helped him cast enough doubt on her accusations for courts and investigators to find him on multiple occasions blameless and let his prolific career continue unharmed. The media was the enemy as much as Allen.

Meanwhile, Mia raised Ronan (changing his name from Satchel) with no contact with his father and as her close confidant, inculcating in him the family's blood score against Allen. Through her entrée as a Hollywood activist, she introduced her son into high political circles, where he would work briefly for Hillary Clinton and for the U.S. diplomat Richard Holbrooke.

Mia Farrow's revival of the charges against Allen in 2013, dormant for more than two decades, in the same *Vanity Fair* article where she dangled the Sinatra angle, was coincident with Ronan Farrow's television debut. In his book, Farrow modestly demurs here, saying he has always tried to distance himself from the Allen situation, and it is only with the heaviest sense of duty that he has taken up his mother's role as the main family prosecutor and spokesperson. But that's almost exclusively who he was as he began his anchor job: Woody Allen's implacable accuser, achieving dramatic notoriety for it, and, as well, possibly, Frank Sinatra's son. (There was an effort to cast Farrow as a would-be diplomat, and he would subsequently write a book about diplomacy—a book moronic in its simplemindedness and probably unpublishable but for his media notoriety.)

As it happens, Farrow's show was quite a dreadful flop. He was hopelessly wooden on camera and absent the boyish charm the network had convinced itself he might offer. His cringeworthiness was made worse by his mother's frequent calls to high-ranking NBC officials to complain about his lighting and the low caliber of his guests. To boot, he was personally unpopular at the network, an entitled name-dropper, which is quite something to be singled out for in the television business.

He was, in essence, fired, but in television custom allowed the gentle landing of working out his contract. He was given a temporary assignment to the *Today* show, with the clear implication that his future at NBC was short-term.

Then Weinstein came into the picture. Here commenced the struggle that is the centerpiece of Farrow's book, an epic journalistic showdown. Him trying to get out the truth about a sexual predator, and the powers-that-be trying to thwart him—hardly an unfamiliar tale in the Farrow home.

For NBC, this—Farrow as crusading investigator—was a confusing development on a number of fronts. First, NBC had fired him. And yet here he was proposing a major investigative effort—an odd bit of not getting the we-don't-really-think-much-of-you message. And, at best, he was a mere rookie reporter, with scant journalism background and little support in the organization—*and he wants to do what?*

And then there's the Allen thing. Certainly, in conventional reporting terms, you'd naturally question the appearance of bias here. This person whose life story was bound up in one of the most controversial charges of sex abuse of all time was now asking—demanding—to represent the network in a dicey sex abuse exposé. (In *Catch and Kill* he dismisses even the suggestion that there might be legitimate concerns about bias as preposterous.) And there was yet another, sotto voce, aspect of this. Many in the news division didn't believe the Farrow family's Allen story. This had become something of a generational divide. Younger people seemed to blindly accept the Farrow version, while older people—and these were older media people running NBC News—were skeptical. Some, in fact, believed the story to be flatly false and that it only achieved younger-generation credibility in a Trumpian way, with the baldness and magnitude and repetition of the Farrow family claims.

Having already hired him (even having now fired him), it was perhaps too late to ask who Ronan Farrow was and how you would measure his credibility *if* Woody Allen was in fact innocent, if Farrow was (either wittingly or unwittingly) part of a revenge plot. But the Weinstein story was awkwardly forcing the question at NBC (more awkward still because the current politics of the Allen story meant you could not ask the questions out loud).

As the teller of his tale, Farrow, naturally, does not allow, or appreciate, that at NBC he might have been regarded as a creepy presence. Instead, it's a conspiracy to silence him. In his telling: Harvey Weinstein, one of the most powerful and fearsome figures in modern media, is on the phone, demanding, threatening, wheedling, as surely he was, and NBC executives gave in to him. That of course might be true *along* with Farrow being a creepy presence few would have reason to trust with this story.

At this point, Farrow shows up at the *New Yorker*. He is sponsored by the writer Ken Auletta, a New York media fixture married to the literary agent Amanda Urban, who was in turn the protégée of the literary agent Lynn Nesbit, a close Farrow-family friend—who took a prominent role as a media surrogate in supporting the 1992 allegations against Allen—and whose daughter was the longtime girlfriend of Mia Farrow and André Previn's son Matthew. (At every turn, the background of this story is about media power and connections.) A further part of the background here is that by this point it was well known that the *New York Times* was rushing to get a story about Weinstein's long history of sexual abuse into print. The story, in other words, had become a foregone conclusion; the fears that various publications, including the *New Yorker*, have had for many years about Weinstein's vaunted reach and threats were evaporating.

The *Times* publishes its story, pretty much demolishing Weinstein, and then the *New Yorker* publishes the Farrow piece, putting a final nail in the Weinstein coffin, if it needed one. Farrow shares in a Pulitzer Prize.

From there, he goes on to claim the central spot on the powerful-men-sexual-abuse beat. His targets will include former New York State attorney general Eric Schneiderman, then Supreme Court nominee Brett Kavanaugh, and then CBS chairman Leslie Moonves.

Farrow's work for the *New Yorker* is notable for being particularly un-*New Yorker*-like. It isn't truly written, it's stripped-down, police-blotter, tabloid stuff (and even in this, Farrow is often paired with other writers). This accusatory-tabloid style gives him a kind of power few journalists ever get—he can break anyone. Just the rumor of Farrow's interest in someone can break them. It's an old-fashioned sort of press power. The accuser is more important than the accusations.

If the fundamental question about Allen's guilt or innocence—and Farrow's unrelenting pursuit of what might well be a false charge—yet lurks, almost nobody is going to mention it.

By the time Farrow publishes his book, the media equation has been entirely reversed. Farrow holds the power and the heretofore powerful men in media are quavering before him. Indeed, the most potent weapon against a powerful man is to accuse him of sexual offenses. There is likely no one who understands this better than Farrow. His book, focusing on the perfidiousness if not corruption of NBC, accuses virtually every ranking news-division executive at NBC of some form of sexual transgression. In the wake of the book, NBCUniversal's top management reorganized the news division, putting a corporate-politician-type without news experience, Cesar Conde, in charge. So the effect of Farrow's campaign against the network will likely be less, not more, news aggressiveness.

In the larger media business, among many working journalists, there has remained a private current of doubt about Farrow. There's the discomfiting entitlement of Farrow's rise with continued resentment at the *Times* about his sharing in the Pulitzer Prize. There's the nagging, if mostly unspoken, weirdness of the Farrow family story: Mia Farrow's brother in prison for sex abuse; her practically teenage marriage to the middle-aged Sinatra—himself a legendary sexual predator; Mia having Ronan's legs broken as a teenager to make him taller; three of Mia's fourteen children dying at young ages under never entirely explained circumstances. Indeed, the Farrow family story, even without the Allen saga, is gothic. What's more, there have been reports about Ronan Farrow's threatening approach to sources and major questions about his article (with Jane Mayer) in the *New Yorker* about a Yale classmate of Brett Kavanaugh's who might possibly, though without supporting evidence, have been harassed by Kavanaugh at a law school party. And there remains Allen.

What if none of the accusations against Woody Allen are true? Allen, after nearly thirty years, continues to deny every meaningful detail of the claims, with no one else coming forward to support them, and with the Farrow children divided over their veracity. But not only that, what if Ronan Farrow has pursued the vendetta against his father knowing it was a likely fake? The account by Ronan's brother Moses (starkly refuting almost every one of his mother's central claims about the alleged molestation), who was fourteen at the time of his mother's accusations against Allen and present at the time of the alleged incident—Ronan was five—certainly suggests you would need to be willfully blind not to have major doubts.

At the same time, even given questions about him, Ronan Farrow's media profile remains unassailable—he's a righteous fighter. You're an outlier—part of the problem—if you question him. Moses Farrow was unable to find an established publisher for his account; instead he posted it on social media.

Ben Smith, the *New York Times* media columnist, tried to chip away at Farrow in May 2020, taking worthy issue with some of Farrow's journalistic methods. But Smith seemed to shy away from asking the larger question that appeared to be on his mind: How exactly did Ronan Farrow get to be Ronan Farrow?

It is undoubtedly heretical to compare Farrow to Weinstein. And yet each seems to have seen the media business as a personal battlefield, a kill-or-be-killed prison yard. And for many, there are similar fears in crossing them—part of the reason so many young actors and actresses have publicly elected not to work with Allen is the fear of Farrow's condemnation.

In 2017, Allen's wife Soon-Yi Previn—in some sense the central character in the events that still pursue her family, but frustrated by the lack of agency she is allowed in explaining those events (Farrow continues to suggest that his adopted sister is intellectually impaired, risible to those who know her)—gave an interview to *New York* magazine about growing up in Mia's house. It's a devastating portrait, echoing the account given by her brother Moses, of extraordinary family enmity and dysfunction, with few fates being as surreal and dark as to be adopted by Mia Farrow. But the piece would have been much more devastating, except that Farrow closely tracked the story—as Weinstein would track Farrow's story about him—threatening and pressuring the magazine, which, according to the writer Daphne Merkin, uncommonly, if not unethically, showed Farrow substantial parts of the story, if not the entire article, before it was published, allowing him to critique it and demand changes.

Two years later, with copies of Allen's memoir *Apropos of Nothing* already printed—and with the publisher contractually insisting that Allen not disclose its publication to even close friends for fear of how Farrow might react—Farrow mounted an overnight campaign that prompted a walkout by the younger members of the publishing company's staff, demanding cancellation of the title. The publisher capitulated and pulped the book.

Yes, Farrow has won. Hands down. And become a great power in the land.

Harvey

The confusion is to have been so lavishly and for so long rewarded for exceptional and inexplicable behavior and then, in a whipsaw zeitgeist change, prosecuted for it. What options are there but to stick with what has always worked for you?

"This book is worth millions . . . millions. You keep domestic, I'll take foreign," said Harvey Weinstein. And I had better agree to the deal now because there were other writers beating his door down. "Everybody wants to write this book. Who wouldn't?"

He was in the second week of his trial in Manhattan Criminal Court, charged with sexual assault and rape. After court he headed up to his lawyer's office on Madison Avenue. In ill-health, perhaps exaggerated on the jury's behalf, the man with a once great entourage was yet, in his walker with the tennis-ball wheels, still trailed by an assistant to whom he shouted questions and orders.

The book was to be the life story of Harvey Weinstein, from rags to riches, and, in addition, a furious attack on his accusers. His assistant was sent off to get the PowerPoint deck that outlined the injustices against him and the lies and hypocrisy of the women out to get him.

I was here out of pity and interest. He had imposed himself, impossible to ignore, on a media generation—the greatest Hollywood figure of his time. And now look at him.

Once, years ago, I had written about him in a way he hadn't liked. He immediately retaliated by engineering an attack on me on "Page Six," the gossip section of the *New York Post*. "Never underestimate the power of

Harvey Weinstein on this page," said Richard Johnson, the editor of "Page Six," when I called to ask what gives. Never underestimate the power of Harvey Weinstein anywhere, was the message.

"I can fuck anybody," he told me, affably, shrugging, when later I asked him about the "Page Six" hit.

He was, he reminded me now in his criminal lawyer's cramped Midtown office at a conference table with sticky residue, his part-time PR guy sitting in, the most successful book publisher of all time. Miramax Books: from nothing to, overnight, more bestsellers than anybody in the industry. And what had he known about the book business? And when all this was over he was going to go back into the book business because everybody else in the book business was so dumb that you couldn't help but make money in it.

Was the enfeebled man in the walker facing life in prison delusional now, or was he *always* delusional—so fiercely able to insist that everything was as he wanted it to be that, life being too short to resist, enough people gave in and agreed with him?

So many women with all their rage directed at him—"Ninety in all, or so, but only thirty-five really matter"—was just the background to larger plans. Yes, the trial was on his mind, but it was one of many projects.

"The book is a focus. We've got to tell this story. We can definitely give an hour a day, more if we have to." He looked to the PR man.

"But—if the verdict goes against you?" the PR man gingerly asked in an effort to acknowledge some reality.

"What—would I have to go to jail immediately?" he asked of no one in particular. "We'll appeal."

"It's possible they might take you into custody right away," said the PR man.

"Wow," he said, taken aback. Had nobody told him what being convicted of violent crimes might entail? Whatever. Prison was not on his mind.

The book was on his mind. But the book was as much an internal monologue as it was an actual book. It was reality as he dwelled in it, the superstructure of how he was reasoning his way out of this, and if it could only be taken, some part of it—he pushed the PowerPoint forward—and, well, perhaps rooted through the British press. Yes, that was the way. The

Daily Mail. "Geordie Greig"—the *Daily Mail*'s editor—"is one of my best friends. He'd pay a fortune for this!" That would certainly send a message. The real story. Why the women were after him. Yes.

Curiously, he was on a first-name basis with his accusers—"Annabella," "Mimi," "Jessica"—as though the trial and scandal and Sturm und Drang were just part of the continuing conflict that, to him, was seduction.

Almost everything he said was cockeyed. His present situation was as stark and hopeless as it could possibly be, and yet his version of it workable, variable. But even if you discounted everything he offered, saw it all as addled or delusional, his voice had a unique, even beguiling, authority. It was confidential, full of intimacy and friendliness. People had tried to explain this before, how out of grandiosity, malevolence, and reality distortion, he yet produced a marked likability factor.

In fact, the book he proposed was not uncompelling. A picaresque account of a man without virtues or advantages, an ugly, unsympathetic man, who by sheer dint of the promoter's drive achieves great success and gets the girl(s). He's an outsider looking in who crosses the threshold by assuming the identity of the insiders, but more determined than they are, stronger than they are, more fantastic than the most fantastic of them. He has ingested the Hollywood mogul myth and become the greatest of them there ever was. Yes, he is not a rapist, he is a *mogul*. The willfulness of people not seeing that elemental distinction is just another part of the inevitable war against him—rape is a mere rhetorical flourish by the other side. Oh yes, and in this book he will name names. He won't go down alone.

As much as such a book might be the true story of the dark heart of American success, and of an industry collectively guilty of everything Weinstein is personally guilty of, it, of course, won't get written. It is not just too dark, and Weinstein a character too repellent, and the industry now bent on protecting itself, but you would have to deal with Weinstein to write it.

Weinstein is himself, by many accounts, virtually illiterate, never reading anything. He achieved his vaunted "taste" as a consensus of other people with vaunted "taste"—an ugly guy, he sought out the cool and beautiful people. And yet, other than the words themselves, he considers himself a writer.

"Virtually everything I've produced, I'm the writer on. I don't get the credit, but I'm the real writer," he assures.

In fact, as another insult, without the writers he's employed, he's had to actually write his own screenplay—which, to prove it, needs to be read on the spot. He calls to his assistant. The screenplay is produced. "Just start it," he instructs. Except that it's unreadable, twice the length of an ordinary screenplay, and without evident point or direction. "Keep going. Keep going," he urges.

Anyway, he can't write his own story and would be a vicious and mortal roadblock for anyone else writing it. But never mind, of course. There is not going to be a story. No one wants to know the real Harvey Weinstein.

Not even Harvey Weinstein. Really, he just wants to talk. Talk is the power. Talk makes things happen. You don't know what is going to happen, but if you talk enough to enough people, something happens, and then, if you're Harvey, you badger and wheedle and hammer and threaten to make it what you want to happen. Sex and movies. And the more you talk, the more random things might happen that you can try to bend to your will. You just hit on them all—girls and everybody else.

His defense is its own admission. "It was transactional." He could force girls to have sex with him because he had something they wanted; he paid them with what he could give them (forget the fact that he often cheated them—that's just the natural give-and-take of any transaction). He was so ugly, and miserable, and unlovable that no one would have sex with him otherwise. That's the admission: no one actually wanted to have sex with him. Ever.

"But is that rape?" he demands. Well, if you have to ask the question—even his PR guy averts his gaze.

Anyway . . . it's too much. All this conflict, more than even he can tolerate, he says, now the martyr. He's ready to turn his back on it all. Just walk away. "What I want to do is just go live in Italy and get away from everything. Maybe make a film or two a year."

Yes, and perhaps fly.

Okay, but here's what he really wants—here's the ask. "I want you to come down and see the show. We'll arrange it. VIP."

"The show?"

"The trial. Come the day after tomorrow. It's gonna be good. And then you'll see if you want to write something."

"I probably won't be writing anything."

"Yeah, well, you'll see if there's something you might want to do for the London papers. I think that's the best way to go. You'll speak to Geordie. We were going to do his book about Lucian Freud, what a beautiful book, as a film. I still want to do it. Anyway, we'll get you in. You won't have to wait."

"If I come, I can wait like everybody else."

"Oh god, no, we'll make all the arrangements. Text me tomorrow afternoon. We'll have major fireworks for you. You're gonna love it. You gotta come. Be worth your while. I promise. It will blow your mind."

Texts followed the next day, confirming times, entrances, point people. Then a request: "Can you call Harvey?" And another: "Harvey needs to speak to you."

And from the PR guy: "Do you have a minute to call Harvey? He just wants to make sure everything is a go and you have all the details."

"You missed a great day," said Harvey when I called. "I should have gotten you there today. But tomorrow will be fantastic. You'll have a good seat. Have you spoken to Geordie?"

"Have I spoken to Geordie?"

"They're going to love this. These girls are so transparent. It's disgusting. What did Geordie say? The *Mail* has got to want this."

"Harvey, really, this is not what you want now. This would not be good for you, in my opinion."

"No, this is important, something like this, in your voice—"

"Harvey—"

"Hey—wait—I know you think I'm a nice guy. Just hanging out. I really am a nice guy. I'm a totally nice guy. But don't give me any of this bullshit. If we're going to do this, you've got to do it. I'm a nice guy, but I can turn into Michael Corleone just like that! Michael fucking Corleone."

"Okay, I'm hanging up, Harvey."

"Why? Why?"

"I'm hanging up now."

Twenty seconds later, the PR guy: "What the hell happened?"

"He's turning into Michael Corleone, he said. I guess that was a threat."

"Oh, damn it. Did he mean it?"

"I don't know."

"I'll call you back."

Fifteen seconds later: "He didn't mean it. He was joking, really."

"Okay . . . but I'm going to pass on this."

"Oh come on, everybody deserves another chance."

"Yeah, but I'm going to pass."

"Oh, jeez."

And then, repeated messages from Weinstein. Apologies. Abasement. Misunderstanding. Under terrible pressure. Another chance. No obligation. Just come. Please.

And then the PR guy: "Harvey's very hurt that you haven't responded to him. Can you just text him and say no hard feelings?"

"That means a lot," said Harvey, who four weeks later was convicted of rape and assault and sentenced to twenty-three years in prison. "Let's at least have a dinner or two down the road."

Jann

Long ago, a glamorous Hollywood producer with a supermodel wife agreed to buy the film rights to my first book and invited me to his East Hampton house for the weekend. The centerpiece of the visit was to be an intimate dinner party for various other glamorous people and the guest of honor, Jann Wenner, the editor in chief and owner of *Rolling Stone*. It is now almost impossible to express how meaningful and central Jann Wenner was then—that summer of 1979. The seventies were Wenner's decade; he was as large as any of the rock stars he helped make. Let me go out on a limb to say that, as an equivalency, at that moment, Wenner, as innovator, impresario, cultural arbiter, and difficult personality, was Steve Jobs–like. So great was his stature that, having done hardly anything very notable in the three and a half decades since, he still remains an important media and social fixture in New York.

Anyway, the dinner party unfolded, the caterers set up, the other guests arrived, drugs and alcohol were consumed, hours passed, and no Jann Wenner. Waiting. You could almost literally see sobriety return, and mellowness and eager expectation, that mood of the socially entitled, turn into anxiety, even fear. And yet no Jann. A call earlier in the evening—he was on his way—and then nothing.

Finally, at about one o'clock in the morning, the glamorous producer, face ever redder, just burst into tears. A total social breakdown. Mortification of the cultural soul. The zeitgeist that had promised to stop and embrace him had instead had second thoughts. Everything lost. Including, a few days later, a victim of an embarrassment never to be spoken of again, my movie deal. Alas.

But in some sense the incident itself was like a movie deal—a Jann moment. That mix of ego and attention deficit and unregulated behavior invariably resulting in disappointment, if not outrage and incomprehension, has long been a media rite of passage.

* * *

Wenner is one of the earliest examples of media owners becoming as culturally significant, and as temperamental, as stars or news makers. Wenner himself—certainly not a star, and not really an editor or writer—has been as much a figure and beneficiary of the promotional ecosystem as he was a facilitator of it. The media as a self-promotional power, as a way to turn cultural ambitions into cultural standing, was in part a Wenner invention (he certainly took full advantage of this development). *Rolling Stone* existed not just as a way to make money from the exploding music culture but to join Wenner to the culture.

That is also the impulse that, late last year, in an article about rape on college campuses, would embroil *Rolling Stone* in what some people believe, forty-eight years after its founding, is its death-knell controversy. The writer Sabrina Rubin Erdely, a freelancer specializing in stories about rape victims, sought to illustrate the popular media idea of a "rape culture" on American campuses. To do this she identified a woman, code-named "Jackie," who claimed to have been raped amid a drunken fraternity party, and, in the you-were-there New Journalism style pioneered in part by many *Rolling Stone* writers in the seventies—Hunter S. Thompson, Joe Eszterhas, Lester Bangs—told in the greatest detail Jackie's story. Almost all of which turned out to be utterly false. Many postmortems followed. The Columbia Journalism School published a formal investigation five months after the story appeared, finding, on *Rolling Stone*'s part, a collapse of virtually every journalistic standard and norm.

But in a sense the most curious element of the affair was never examined: Why was anyone taking *Rolling Stone* seriously in the first place? How in hell was it still thought of as consequential and authoritative?

Whatever it once might have been—and we will get to that—it wasn't that anymore. Not only had it lost its importance and power in the music industry, but the music industry itself, from where *Rolling Stone*'s influence sprang, had declined to a mere shadow of its cultural relevance. As celebrity and fan media, *Rolling Stone* had been eclipsed by a large number of other titles and outlets. As an alternative voice, well, the internet had happened. And as a rich and profitable independent media company, *Rolling Stone* had declined to a fraction of its once-vaunted value. Who cared about it anymore?

And here's something else that failed to come up in the endless, deep examination and ontological questioning of its journalistic methods: *Rolling Stone* has always been filled with tosh. You might even go so far as to say that one of its main accomplishments, its publishing genius, was that it made up its own world.

Certainly, I don't think it would be too controversial to say that almost everything it ever wrote about the music and entertainment business was written to a purpose and effect that had almost nothing to do with, strictly speaking, journalism. In part it had to do with Wenner's own relationship with an industry he wanted leverage in. And in part it had to do with the kind of reality, more coherent, more attractive, more romantic, that Wenner wanted to project.

The socially ambitious Wenner extended this reality distortion to a wider cultural reach, and, most ambitiously, to politics: Hunter S. Thompson covered the 1972 presidential campaign and, in a 1976 anointment in *Rolling Stone*'s pages, gave Jimmy Carter (Jimmy Carter!), many people believe, the liberal credibility to win the nomination and presidency—turning Wenner into a kingmaker.

Rolling Stone's journalism was reality distortion. That's what its self-description, *gonzo*, actually meant, and for many years, it was quite a singular virtue. Wenner's contribution to journalism was never to uncover truth, or to establish the record, but to allow a particular cadre of oddballs, some inspired, some demented, many just screwing around, to create a kind of narrative that wasn't much available in other venues and whose originality and lack of journalistic constraints helped define the magazine, if not the truth.

Putting aside journalistic responsibility—not an issue that raised its head very often in *Rolling Stone*'s first twenty years—Wenner is, for better or worse, one of the last people to believe in the act of publishing as an effective world of make-believe. The *Rolling Stone* world, its rock and gonzo ethos not all that different from, say, *Playboy*'s libidinous world, did not exist, except in *Rolling Stone*'s pages.

Inevitably, perhaps, Wenner came to take this world very seriously. Well, it is unlikely he took his music journalism very seriously, and it is unlikely he took many of his journalists, most of whom he fell out with, too seriously, but he did take himself very seriously.

He created a fantasy world both for his ever-younger readers and to accommodate his own dreams: he was a media personage, a mogul, a sybarite, a contender to be—before much richer people made him look ever more small-time—the most freewheelin', I-can-have-everything, I'm-a-star glamour-puss on earth.

He was a feudal baron, media nobility, running *Rolling Stone* as a kind of eighteenth-century kingdom over which he had absolute control. Indeed, as *Rolling Stone*, once a singular power in the music business, managed to misread and miss out on every important trend in music's changing universe over the past generation, its own internecine conflicts and Wenner's authoritarian management style yet continued to make big media news.

Nothing about *Rolling Stone* was as important as this fact: it was his.

This produced not only a bizarre journalism result—page after page of inconsequential celebrity and fan news, broken by a long-form report on a weighty social issue—but an eccentric business outcome. During the eighties and nineties, virtually every independent magazine in New York (in the seventies there may have been as many as twenty-five important independent titles) was merged with or acquired by a handful of big publishers. Except *Rolling Stone*. Indeed, no period had seen as much turmoil and transformation in the publishing business as this one. It affected every enterprise in the industry. Except, somehow, *Rolling Stone*.

In a way, this is sort of heroic. Much of the consolidation in the business was damaging to the unique identities of the magazines that lost their independence. On the other hand, you start to look mighty foolish if you think you can wholly ignore radical and tectonic shifts in your business.

Rolling Stone was ever courted. Everybody tried to buy it. At various points the business might have been worth as much as a billion dollars, and, in eighties dollars, on an inflation-adjusted basis, much more. But Wenner, who was as money hungry as anybody, held out, even as it was clear the industry was changing in a way that would make it vastly harder for *Rolling Stone* to make big money, and as the magazine itself became less relevant. Why?

In 2005, a lifetime since he failed to show up at that East Hampton dinner party, he called me in to discuss moving my column from *Vanity Fair* to *Rolling Stone*. He could not have been more courtly in his manner or generous in his offer, but he did say that I should understand that *Rolling Stone* had a point of view—"an agenda," he actually called it—and that writers at the magazine had to follow it: that is, although he didn't quite put it as such, a mishmash lefty tilt and a careful bow to friends of Jann. Now, in the scheme of things, *Rolling Stone*'s agenda hardly amounts to a hill of beans and I do not mean to make this a journalistic issue or to be shocked at all. But what I think is notable, even quaint, is that, in some screwball way, Wenner probably turned down vast riches for his agenda—not even so much a political agenda but an agenda that gave him the right to set his own agenda.

Curiously, Wenner—who last year agreed to cooperate with the writer Joe Hagan on his biography—is trying now to transition what is left of *Rolling Stone* from his own day-to-day management to that of his twenty-five-year-old son, Gus. Perhaps that is another reason Wenner has held out and held on. You aren't really a king if you can't pass on your kingdom.

Indeed, various inside reports credit Gus with responsibility for the rape article—a like-father-like-son approach to journalism and agendas and an effort, however much a lazy one, to stay on the side of the liberal angels, however unexamined, of the moment. And many believe that the reason nobody in the chain of command, neither writer nor editors, was fired in the aftermath of the discredited rape story is that true responsibility would have then quickly found its way to the heir and, hence, to his father.

That's not the way you want it to end. Even if end it must.

Hitch

Christopher Hitchens, my former colleague at *Vanity Fair*, was diagnosed with cancer in 2010. But even before his illness, and his death almost two years later, he was on his way to sainthood.

His beatification probably started with a ten-thousand-word profile about him written by Ian Parker in 2006 in the *New Yorker*. "A portrait," according to Parker, "in the shadow of a gigantic self-portrait." Hitchens had occupied a pretty conventional slot as a left-wing writer in a period when the Left was in decline and the free-market ethos was on the rise. By 2003 and 2004, however, he had become one of the more prominent left-wing converts to the Iraq War (perhaps the only one). This conversion was the subject of the *New Yorker* story. But the profile went easy on his politics and celebrated Hitchens's lonely battles, warriorlike contrariness, and determined originality in a time of uptight conventionality (everybody had stopped drinking and smoking, but not Hitch). His I-stand-alone notoriety continued with the publication of his 2007 book *God Is Not Great*, which became his first bestseller. His stature further rose with a second bestseller, a memoir of his against-the-grain life, *Hitch 22*. And then, on the heels of his memoir, came his fatal illness, chronicled in print and in public forums. Fevered encomiums followed.

This transformation from political irregular and hack polemicist to towering moral figure was curious, if not amazing, to many people whose careers had intersected with his. How did the character actor become a leading man? How did the fool become a sage? And what about the bad stuff? Not just his full-throttled embrace of the Bush war but, before that, his casual and convenient betrayal of his friend the Hillary Clinton aide Sidney Blumenthal, back in the Monica Lewinsky days. Or his weirdly tolerant relationship with some of the era's most infamous Holocaust deniers. These are the kind of epochal contretemps that, in the chattering class, usually make for deep enmity rather than enduring love. Then, too, how has this uniquely British figure, full of British class issues, British political hairsplitting, British literary conceits, and plummy accent to boot, become, in his transmutation, a super-American—a gunslinger journalist?

He was, self-styled, a writer engaged with his time, a bookish man called to join the day's great and bloody battles of conscience. But really his issues were largely of another era: internecine squabbles on the left, a Cold War attention to the world's geo-sectarian divisions, God's existence . . . or not. He never much grappled with technology, or money, or media, or the environment, or racism—factors that, surely, were remaking the world a lot faster and a lot more profoundly than his longtime preoccupations.

He saw himself as a sixties guy, even making the case that he was a significant figure in the tumultuous period from 1966 to 1968: "I did my stuff in helping my American comrades discredit first President Johnson and then President Nixon." Although, in fact, he was still a teenager in 1968. ("If you remember the sixties," in Robin Williams's famous formulation, "you weren't there.") Walking into a Hitchens "event" in recent years could seem like having been dropped back into the late-sixties maelstrom: Hitchens, sometimes with his wife Carol Blue, falling rock star–like from a limo, feet bare and bottle in hand, with these events often breaking down into obscenities and name-calling.

His frequent public forums—in which Hitchens's British-style debating skills were presented as a sort of miracle—had become a significant and profitable part of his career. He had a cast of agents and hucksters who would organize and promote these events in cheap venues, reserving him a cut of the door.

In American media culture, he took a place last occupied by the conservative pundit William F. Buckley Jr., who regularly wowed middle America with his hauteur and erudition on his talk show *Firing Line.* Of note, Hitchens seemed almost invariably to be matched in his debates with lesser lights—it was Hitchens among the stupids.

I was always on reasonable terms with Hitchens—or certainly had the

younger man's good grace to mostly shut up while he talked—and once, at the height of the Iraq War, he asked me to moderate one of his public debates.

The other protagonist was probably demented (if not homeless) and borderline coherent. Still, it was a packed house. Hitchens arrived drunk—though I wondered if it was more pretend drunk because he kept talking about how drunk he was—but at some point he certainly was drunk.

I'd say he had only partial awareness of the event itself. The famous adlibber seemed to stay focused because his lines were carefully memorized. The other debater kept interrupting with obscenities and catcalls and, trying to be a diligent moderator, I kept stopping the debate and returning to where the interruptions began. A swaying Hitchens would back up to the cue and repeat his lines verbatim.

Eventually it became impossible to continue—although Hitchens himself seemed immune to the insults and commotion. But I finally said, in some despair, "Christopher, let's just go." When he hesitated, I said, "Well, I'm off," shaming him, it seemed, into following me. But then he shortly doubled back, delivering himself, in some obviously blissful sense, into the passion of the crowd.

When last seen, he was, in rave fashion, at the center of a group of young men worshipfully levitating him, while others catcalled and gestured obscenely from the sidelines.

In contrast to his Hunter S. Thompson persona as a connoisseur of chaos and self-destructive excess, he also styled himself as a public intellectual. He was, or fancied himself to be, disciplined, precise, scholarly, even pedantic when it came to spelling out both arcane facts and moral imperatives. He was not, though, an academic or scholar in any actual or formal sense. He was more accurately an autodidact—with the autodidact's self-justifications and disproportion.

Along with his many books, there was a near-daily production of columns and book reviews. Much of the work was repetitive and boilerplate, the same subjects recast for different outlets. The myriad essays tended to the pontifical, full of moral dudgeon and high virtue and not a lot of surprises—nor much humor. Nevertheless, such output had the effect of making the game look easy. It was writing that probably appealed more to would-be writers than to readers.

In all his manic industry, he produced no memorable book.

He wrote short admiring books about George Orwell, Thomas Jefferson, and Thomas Paine as well as pamphlet-like books attacking Henry Kissinger, Mother Teresa, and Bill Clinton, but no true biography. Most of his books are cobbled-together collections, or pieces of columns. There is no narrative long enough to justify his reputation as storyteller or polemicist. He proudly told people his God book was written in four months.

In a sense, Hitchens's most self-defining book, or his key personal positioning statement (though all his books are strong on personal positioning), is his short *Letters to a Young Contrarian*.

The conceit of the book is that he is the teacher and that an admiring and precocious student has asked for his advice—a setup that only the young and admiring might find credible ("You rather tend to flatter and embarrass me, when you inquire my advice as to how a radical or 'contrarian' life may be lived"). The book is modeled on Rainer Maria Rilke's *Letters to a Young Poet* but, hopelessly cloying, feels more like Khalil Gibran's *The Prophet*.

The book's message is . . . well, nothing more than that young people should challenge the conventional wisdom and question authority. It is also defensive and self-aggrandizing as it lays out the case for being Christopher Hitchens. (A Hitchens aside that might have been directed at Hitchens himself: "If you have ever argued with a religious devotee . . . you will have noticed that his self-esteem and pride are involved in the dispute and that you are asking him to give up something more than a point in argument.")

It quite ends up making the case against him. Hitchens was really not a contrarian—at least not a contrarian in the sense of someone with exceptional, divergent, surprising, and lonely opinions—but rather doctrinal and partisan. What's more, he mostly gave offense where no offense would really be taken—or where he could be guaranteed a phalanx of defenders. Mother Teresa was one of his theoretically courageous targets—except who cares about Mother Teresa?

His God book followed Richard Dawkins's *The God Delusion*. Atheism was already a bestselling view. The God book is also a particular sleight of hand. It makes a persuasive case against a deserving target, so you might forget that virtually the entirety of the Hitchens-reading audience is comprised of nonbelievers—nonbelievers who have not even had to have a crisis of faith. The God question may have been a lively and risky one in the sixties, but now belief in God is more a demographic condition than a philosophical argument. (Hitchens seemed to enjoy debating the red-state faithful—again, Hitchens among the stupids.) Still, it was, in its embrace of conventional wisdom, a major commercial success—and, in that sense, a further self-justification.

His crowning work is his memoir, which, released days before his illness was diagnosed, takes on a special poignancy. It's an old-style memoir full of avoidance and self-congratulations. Hitchens does have a painful story. His mother commits suicide in the first chapter—but this is dispensed with forthwith as mere background to Hitchens's own greater experiences. He confesses his youthful homosexuality—but really it's not so much a confession, but a dismissal: everybody did it, pay no attention. (His friend Gully Wells, often thought to be the model for the protagonist in his friend Martin Amis's first book, *The Rachel Papers*—and, as the ever-name-dropping Hitchens reminds us, the stepdaughter of the famous philosopher A. J. Ayer—widely pointed out to friends after the book came out that Hitchens was "gay much longer than all the other boys who were gay." But that is not a conflict in the book.) The book, much of it about the quarrels on the left, circumvents the personal—or emotional. While it's a birth-to-almost-death autobiography, great parts of his life are excised from it, including an eight-year first marriage that produced two children.

It's like a presidential memoir. A keepsake book, a gift book for believers. And what you have to believe in is Christopher Hitchens. As death approached there were ever-more believers.

The book is also about social climbing. In an obvious sense, Hitchens's entire life is about social climbing.

He turns the when, the how, the what-if of the almost-missed chance, the luck of not saying the nasty thing he might have been expected to say, of his first meeting with Martin Amis into a Proustian moment. (Hitchens denies in his memoir that he had a sexual obsession with Amis, but it sure sounds like he does, and his friend Gully Wells has spread it about that he was hopelessly smitten and for years mooned around about Amis.)

The background to everything he writes is about who he knows and who he met when—and how fortuitous each of these meetings turned out to be. The entire Hitchens oeuvre is an orgasm of name-dropping: "My late friend Ron Ridenhour, who became briefly famous . . . my dear friend Salman Rushdie . . . my dear friend Ian McEwan . . . [I first met] Thabo Mbeki, now the president of South Africa . . . I first met Kim Dae-jung, now the president of South Korea and a Nobel Laureate for Peace . . . my Chilean friend Ariel Dorfman . . . my friend Peter Schneider, the great novelistic chronicler of Berlin life . . . my friend Adam Michnik, the Polish dissident . . . my friend Martin Amis . . . my friend Salman Rushdie [again] . . . my old friend Edward Said . . . I was to become very close to Jessica Mitford . . . my Argentine anti-fascist friend Jacobo Timerman . . . my later friend Jessica Mitford [again] . . . our dear friend Anthony Holden . . . my friendship with Brian and Keith McNally . . . my friend Martin Amis [again] . . . I knew Susan [Sontag] slightly by then . . . I was introduced to Salman Rushdie [again] . . . my friend Marina Warner . . ."

The obvious point—the instructive point—is that this is how Hitchens, the son of a career naval officer, navigated his upward trajectory through the class system. He made himself the consummate insider. I can't think of a more clubby writer than Hitchens. And clubby in that very British sense of ever trying to be a member of a better club.

He was off to boarding school at age eight. He was bisexual until he wasn't (that particular form of upper-class British sexuality). He was hermetically Oxbridge. Of course, he was a lefty in angry (and fond) opposition to clubby Britain. His intimates were also other lefties all drawn from a *Brideshead* set. Save for Saul Bellow and Gore Vidal, practically all his literary models were sniffily British. His style of journalism, that particular, opportunistic, cynical British form (ridiculed by the British, too), was all about parachuting into a foreign country and acquiring instant expertise. Rejecting Britain, he became an exaggerated figure of Britishness. And although he professed a constant formal love for America, he couldn't help his condescension and contempt—which was probably appealing, too, for Americans.

Notably, many of those in Hitchens's set moved to America—Britain being too small for them and their ambitions. Anna Wintour, whom Hitchens almost married, became the editor of *Vogue*. Gully Wells and her husband at the BBC got a house in the West Village, and Hitchens lived in their basement. Later, he moved into the basement at Andrew Cockburn and his wife Leslie's place (Cockburn ultimately fell out with Hitchens). Salman Rushdie moved to America, too. And finally, Amis followed.

This pack of media Brits formed a movable power clique, always promoting one another. (There is a point here, too, about America as a fading literary superpower and their opportunities in this vacuum.)

Of note, somehow Hitchens, for a long time the runt of this Brit-lit pack, the courtier and designated promoter, emerged as its most famous member.

He was a bully. This may have been because he was so often drunk.

But it is also because to him—both as a matter of character and, no doubt, owing to his long years on the left—this was a binary world, good and bad, right and wrong. In that, he had the appeal more of a Fox News personality than of an essayist dwelling in the gray areas.

Still, he was theatrical or clownish enough to be forgiven for his often near-violent opinions—"Oh that's just Hitch." Except he wasn't just theatrical. He wielded something close to an actual stick. He could be dangerous.

There was his malevolent animosity toward Bill Clinton, a companion piece to his blithe satisfaction, at age fourteen (repeated with renewed satisfaction in his memoir), over JFK's assassination.

His issue, and his near-violent reaction, was about the relativism of American liberalism—its crafty compromises, its moral triangulation, its Clintonianism. The purity (and verbal violence) of the American right was much more to his temperament. Clinton, the master relativist, caused Hitchens to froth wildly.

Part of this was sixties stuff. It may be that Hitchens, nearly three years younger than Clinton, resented the Oxford upperclassman's greater sixties status. (Hitchens seemed to have a minor obsession with whether or not he was ever in the same room as Clinton at Oxford—naturally, he concluded he was.) Hitchens accused Clinton of informing on American antiwar students during his time in Britain.

Conspiracy lurks behind almost all of Hitchens's causes and passions.

This was the apparent background to Hitchens's decision to testify against his friend Sidney Blumenthal (his best friend!), who had testified that he had not besmirched Monica Lewinsky to the media. Hitchens said, no, that wasn't true—Blumenthal told *him* that Lewinsky was a stalker.

And suddenly hundreds of thousands of dollars in legal fees, as well as possibly his freedom, hung in the balance for Blumenthal because of a gossipy lunch.

Hitchens's rationale was straightforward: he had to turn on his friend to help get Clinton.

Then Iraq: Hitchens took up his defense of the war when it still looked like it would be a certain American romp. He was very vocal about his view of the war's righteousness for another year or so, becoming a sort of mascot of the neoconservatives, and then gradually quieted down as everything went wrong.

Then the Holocaust: for reasons involving the Left, Israel, the British ambivalence toward Jews, and perhaps his own later-in-life discovery that his mother was Jewish, people who walked the thin line of Holocaust revision and outright doubt held great fascination for him. But if you tried to call him on this (indeed, he was probably not a Holocaust denier as much as a Holocaust-denier enabler), he threatened suit. On top of everything else, the thin-skinned Hitchens was litigious—he'd cost you money if you crossed him.

Again, all this might have more logically left him as a controversial and divisive figure. In a sense, though, if not by plan, then by remarkable instinct, he was saved by God. He was forgiven his right-wing doctrinal alliance because he was now challenging the right's belief in God. (At the same time, he mitigated this affront to his new friends on the right by liking the Islam God even less than the Christian one.)

Hitchens was a great social figure. In a way, he was accessible to all. But I always found him perplexingly impersonal. There was the wall of all that verbiage. Off the page and in person . . . blah blah blah . . . and always repeating his own columns. Drunk, he'd reprise them, in the same conversation, again.

I never had any sense of whether Hitchens was happy or despairing. Lonely or content. Satisfied or self-loathing. But certainly being drunk so much of the time would not suggest he was tip-top.

It was an external life. His greatest effort always seemed to be to live in public, with the effort itself being more important than the nature of the opinions or controversy that got him there. This made him something of an object of curiosity and admiration in a time when more and more (if not most) writers were losing their platforms and retreating to the edges.

I think it is probably not a coincidence that as the existential crisis of journalism became more severe, Hitchens became an increasingly salutary and reassuring figure. In spite of it all, he continued and thrived. This is another version, of course, of being famous for being famous.

He became a model for the large numbers of young people who wanted into the game (confusingly, as the business shrank, more people sought to be in it). Not only did his example suggest that there could still be a livelihood living by one's pen, he showed that there could still be great romance to it—and damn the internet.

He spoke his mind and lived his life with profit and impunity—or so it seemed.

Arianna

I simply do not feel the bad things it would be so easy to feel about Arianna Huffington. The bile, the resentment, the envy, the desire to wound, or at least the dream of wounding, that accrue around the inflated, the pretend, the scheming, and the ridiculous just isn't here.

Of course, now I have implied that Arianna is all those things. Well, perhaps. But if one person must be . . . I feel much better that it is Arianna. Which is, in a sense, her talent, to be so transparent that she is not only forgiven but actually understood.

In five years, she has upended the news business in America and has become one of the country's most famous women. Her news site, the Huffington Post, started with the deliberately craven and unintuitive concept that Arianna could convince her celebrity friends to write for free, and that if you had celebrities doing it, everyone else would, or at least everyone else who wanted to do what celebrities do. It worked. Celebrities, it turns out, are desperate to be noticed. They have opinions. And they need help using the internet.

But mostly they know Arianna. Indulging any doubts you might have, you still couldn't question her tirelessness (one of her pet issues is the importance of sleep). Suddenly, wherever there were celebrities, through whatever means they might be contacted, Arianna was there, asking them to blog for her. She would say "blog" in a fashion that seemed akin to asking people to pray for her (how could you refuse?) or, with the pitch of her peculiar accent, do yoga with her, or—such was her fervency—as an invitation to unimagined new pleasures.

She called me, she wrote to me, she met with me, she waited around corners to beseech me to blog for her—and there wasn't a chance I would (although, in fact, later I did). It was nuts. Nuts it worked, nuts she would pursue it so relentlessly.

But perhaps she was born to this mission. Not only was she indefatigable, but she had a fabled Rolodex. Her career—a monument to charm, tenacity, and tirelessness, even before she started the Huffington Post—was built on the simple premise that the process of becoming well known is precisely connected to knowing people more well known than you are. They pull you up.

Now, many people do this. They network, which has come to have rather positive, even democratic, connotations; or they social climb—at least in the eyes of the envious and disapproving—with its negative emphasis on artifice and status. It's a means to an end.

Few people truly appreciate the art—the pleasure—of knowing the right people. The right people cut through the barriers to happiness like a knife through butter. Knowing them is the real job—amassing them, following up with them, finding common ground with them, sustaining their enthusiasm for you.

It's notable that Arianna comes out of Britain, where the penalties are so much greater if you actually get caught social climbing. On the other hand, the best climbers I know in New York are Brits. They mobilize. They use, well . . . social skills.

Here's a premise: Americans don't have good manners—that is, a prescribed way of behaving that mandates a prescribed way of behaving back.

Americans, for instance, do not give dinner parties. This includes even most social-climbing New Yorkers, unless they have fabulous staffs (or access to a corporate caterer). In the most status-conscious city in the world, we are all afraid to entertain in the home.

But not the Brits in New York. They invite you for supper, a rare, peculiar ritual (the emphasis for Brits is on the invitation and conversation, not the food, or even, it often seems, on cleaning the house). In return, they expect you to invite them. And if that doesn't happen, at least they expect you to spread the word that there is an invitation to be had—and New Yorkers queue up for a dinner invitation.

* * *

Arianna Stassinopoulos arrived in New York aged thirty. She was born in Athens and moved to London as a teenager, where she cut an impressive path—through Cambridge, where she headed the Cambridge Union, then as a TV guest and talking head, and then as the girlfriend of journalist Bernard Levin, twice her age, who ultimately declined to marry her. So, husband hunting in New York, she rented an apartment and . . . threw dinner parties.

I could call up Arianna and confirm the best story I know about these dinner parties. But I don't want it not to be true. I tell my children this story as an example of savvy and pluck. (I have heard it from three different people.)

Arianna set about having dinner parties, inviting the most prestigious New Yorkers who would come and, at an appointed hour, she would deliver an impromptu toast, fifteen minutes or more of sweeping, seamless, knowing, witty observations, the likes of which no awkward table in New York had ever heard before. Grown men, those attracted to ambitious women anyway, swooned. When, ultimately, it got out that these toasts were written and rehearsed, that only added to the allure. Indeed, this is what I tell my children: it's not the effortlessness but the effort that goes into making it effortless. In praise of artifice, if you will.

Indeed, hers is a story of effort and effortlessness. She achieved note as a conservative polemicist, without ever really—or at least not earnestly—writing polemics. She wrote two biographies, one of Maria Callas, the other of Pablo Picasso, each disputed by scholars and professionals—but no matter.

Six years after arriving in America, she married Michael Huffington, heir to a natural gas fortune, and settled with him in California. She put Huffington and his fortune to work, getting him elected to Congress. Two years later he—with her by his side—ran aggressively for the Senate. There are stories here of the harridan conservative wife taking over the campaign. It was her cause.

But Michael Huffington lost. And was gay. (It was always quite unclear for which reason she divorced him.)

And then Arianna became a liberal.

I perhaps have not described her conservatism enough to suggest the full extent of her conversion. She was nothing less than the go-to conservative woman. She was strident, pugnacious, dismissive, witty, and absolutely on the conservative line. Her becoming a liberal is only slightly less dramatic than Sarah Palin becoming one. Honestly, there may have never been a public conversion so extreme.

So you would think this might warrant some critical attention. What happened here? What psychic upheaval or bit of incredible flimflam had we witnessed?

Cynically speaking, it seemed as if Arianna had, mirabile dictu, recognized not so much her true beliefs but her true temperament. She not only became an unreluctant liberal, she became a Hollywood liberal. It was as though she had compared the two. On the one hand there were the California conservatives—grim, suburban real-estate salesmen, destined to never prevail in California politics. On the other there were rich, glamorous movie stars and studio executives, comprising the true California Establishment. Comparing the two, she made her choice.

And who was going to fault her? Certainly not the liberals grateful for any converts from the hastening conservative tide. Indeed, Arianna, with her community property state portion of Huffington's wealth, quickly became a liberal fixture and, with no embarrassment at all, a flaming liberal television talking head.

Whatever lingering doubts and suspicions there may have been were overcome by her enthusiasm. There wasn't an ambivalent bone in her body (this, in itself, may be the secret of her success). Overnight she was more liberal than the liberals. And she was—her leitmotif—more tireless. She is the Energizer Bunny. And, honestly, so good-humored about it.

I first met Arianna in 2000. She had cobbled together a quixotic counterconvention to the official Democratic and Republican nominating rituals. You had to admire her for the niftiness of the idea and the sheer doggedness of pulling it off. She was backer, stage manager, and host. It was Arianna and her ragtag band of lefties.

Arianna defined engagement in a curiously post-political sense. She had more energy than, specifically, ideology. She was a self-promoter. She was less a rebel without a cause than an Establishment figure without a platform.

She published books of no intellectual or polemical consequence, but they had a self-help ring of sprightliness and verve.

And then, during the 2003 recall election of California's hapless governor Gray Davis, she briefly ran in the primary to oppose Arnold Schwarzenegger. With single-digit polling figures, she awesomely shoehorned herself into what seemed like every photo op in the campaign. This was kooky but endearing.

* * *

Like so many internet notions, the Huffington Post was born out of idleness and a gift for self-promotion. The Drudge Report, retailing conservative talking points and other people's news, had become influential. So why not a liberal Drudge? Why couldn't Arianna become the liberal Drudge? Plus, she had this sweetener idea about getting celebs to blog.

She may not have been the least credible figure in digital America but, as a fifty-four-year-old woman in Chanel suits, she was among them.

But she was tireless. She went everywhere with her missionary zeal about blogs. Never was the word *blog* said so often as in a conversation with Arianna. You could, according to Arianna, remake yourself, and save yourself, and, possibly, immortalize yourself with a blog. It was easy. Blogs were, well, blogs. You could dash them off.

And, somehow, as testament to the ease and naturalness of blogging—the pure pleasure of it—she wouldn't pay you.

Three years after its launch, the Huffington Post, with its tens of millions of unique visitors every month, was rivaling, at least in the conversations of media sophisticates, the *New York Times*. It was the new liberal voice in America.

Among the bigger compliments, Arianna's longtime rival in America, that other Brit and the once undisputed queen of media in New York, Tina Brown, started a rival site, the Daily Beast. The comparison was instructive. Tina Brown's approach had always been exclusionary—I'm simply more exclusive than you. Arianna's was embracing—literally everyone could do it; it was a big blogging tent. What's more, Tina Brown always showed the strain of the hustle, was wounded by the resentment and envy and bile that accrued. Arianna loves the hustle; not noticing or caring about the spite, it simply doesn't exist. Everyone loves Arianna.

Judith

Somehow Judith Regan—the most famous book publisher of her generation, and the would-be Nancy Drew ready to finally close the O. J. Simpson case—has always gotten away with her obscene, grotesque, often funny, Jewish-obsessed, not just politically incorrect but reprehensible, probably slanderous, not necessarily truthful monologues (definitely monologues—she doesn't really engage in conventional conversation). Neither corporate America nor upwardly mobile society objected or, even, seemed to blanch. Her diatribes were part of her charm—or at least part of the forcefulness of her nature (if you didn't find her charming, you certainly found her forceful). I do know that one of her former lovers, no shrinking violet himself, says he finally broke up with her because he couldn't stand her Niagara of obscenities anymore, but the stuff about Jews, for instance—one of her perennial themes is that Jewish men run the media world and they need special handling—never bothered him (he's Jewish).

The Jewish thing just got crowded into all the other taboos Judith was verbally violating. And, anyway, Jews really aren't the issue for her; authority is the issue. Judith hates authority (and, conversely, loves power). She's got an eight-hundred-pound chip on her shoulder. And the chip is part of how she's made money—she's tapped into a vein of American resentment and victimhood, plus she's been able to bully her way into the market—and making money gives a pass to even the worst manners.

Also, her world, on top of being so profitable, is clearly such a harrowing, bleak, sordid place—Hobbesian with a twist of sexual perversity and degradation—that I don't think anybody wanted to look too closely at it or risk getting drawn into it.

Judith (she used to be Judy) and I went to college together. We were great friends for twenty-five years before—as with so many other people in her life—having a falling-out. The proximate cause was my wife's law firm's involvement at one stage in Judith's harrowing, bleak, and sordid divorce from money manager Robert Kleinschmidt—among the most contentious in New York State history. Likewise, Judith may have been one of the most contentious clients in legal annals. Lawyers are her enemies. It was a lawyer at HarperCollins, the division of News Corp that employed Judith, who provoked her final, allegedly anti-Semitic sally.

Judith's college boyfriend was my best friend. After college, she moved in with my friend and his wealthy parents in their fabulous Manhattan apartment, overlooking Central Park. My friend's father—Jewish and a lawyer—didn't like Judith very much, and she didn't like him. There were a lot of class issues and nuances here, which came out in running commentary—profane, angry, scurrilous—about the rich, the Jews, and lawyers, delivered to me from pay phones around the city. I confess I found it entertaining.

On several occasions, we almost got involved. Aside from her being with my best friend, I sensed, even then, that it was not a good idea to be on the descriptive end of her running commentary (from Judith, I know things about the intimate behavior of other men—when they cried, how they begged, where they like to insert sharp objects—that may have altered my fundamental view of humanity). Years later, she told the *Washington Post* that I was gay, that I had a thing for her college boyfriend. I got off easy.

Anyway, she isn't just preoccupied with Jews, or not principally. She can square off against all ethnicities, sexual orientations, and gender types (she actually manages to be both anti-women and anti-men). She grew up on Long Island, in Bay Shore, and glommed a working-class, ethnic sensibility—Archie Bunker, but her Archie Bunker wasn't written by liberals—onto the body of a very pretty, perfectly yuppie-ish Vassar girl. It was a striking juxtaposition. Powerful. Over the years it became part shtick, part expression of an always increasing anger, part stay-out-of-my-way corporate-bureaucratic strategy, part reflexive garrulousness. She just can't stop talking. Anybody who's ever come in contact with her has been exposed to the bilious, vitriolic, manic, gynecological, anti-everybody-and-every-propriety conversation—if not awed by it. Everybody at Rupert Murdoch's News Corp, which gave Judith her great platform, her carte blanche, was used to it, inured to it. "Sure, absolutely, no question, we've heard this all before, but there comes a tipping point," says a senior News Corp executive about the charge of anti-Semitism that finally got her fired when I press about why now, why the company hadn't gotten rid of her years ago.

You can reduce the most difficult employee who ever existed to just an HR problem. Or you can see her in more codependent terms: she's not just a News Corp employee but its creation—unlikely to be tolerated anywhere else.

Or, maybe, she's the last of the tabloid originals, a throwback, full of piss and vinegar, larger than life, finally subdued by the bland bureaucrats of corporate media.

At any rate, what's different about Judith's behavior now is that less than a year ago, after twelve years at News Corp, in a state of pique and hubris notable even for her, she relocated her publishing company, Regan-Books, to Los Angeles from New York, a move the *New York Times* found significant enough for a front-page story.

In the *Times*'s view, Judith's move to Los Angeles was a harbinger of a major shift in the media landscape. Although various book people had tried before to figure out a reliable way to transmute books into more remunerative media, to morph themselves from publisher to producer, to go Hollywood, and had failed, this was Judith Regan.

She had, the *Times* implied, supernatural powers in the book business. This is partly because she screamed so vulgarly and violently—demanding and achieving so much attention. But, as well, because she had a different idea about what a book was—a less sentimental idea. Her books were concoctions she controlled. They were often her idea, written by her ghostwriters (once she had the very unlikely idea that I should ghostwrite Howard Stern's book: "You'll sit next to Howard by his pool on Long Island and write while he talks," she instructed, which is when I begged off), propelled by her publicity acumen. She dominated tone, sensibility, drama, taste—the whole production. She was the Phil Spector of publishing.

What's more, she herself was—or thought of herself as—a media poly-morph. She'd wanted to be a television personality before she got side-tracked into books—she was hungry for television. She'd once worked for Geraldo. Ideally, she'd be Barbara Walters. True, she'd had a show on the Fox News Channel, in one of its least-watched time slots, and while on-air she was charmless, that had not dissuaded her from thinking of televi-sion as her inevitable future. (In the mid-nineties, Judith, with the British newspaperman and television presenter Andrew Neil, was handpicked by Rupert Murdoch to be the coanchor of a later-aborted Fox network com-petitor to *60 Minutes*.) She'd not only create content but personify it. Be the brand. This is, anyway, how the *Times*, influenced by Judith's publicity talents, saw her move to Los Angeles.

But perhaps more to the point, one the *Times* entirely missed: she had become anathema at HarperCollins headquarters, in New York—she needed to get out of Dodge.

Among the major bullet points on the résumé of Jane Friedman, Harper-Collins's CEO—who finally fired Judith before Christmas and who, for the ten years she's run HarperCollins, has, by most accounts, been waiting to fire Judith—is that, in addition to taking the book publisher from an also-ran to a leader in the business, she's existed with Judith for so long. Fried-man makes lemonade from lemons. Indeed, Friedman has long suggested to Murdoch that to the extent that Judith was valuable to News Corp it was because she could keep Judith under at least some minimum amount of control.

But Judith had Murdoch's ear, too—although up until what point is a subject of some revision now. And Friedman would have known what wounding things Judith would be capable of saying about her (it's impossible to look at a person in the same way after one of Judith's verbal maulings).

It was the diva against the corporate good girl. (There is another view, which sees Friedman as also a diva, but all other divas are oppressed by Judith's diva.) A match, which, arguably, because of the fallout from the Bernard Kerik affair, Judith had started to lose, and losing is not really an option for Judith—she'll always strike back.

In the tumble of ethics charges that surrounded Kerik, former New York City police commissioner and business partner of Rudy Giuliani, when he was nominated by President Bush to be the homeland security chief, in December 2004, it was reported that Judith was one of two mistresses (he was cheating on his wife with Judith, but on Judith with his other mistress), trysting with him in a special ground zero apartment and working out in the gym with him. It seemed to be part of her tough-guy thing: men are brutes, so go with the most brutish of them.

Indeed, when Judith lost a cell phone on the set of her TV show, she was able to have NYPD detectives sent out to the homes of the production-crew members she suspected of having snatched it.

Before Kerik, it was hard to actually tell Judith's story: the raging, sexually explicit, pretty clearly bonkers Judith story. That's the dialectic: if you are a success, especially a corporate success, you cannot also be out of control and beyond the pale. Even if you appear that way, it must be that you are crazy like a fox. The success, and her own publicity about her success—she's consistently had more books on the bestseller list, from authors Rush Limbaugh and Howard Stern and Oprah favorite Wally Lamb to the Zone Diet series, to Jenna Jameson's *How to Make Love Like a Porn Star*, than any other book editor—made the HR complaints, employee settlements, and earlier suggestions of anti-Semitism just sour grapes.

But the Kerik debacle officially made Judith a tabloid figure. "Judith" became a punch line.

Before she made the move to Los Angeles, a rival publisher signed up a presumed roman à clef about her, *Because She Can*, by Bridie Clark (who once worked at *Vanity Fair*), which appears this month, a kind of *Devil Wears Prada*, except that Judith would likely not be played by Meryl Streep, that former Vassar girl, but, more to type, by Roseanne Barr.

The move to Los Angeles could be seen as an attempted end run around Jane Friedman and HarperCollins, as well as around the fallout from the Kerik publicity, as well as, by the by, a transformative book-publishing strategy. It was, too, an effort to find a place more hospitable to her style—in Hollywood they understood executives with, well, flair.

It was also an ambitious corporate move. Her goal, however vague in its exact designs, was to create an independent News Corp division. No more HarperCollins. No more Judith Regan, book publisher—she changed the name of the imprint to just "Regan"—but Regan as mogul and personality.

It is important, however, to keep in mind that Judith does not seem to have considered business plans as much as crises, battles, enmities, clashes of egos, and attendant publicity, from which a direction, often an impulsive one, emerges. The value of this counterintuitive corporate behavior is that, for at least quite a number of years, it seemed to hold the interest of the boss.

That's the media nexus: Judith and Rupert. It's hard to imagine her fantastic and improbable career having been possible without someone exactly like Murdoch in her corner. If people at News Corp think Rupert is on your side, seas part.

Now, it is true that Judith made Rupert money, but in the scheme of things—News Corp is a $71 billion company, against ReganBooks's $80 million in a good year—the money doesn't begin to explain the exceptions that were made for her, the ways she was coddled, the advantages she was given.

Even before she began making money for him, Murdoch was enamored of her. The deal she made when she came from book publisher Simon & Schuster—where she famously claimed to have stored, several years before Monica Lewinsky, one executive's DNA sample—included not only an imprint and promises of a television show but also a substantial personal stake in her enterprise. (This minority stake was bought out a number of years ago by News Corp.)

There is, too, a kindred-spirit thing. Murdoch remains a tabloid guy. There may not be too many people who have his certain feel for the meretricious nitty-gritty of mankind, but Judith is one of them. Perhaps for some of the same reasons he accepts the multimillion-dollar losses of the *New York Post*, he indulged Judith. They both have a kind of soul. Murdoch, according to a former executive at News Corp in the early Judith years, used to laugh at her but, at the same time, deeply enjoy her provocative, populist, tabloid instinct, which so tweaked the noses of the book-publishing crowd. (Murdoch's former wife Anna is said to have disliked Judith because she regarded her as a bad influence on her husband, indulging his down-market tastes.)

And then there's the sex thing. Judith's sex talk is not only unstinting, disturbing, and subversive, but also what makes her sui generis. She's vulgar but uncommon. Powerful men—the list is long—can't resist Judith's vagina monologues. Perhaps because her sex talk is not just dirty but, fundamentally, about power. And control. ("What's my secret?" she once snarled at me. "I'll tell you my secret. I never let them come!") To hear it is a kind of privilege of wealth. You're in the presence of something sexually spectacular. Power of the highest order. A friend of mine with whom she was once involved, a famously tough executive at the top level of a giant media conglomerate, mused, "I thought Judith was me in a skirt."

"She talked back to him. He liked her swagger," says an observer to Judith and Rupert's relationship.

For most of her time at News Corp, Judith had her special edge with Rupert, which cut through the company like butter.

Part of the tortured explanation at News Corp for how the O.J. business happened involves separating Rupert—who is said to have soured on Judith during the aftermath of the Kerik affair—from Judith. Rupert, one News Corp source says, started to regard her as a "really embarrassing aunt you keep at a distance." She wasn't invited, for instance, to the most recent gathering of major News Corp executives this past summer in Pebble Beach. "He did not seek out or relish her company" is the official, dyspeptic status report on their relationship. Murdoch maintains he spoke to her only "once every couple of years."

And yet, Jane Friedman, whose formal approval Judith needed to relocate her office to Los Angeles, is said to have believed that Murdoch had sanctioned the move. And, too, Rupert personally approved the O.J. deal.

True, there's now an effort at News Corp to mitigate his approval. Judith, a News Corp official explains, "laid it out in a cursory fashion" to Rupert. He didn't "look at this thing in an organized fashion." Judith "got Rupert at an opportune moment. He didn't have all the facts at his disposal." Still, the official, unavoidable News Corp admission is that Rupert made the decision to go forward.

And yet, come on, if you're Murdoch and News Corp and you've got O.J., by whatever ruse or circumstances, on the brink of confession, why wouldn't you go forward? Murdoch may well have turned on Judith, but he would not be cold to potentially one of the greatest tabloid stories ever told: the O.J. confession (Murdoch once published what he thought were Hitler's diaries, which, alas, were fake).

Judith certainly needed O.J.—and knew his value. (She'd published one of the most successful O.J.-related books, by assistant prosecutor

Christopher Darden.) She needed Rupert, too—and an O.J. confession was plausibly a way back into Rupert's tabloid heart. What's more, she needed, after six months in Los Angeles, to truly demonstrate the synergy, multi-media thing. And, then, she was fifty-three.

Again, Judith would make the valid point that if she were a man, fifty-three would hardly be any sort of an issue. But it is hard to turn yourself into a TV star at fifty-three (actually, even for a man it would be hard). And if one of your trademarks is sex talk, the context perhaps changes, cruelly changes, you might say, for a woman at fifty-three. Indeed, acknowledging this, or trying to turn the tables on this, Judith last summer did a radio show—she's recently launched a satellite-radio program for herself—on the end of sex.

She wasn't wrong to think that getting an O.J. confession would offer her a mighty star turn—and certain renewal. No matter that she had to finesse O.J. into confessing. And finesse News Corp into thinking that she had a confession—Murdoch insists she told him O.J. would confess—or, at least, that the drama of it all would be so big that it would overshadow the devil in the details (i.e., that there might not be an actual confession).

And not just a book, but the television interview. This was the Barbara Walters moment. Judith began looking for the most prominent exposure—and best deal—for the interview. Apparently, her model here was the hugely successful, twenty-seven-million-viewer Martin Bashir interview with Michael Jackson, which ABC aired and in which Jackson confessed to sleeping with young boys. And ABC was seriously interested in the O.J. project. During the course of the two-month negotiation, Barbara Walters considered doing the interview (she has since minimized her interest). This became part of Judith's ultimate justification. The Barbara Walters standard: "Barbara Walters interviews murderers, dictators, and crimi-nals," Judith said, defending the O.J. project. And Barbara Walters might have gotten away with doing it. Her imprimatur might have made it less craven and feral. But News Corp people say that what happened at ABC is Judith began to insist she was the necessary interviewer—that only she could do it! The discussions with ABC ended.

The Fox network took on the project with Judith as its central fig-ure—if she wasn't exactly a television celebrity, she was, after all, a News Corp celebrity—apparently without dissent from anyone at the network or at News Corp, and with approval from News Corp president and COO Peter Chernin.

The appetite for O.J. and television confessions being constant—and who would have thought otherwise—Fox had every right to expect that an O.J. confession might do some of the biggest numbers of the year.

The furor over the book erupted, in the week before Thanksgiving, without anyone seeing it. Such sight-unseen contretemps are usually hyberbolic—media hysteria exaggerates reality. But in this instance, the book itself—beginning to circulate within News Corp just before the holiday—is vastly more cynical and bizarre than the reports. It almost presents as a comedy: not O. J. Simpson confessing to the murder of his wife and her friend, but Simpson coyly speculating on how he might have murdered them if he had, but of course he hadn't. *If I Did It* is so without context, other than as a run-amok, phantasmagorical marketing-and-merchandising scheme, that all you do, as you read it, is consider the psychopathology of how it ever came into being. What's more, it's amply evident that even the confession that exists in the book as a "hypothetical" is a pulp artifice—the book's aw-shucks Holden Caulfield/Huck Finn voice changes in the murder scene to Mickey Spillane—as concocted as everything else, in the end much more the work of a desperate bookseller than of even a money-hungry murderer.

Murdoch was at his ranch, in Australia, when the announcement of the book and the interview was made, on November 14. Gary Ginsberg, a senior News Corp corporate strategist and one of Murdoch's key lieutenants, was on his way back from Australia. By the time Ginsberg landed, his BlackBerry was going crazy, and, in some sense, the tabloid landscape had changed in America.

O.J., who had begun the current tabloid epoch, was in a sense ending it, causing a sudden, mass reversion to a shocked and appalled bourgeois sensibility. Judith's market value took a direct hit.

While this was evident to Ginsberg, it was not yet evident to Judith. She continued to work the publicity levers—negative publicity, after all, can be more positive than positive publicity—once again creating an O.J. circus. What could be bad about that?

The money, however, was the smoking gun. By agreeing to an indirect-payment scheme to a purported third party, News Corp, a Fortune 100 company, through ReganBooks and HarperCollins, appeared to have conspired with O. J. Simpson, the most notorious living American, in an effort to bypass or, even, defraud his creditors.

O.J.'s victims' families—the Browns and the Goldmans, astute media practitioners (who, in a civil suit, had won a vast monetary judgment against Simpson)—went into action. They wanted not only the dough but moral attention (or just attention).

Affiliates began to react—expressing distaste and reluctance to air the two-hour interview.

What's more, Fox News, in an almost insurmountable internal political complication for Judith, turned its vaunted media venom on the project. The possible reasons for this slap were varied: reported tensions between Fox News chief Roger Ailes and Chernin, who'd approved the Fox-network interview; an effort to distance Fox News, with its version of heartland moralism, from the Fox network (always a tetchy branding issue), with its outré-ness; and Ailes's antipathy to Regan—he'd moved her talk show off the air (once they had gone on a date together, which Ailes has reported to be the scariest evening of his life).

Then, in an impulsive act to justify the project and further fan its flames—and, too, emphasizing her own central role in it—Judith released a statement, a remarkable statement. Now, for years Judith has been promising her own book. Its theme has always been women and their strategies against men. The book has never been written, in part because, while Judith may be able to edit someone else's book, her own voice veers to the unhinged. Her statement—about a former lover who, she claimed, had abused her (distinct from her former husband, whom she regularly and epically ranted about), and who somehow, in her mind, seemed now interchangeable with O.J.—released first to the Drudge Report and then reprinted in Murdoch's *New York Post*, among other places, was not unreminiscent of Unabomber Theodore Kaczynski's manifesto.

For News Corp the statement was heaven-sent. It meant that it was squarely Judith's mess. She was hanging it around her neck. The subtext was clear: I have lost my mind and all objectivity. It was, in the incredulous News Corp view, a professional suicide note.

News Corp began to formally wash its hands of the project.

Ginsberg and News Corp general counsel Lon Jacobs and HarperCollins counsel Mark Jackson spent the weekend in secret meetings in Indianapolis with representatives of the Brown and Goldman families trying to come up with a deal that would disgorge all of the book and television earnings to the families.

But by Monday morning, with more affiliates in retreat, and without a joint agreement with the families (the next morning Denise Brown went on the *Today* show to accuse News Corp of trying to buy the families' silence), it became clear to everyone—including Judith, who shot an e-mail to all concerned saying she no longer wanted to publish the book—that the project was dead.

It was only later in the day that Judith came to understand that the company was killing not just the book but the television interview. She would not become the heroine of one of the greatest melodramas of the age.

Part of Judith's appeal, if you will, is knowing that, at this point, she won't try to save her job. No false contrition. No effort to reach out, heal. She will, reliably, set fire to the house.

The people at News Corp just sat back and watched.

She used her Sirius radio show to attack the company. She raged to anyone who would listen. She was an open wound, a jihadist, and, finally, an entirely isolated figure in the company.

Two days before she was fired, *Publishers Weekly* did a story about an upcoming novel ReganBooks was publishing about Mickey Mantle. The book (since canceled by News Corp) apparently has Mantle in various imagined sexual situations. But according to a News Corp source, Judith hadn't even read the book—the exact detail that finally made Rupert blow his stack and decide he was finished with her.

And then there occurred, as they have over a dozen years so often occurred, the raging, loaded, fraught, contemptuous, abusive conversation—this one, allegedly anti-Semitic, with Mark Jackson, the HarperCollins lawyer.

It's a dicey stage, the actual firing, or its cause, or explaining it is dicey, because it's what the defamation and breach-of-contract lawsuit promised by Judith's lawyer, legendary litigator Bert Fields, will hinge on. (Fields is the Hollywood lawyer who was questioned in the Anthony Pellicano wiretapping investigation; Judith is a longtime friend of both Fields's and Pellicano's.)

Had the decision to fire her already been made and was the allegation of anti-Semitism a convenience, a trumped-up thing, as Judith has suggested?

It may be the longest firing in corporate history. The life-is-too-short desire to do something about Judith, to be done with her, to expunge her, had existed, after all, at HarperCollins and News Corp for nearly all of her tenure, just waiting for the wherewithal. Or waiting for someone to seize the day more forcefully than Judith was always seizing it.

The purported anti-Semitic moment that became the cause of her termination—the language of which will be debated in depositions possibly for years to come—was a ritualistic one. They must have been waiting for it, could have counted on it like the sun rising, Judith's going bananas.

When she did, Jane Friedman went to Murdoch—one can only imagine with what satisfaction—and, finally, he ended it.

Still, Judith may be right in her technical defense—her bizarre equation of what was being done to her with the Holocaust, and, hence, that the Jews at HarperCollins should therefore be sympathetic to her, might not, on its face, be anti-Semitic (although it's certainly something off-kilter). The people at HarperCollins may just have gotten too enthusiastic, heard the word "Jew," and pulled the trigger, because Judith's verbal path here is so well worn.

After all, were they really firing her for her inappropriateness? Or had the triumphalism of her inappropriateness finally, after years of effort, been beaten back by the power of conventionalism? Were they firing her for being who she was?

Anyway, the strange, singular, disturbing, mad, and in so many ways inexplicable career of Judith Regan at News Corp had come to an end.

Tina

One morning a few months ago, I finished my run and, following my usual routine, picked up a newspaper in the lobby of the Carlyle Hotel. On my way out, a woman in an outsize raincoat, with a refugee-like scarf around her head, weaved toward me. She seemed confused, or in some distress, or so nearsighted as to make you think immediately of Mr. Magoo. She reached out to steady herself on me and, in an English accent, which made her seem somehow even more befuddled, asked, "Do you know the way to Madison Avenue?"

"You're actually *on* Madison Avenue," I replied, looking at her closely and realizing, suddenly, that the discombobulated woman was Tina Brown.

This story, which I've been dining out on, and which everyone I've told has enjoyed enormously, is an example of backlash. You could not have told this story a few years ago. People would not have been receptive to it. It would have said more about the teller (that you were envious of or, worse, unknown to Tina). Or it would have been understood in a different way. It might have even seemed charming, humanizing (at the height of her power, people often spoke of her vulnerability).

Whereas, at this moment, everyone understands it as caricature. Belittling. Farcical. Possibly exaggerated. (Was she really weaving? Really wearing a scarf like that?) It fits the current thinking: Tina Brown is a lost figure who can no longer even find her way to the main thoroughfare of her life and career.

But now, partly because of a new book, *Tina and Harry Come to*

America, I find myself feeling more than a little guilty about telling this story (and not once, either—I've retailed it everywhere; of note, if not necessarily in my defense, the only people I know who haven't participated in the Tina-bashing craze are people directly on her payroll—and many of them have found it an irresistible diversion, too). The book codifies and collects every aspect and tonal shift of the revisionism directed against Tina Brown and her husband, Harold Evans. Its focus (not unlike my Carlyle story) is the morphing of the couple's fabled acuity, style, and ambition into nearsightedness, frumpiness, and profound lack of direction. It is, although the book's author, Judy Bachrach, may not necessarily realize it, about a perceptual transformation. And while I don't know if their fall from grace is as world-class as the book makes it out to be (on the level of Nixon's and the Clintons', the book suggests—it even has Hillary bashing Tina), or even how noteworthy it is to people outside the media community, it certainly makes you think that, as backlashes go, it's really up there.

* * *

The book, which details the couple's professional, social, and sexual histories (here is a universal lesson: whoever you sleep with will someday talk about it—plan accordingly), is of course itself part and parcel of the backlash. It's published by Simon & Schuster but is in the style of the Regnery Press books about Clinton—an unrelenting, not-very-nuanced indictment of character flaws, professional conflicts, compromises, and a host of other unkind social acts written for an eager, and bitterly predisposed, audience.

As compelling as all these tidbits are, there is, clearly, no smoking gun here. There's no deed, or event, or betrayal that provides a clear explanation for why the crowd would want to tear Tina and Harry apart—why they should have become such a cautionary tale. They really have not behaved differently from most other hyper-dedicated careerists in Manhattan (most of whom have not yet been shunned by polite society).

In fact, what the book outlines is a Horatio Alger story of get-up-and-go, shoulder-to-the-wheel, how-to-do-what-you've-got-to-do-to-get-ahead-in-the-media-business savvy. I'd recommend it to anyone who is starting out. It's a fine manual.

Rule No. 1: Don't sleep with just anyone; make your couplings count (Tina's college-age liaisons included Dudley Moore, Auberon Waugh, and

Martin Amis and culminate at the age of twenty-one with Harry Evans, a national monument in British journalism).

Rule No. 2: Learn how to give a party (which is different from learning how to party).

Rule No. 3: Cultivate the press (publicity being the currency of our time)—best done by throwing parties.

Rule No. 4: Get to know some celebrities (which takes work, but it's easier than you think) and invite them to your parties.

There is the strong suggestion in the book, and on the part of the many people I know who obsessively rehash Tina's and Harry's careers, that there is something shallow, vulgar, and possibly immoral about all this. And yet there is virtually nobody who is a success in the media business (Tina and I are the same age, and I found myself, as I read *Tina and Harry Come to America*, awed by her precocity—with just a little more energy and fortitude, I could have, I think now, learned how to throw a party) who hasn't followed some of these precepts. Tina (and it is always Tina, more so than Harry) is in a terrible trap. We are enamored by her because she was such a success; we are repelled by her because of what it took to be a success (there's surely a woman's point to be made here—a man is respected for his wiles, a woman trashed for hers).

The media class is not usually so ambivalent about success, but success (no matter how much you've had) becomes something else when it's coupled with failure. And *Talk*, Tina's current magazine, seems stubbornly unable to succeed.

Certainly, it feels like a magazine made by first-timers. It doesn't seem to be able to answer the most basic magazine-craft question (it doesn't seem to have ever even asked it): Who's it for? What's more, it may never be able to surmount what is perhaps a structural flaw: the perception that it is always doing double duty as the house organ for Miramax, which funds it.

And yet creators of magazines create bad magazines. It goes with the territory. The most fabled among them, Jann Wenner, Clay Felker, Hugh Hefner, all made stinkers. They got laughed at but were spared the moral condemnation that Tina has attracted.

* * *

Psychoanalyzing the backlash, we're bound to get to the formulation that it's not about them; it's about us.

There was an obvious codependence. We were each other's enablers. It was an age of excess, of overweening ambition, of greed, and phoniness, and sucking up, and the glorification of strange, obnoxious, preening, uninteresting people. And Tina Brown and, by association, Harry Evans have the misfortune of coming to stand for all this (not to mention having made us participate in it).

I wonder, too, if the backlash doesn't also say something about the general-interest-magazine business. Tina's *New Yorker* and *Vanity Fair* may have been the last gasp of the magazine as social chronicle. By spending huge amounts of money and through constant vainglorious acts of self-promotion, and by creating a subculture of editorial dirty pool (if you could help the magazine, or Tina and Harry, you were stroked; if you couldn't help or hurt the magazine or them, you were fodder), she supported a dying genre. Everyone in our business cheered her on, hoping out of self-interest that she would succeed, but when she didn't (and, I might argue, she couldn't), we all distanced ourselves from her embarrassing and desperate acts.

Likewise, she helped import to New York, and the constricting publishing business, an English sensibility. Because in the publishing world there is so little room to maneuver and there are so few opportunities, it was fertile ground for the development of a class-based, hierarchical structure, which she at *Vanity Fair* and the *New Yorker* and Harry at Random House reigned over. In this system, you're always kissing up to the people above you, but at the least sign of weakness (places in the firmament being so scarce), you rip them apart. The fact that she has run three magazines that compete with each other only increases the strain. Indeed, the author of *Tina and Harry* is a *Vanity Fair* writer—the perception, certainly at *Talk*, is that when Tina goes down, *Vanity Fair* and its editor, Graydon Carter, go up.

Then there's the Hollywood thing, which was the magic potion she poured on a magazine (and which fit the spirit of a self-aggrandized era).

Her father, George Brown, was an English movie producer; she came of age when the movies were the hottest part of media (she also had a foreigner's awe of Hollywood); she transposed British class hierarchies to America by elevating Hollywood celebrities; and, most recently, she's married herself to a movie company. But now, as the result of various cultural transformations (for instance, technology, which Tina has seemed really dim about), the movies have become peripheral and disposable (certainly *Talk* magazine often seems to be a cavalcade of celebrities no one could care less about); it's a bottom-of-the-class business. It isn't where the heat is; nobody takes movies seriously anymore. Hollywood, which once made Tina look hip and powerful, now makes her look craven and silly—and like a dumbo for not getting that it's so over with.

* * *

Ironically, Tina and Harry turn out to be bad at playing the media game (doubly ironic because they had the game fixed for so long—no one would say anything bad about Harry and Tina because everyone was on their payroll or invite list).

They have, it turns out, no appreciation of the rhythms of thrust and parry. Bad press sticks to some people (and then it increases geometrically), while other people brush it off. The process of brushing it off involves a certain level of self-confidence—you have to be able to not take it seriously. Whereas Tina is always chewing over her bad clips, calling reporters and attempting to recast quotes, having friends call reporters, deploying PR agents. And Harry, while in one life a crusading journalist, is, in another, an enthusiastic libel plaintiff.

They wound easily. They're paranoid. They're Nixon-like. They're thin-skinned.

Worse, they set themselves up. You don't throw the party of the century (her big do at the Statue of Liberty) to launch a fledgling magazine—I mean anybody who knows anything knows about managing expectations.

It is the self-confidence issue, though, that may go to the heart of the matter. To some degree, I wonder if this doesn't have to do with a structural anomaly of their success. Tina, especially, achieved massive notoriety of the kind associated with the biggest payday (hence engendering the most resentments). She should have been rich. She became an international brand name. But because she was, in reality, just an employee (and at *Talk*, despite her best efforts to become a mogul, *continues* to be just an employee) and because her successes, at least from a P&L standpoint, have been mostly illusory, she never made her fuck-you money.

And the money is where the confidence and the respect come from—it redeems you. Not having the money means you're just a sucker. Which is, in essence, the social rule propounded most forcefully and unforgivingly by Tina Brown.

Ingrid

When Ingrid Sischy found out I was going to Nice this summer with my family, she had Elton John make us a reservation at a hot restaurant. On another occasion, when Ingrid and I were walking along talking about art and pop culture and I made a point that struck her as something she wanted to pursue, we rushed right over to Jeff Koons's studio to talk about it with him. Then, a few weeks ago, she took me to all the fashion shows. One evening, I went to a screening Ingrid was hosting and brushed up against Uma Thurman. The other day, to make a point about *Interview*, the magazine she has edited for the past ten years, and the artistic and cultural worlds it covers, Ingrid called up the fashion designer Helmut Lang, the artist Francesco Clemente, the independent filmmakers Todd Solondz (*Happiness*) and Kimberly Peirce (*Boys Don't Cry*), and the supermodel Veronica Webb, and they all came over to discuss these issues for a few hours. ("What a group," said the celebrity photographer Patrick McMullan, who poked his head into the room briefly. "I'm so excited.")

Thinking about the life Ingrid leads (and of myself dropped into it), I thought of Fellini's *La Dolce Vita*; but that dwells too much on the emptiness of the glitzy life. Then I considered the Woody Allen movie *Celebrity*; but that's a fairly vituperative vision of this world. Finally I thought of Almodóvar and his sentimental take on fame; he could possibly balance the workaday normalcy of Ingrid's world with, at least for me, its vivid, surreal quality. Imagine having instant access to anybody famous and talented you might ever want to talk to, and, most surreally, finding that they are all very decent-, modest-, humble-seeming people (at least around Ingrid).

I first met Ingrid when *Interview*'s PR people were shopping around for a story to commemorate the magazine's thirtieth anniversary. I was interested for two reasons: first, because any magazine that survives so long and in such a consistent form has accomplished something big; and second, because I had absolutely no idea who reads *Interview*. It thrived, but not necessarily by any obvious logic.

At our first talk, Ingrid and I had a college-dorm sort of conversation about our families, our aspirations, and various artistic and moral issues (Ingrid is a South African Jew who immigrated with her family at the age of nine to Edinburgh and then as a teen to Rochester before going off to Sarah Lawrence). This led to another talk and another and another. I was not unmindful that as the thirty-four-year-old editor of *Artforum* in the mid-eighties, Ingrid was interviewed by the *New Yorker*'s Janet Malcolm; the interview, which became the basis for a two-part profile, stretched on for more than a year. I found I, too, was delighted to keep going. She's warm (almost flat-footedly decent and earnest); she listens; she's motherly; and then there's the fact that she could be talking to someone incredibly famous, but instead she is talking to you.

Ingrid and *Interview*'s place in the fame game is a curious one. Access to celebrities is a complex and expensive process of negotiation and court-ship for most magazines, and often involves the exchange of various inducements. But inch for inch, *Interview*, with its fairly paltry 170,000 circulation, and with far less valuable inducements to offer, gets many more celebrities than any other magazine—the hottest ones, the hippest ones, the hardest-to-get, most furtive ones—which seems to piss many other editors off. (I'm not the only one who asks: "Who reads *Interview*?")

On the other hand, Ingrid, who resembles one of those normal-people sculptures, the kind that scare you in a museum, by the artist Duane Han-son, is not rich; she is not very famous (a usual perk of hanging around the famous) herself; and to the degree *Interview* has been a success, it's been a quirky one (many non-*Interview* readers treat it as a faded flower).

Ingrid sets up a dialectic in the world of popular culture in which there are locals—the authentic, indigenous peoples—and then the great mass of tourists. Tina Brown is a tourist, a voyeur, an exploiter, a tour-guide operator, even (indeed, Tina would often ask Ingrid, a *New Yorker* contributor, to bring various hot people to events she was hosting). Whereas Ingrid runs the local paper here in fametown.

For instance, Sean Penn called Ingrid up one day and asked her to have a drink with a musician friend who had just released a record that wasn't doing very well and that the label wasn't supporting. Ingrid said she couldn't because some friends were coming over for dinner, but, she told Penn, his friend could stop by. So that was the evening k.d. lang, Julian Schnabel, Valentino, and the photographer Steven Klein, all dining in Ingrid's small place in the West Village, first heard Jewel sing (Schnabel had to run around the corner to his house and get a guitar). And that was how Jewel got her first magazine story, which Klein photographed for *Interview*. This is what happens in a small town.

Ingrid, who at twenty-seven became the editor of *Artforum* and possibly the most influential voice in the rise of a generation of painters that included Schnabel, Keith Haring, Jean-Michel Basquiat, and Kenny Scharf as well as Clemente and Koons, seldom discusses fame itself. She talks about the work, or "the work." It's old-fashioned; it's European; it's like when people took movies seriously—the celebrity as auteur. She can talk about Mark Wahlberg with interest. She de-commodifies the famous (*Boys Don't Cry* director Kimberly Peirce complains, in our discussion, about other magazines' "using your commodity to sell their commodity").

In a way, Ingrid is the champion of people who you might not immediately think would need a champion. *Interview* is, she says, "where people who choose the life and the world of fame can feel safe." In a sense, *Interview* functions as—and this starts to get at who exactly reads *Interview*—a trade magazine for the famous, or for those who would like to be part of the fame profession (from publicists to casting agents to actor-bartenders to, Ingrid notes, "pretty boys who've just hit town"). She invokes, too, that young person out there in Nowheresville, full of heart and imagination, quite likely gay, who in *Interview* will see his or her escape route and career possibilities.

* * *

When Drew Barrymore was all but washed up in the early nineties, *Interview* did a nude series with her, which got the interest of other photographers ("big-league photographers," notes Ingrid) and caused many other magazines to feature her, thereby reviving her career. Bruce Weber first photographed Marky Mark with his pants below his Calvin-labeled underpants in *Interview*, which became, after this, the emblematic Calvin ad campaign. Leonardo DiCaprio got his first cover photo in *Interview*. So did Lil' Kim and Chloë Sevigny and Christina Ricci and Edward Norton and tons more.

Interview does for fame what socialist realist propaganda sheets in the early part of the century did for revolution.

It's a visual viral thing. It is also, arguably, a visual viral gay thing ("pansexual," says Ingrid), a message *Interview* sends better than other publications.

* * *

At my afternoon tea with Helmut, who ran his first advertisements in *Interview*, and Francesco, whose work often appears in the magazine, and Todd and Kimberly, both of whom credit *Interview*'s support in the not necessarily likely success of their films, and Veronica, whose post-supermodel life involves writing for *Interview*, I brought up what I find to be *Interview*'s resolute lack of irony.

A funny thing, I thought, had happened. *Interview* began thirty-one years ago as Andy Warhol's flight of fancy; like his mock films, his mock magazine offered unfiltered conversations, which in no small way celebrated banality ("Hi." "Hi, Andy." "When did you get to town?" "Yesterday." "Any jet lag?"). No irony was Warhol's irony.

Now, while much of that affectlessness remains three decades later, it no longer functions as a comment on itself—not Woody Allen mockery or Felliniesque ennui or even Warholian drollery—but, rather, almost as a clubby thing. This is the way the talented, beautiful, hip, and celebrated talk among themselves. *Interview*, which had opened the doors to introduce celebrities into every aspect of American culture (*Interview* is certainly the godfather of *People* and every publication Tina Brown has had anything to do with), had, in a way, shut the doors. It's them (the locals) on one side and us (the tourists) on the other.

At tea, everyone sort of agreed that *Interview* represented a kind of club, although no one wanted to call it a club ("a community," someone suggested; "a current," said someone else).

But I didn't get too far with the irony issue, because the conditions for irony presuppose that you're on the outside looking in, or at least you're ambivalent about being on the inside. But at the tea, nobody seemed to feel ambivalent enough about being included here to see the need for irony—or to see its absence. ("The judgment is implied by the context," said Francesco, defending the magazine's tone. "Why does everyone have to be labeled?" complained Helmut. "To allow something to be what it is is also an act of criticality," said Kimberly.)

And then, too, there is Ingrid's wholesomeness. Irony, ambivalence, and modern self-loathing of any sort are not Ingrid's thing; she isn't brittle. She occupies a pretty firmly contented space.

* * *

As I was saying to Elton John (after thanking him for my wonderful dinner in Nice), there is something really down-to-earth about Ingrid. "She isn't a celebrity editor," said Elton, who seemed, I thought, to know a lot about the magazine world (but then, celebrities would obviously know about celebrity magazines). "She isn't a Graydon Carter or Tina Brown or Anna Wintour," Elton noted positively.

In the myth of the celebrity editor, Tina and Graydon and Anna have easy access to the inside, and they use this access to bring a bit of what happens in this world to us. Partly out of their efforts to get the access they claim to have (which is much more difficult than they would like us to think) grows the culture of celebrity, the climbing, promoting, reputation negotiating (who's in, who's out), and sucking up.

None of this (this "negativity," as Elton says) is part of Ingrid's MO, or, in fact, her personality. There really is not a sense when you're with Ingrid or even when you're reading *Interview* of celebrities and noncelebrities, or, as they might say in art criticism, hierarchality. In a way, Ingrid and *Interview* occupy a much more generous world than the one in which we live. There are no celebrities in Ingrid's world, because everyone is a celebrity; no talented people, because everyone is talented; no beautiful people, because everyone is beautiful.

But let me run; I have Miuccia Prada calling.

Murdoch

Rupert in Love

At a particularly dicey moment in my own love life when I was interviewing Rupert Murdoch a number of years ago, I tried to get some advice from him about, well, about anything a man with three wives, the latest the age of his children, might offer. This is what he said: "Women. What do I know? Women." Then he lifted up the end of his tie, quite a fashion-forward one, and studied it closely. "My wife," he said, "gave this to me. So I wear it." I can't make out what else is on the recording, just mumbles and sighs.

Among the many unexpected aspects of the epochal Murdoch saga, from Adelaide to global conquest, is his emergence as a lover and connoisseur of beautiful and charismatic women, with Jerry Hall, that most famous of rock chicks (ex Mick Jagger, ex Bryan Ferry), his latest consort.

His increasingly public relationship with Hall has been largely treated as either an affront to rock 'n' roll or one of those sexual heehaws that happen in the lives of old billionaires. But, in fact, it is better seen as another revealing and quite consistent part of the Murdoch persona. His pursuit of beautiful women has shaped him and, therefore, in some sense, our time.

His search for sex, glamour, and companionship—he has very much sought all three together—has always been in plain sight, and yet, given his more famously hard-hearted, bottom-line, grumpy lack of sexiness, this has seemed so uncharacteristic as to be entirely discounted in the Murdoch story. When he abruptly announced the dissolution of his thirty-year marriage to his second wife, Anna, in 1997, nobody speculated that there might be another woman involved—however much another woman is pretty much the only reason a post-middle-aged man leaves a long marriage (particularly a billionaire, particularly in California, a community property state).

Shortly after the marriage dissolved, his oldest daughter, Prudence, took her seemingly bereft father on a sailing trip without it crossing her mind that his frequent apologies about having to take private phone calls might have any connection to his marital woes. When, not long after, he called her at home in Sydney and mentioned, by the by, that he had met "a nice Chinese lady," Prue got off the phone, whooped, and ran upstairs shouting to her husband Alasdair, "You won't believe it!"

As it happens, his first marriage, to Prue's mother, had hardly been less of a shock for the Murdoch family. Rupert then, at age twenty-five, was the scion of one of the most important families in Australia. While he was making a reputation as a boy publisher, it was his mother and two sisters who represented the Murdochs' social standing and the good name of patriarch Keith Murdoch who died a few years before, and who now formed a protective cocoon around the family's only male heir.

Imagine the horror when Rupert ran off with an airline stewardess. "It was," his mother said to me, dryly, in an interview fifty years later, "unexpected."

In the face of withering, if not implacable, opposition from his mother and sisters, he married Patricia Booker anyway, displaying his essential dual nature: while seeing himself as a model son whose first loyalty is to his family, he would yet do what he wanted to do.

His eleven-year marriage to Patricia, which produced Prudence in 1958, and which was compromised by his unceasing travel as he built the Australian leg of his empire, came to an end in 1967 when he spied Anna Torv, a trainee or "cadet" at his Sydney paper, the *Daily Telegraph*. Once again, he defied his mother, Elizabeth, becoming the first of a long line of solid Presbyterian Murdochs to be divorced.

Both Patricia and Anna were particularly comely figures—"my son is susceptible to attractive women," noted his mother acidly—with Anna being the more comely. Indeed, Rupert's next three children, Elisabeth, Lachlan, and James, as young wealthies growing up in New York, all had a near-model look that did not come from their father.

Murdoch in the seventies and eighties, full of ambition and entitlement, bore an awfully close resemblance to a jet-setting, international-empire-builder playboy. But this was also in another sense his guilty fantasy. That is, he would have liked to be much more of a rogue than he was.

There are his "Page 3" girls at the *Sun*, partly born out of his admiration for or envy of sixties girlie publishers Hugh Hefner and Bob Guccione. He had a serious extramarital flirtation in the eighties—the only one I uncovered in my research for his biography—but posthaste he introduced the woman to one of his business associates, whom she married. Petronella Wyatt, the daughter of his friend Woodrow Wyatt, and a friend of Murdoch's daughter Elisabeth, would, years later, recall his ogling attention to her as a teenage girl. And then, beginning in 1985, there is Hollywood. His purchase of Twentieth Century Fox was in part motivated by what motivates every outsider to overpay for a movie studio: "Girls, what else?" said John Evans, a close Murdoch lieutenant and confidant at the time. There was even a secret face-lift in the late eighties (which will dramatically fall into deep crevasses). Still, at the same time, there was Anna Murdoch's iron will that Murdoch, in one sense less international playboy and more Dagwood Bumstead, bends to and cowers from.

His daughter Elisabeth much later recalled how her father is easily dominated by women, describing him essentially as a conventionally henpecked husband. Indeed, Murdoch is conflict averse within his family and ever placating. Many of his most conservative views are in fact Anna's, a serious Roman Catholic. At several points he considered converting to appease his wife. Their social life was entirely run by Anna—a kind of Nancy Reagan, benefit-affair, dinner-jacket social life, which he submitted to and bitterly complained about.

Murdoch appeared to be the model of the conventional husband—and, too, appeared to be the kind of conventional husband in the deepest hell of repressed desire. Many of his closest lieutenants recall Murdoch on the Twentieth Century Fox lot, where he was based in the early nineties, as an unhappy, lonely figure who did not want to go home at night.

Then, in 1997, on a visit to Hong Kong, Wendi Deng, an employee at his office there, struck. His sudden metamorphosis, almost superhero-like, into an international Don Juan, and apparent immediate willingness to compromise his fortune, family, and reputation, perhaps only made sense as the product of some truer nature. Or, the wiles of a savvier player: Wendi, opinionated and domineering.

But was it love or obsession? Defy-the-world stuff. His mother barred Wendi from her door. His children stopped speaking to him. His associates tried to undercut her. He was putting billions at risk—really his entire business. But Rupert and Wendi were locked together, physically holding each other. Moony hand-holding stuff. Stroking. Snogging. Him rushing into her arms as he leaves the stage after an annual meeting. Rupert is one of earth's most compartmentalized men, and here he was in the love compartment. Indeed, he so turned over his life that he would never see his former wife Anna again. His life became Wendi's life. Where they lived, how he dressed, who they saw. A rebirth for him. Or a weird, and for everyone around him, eye-rolling, body snatch. Wendi talked to a friend about Rupert and Viagra. There was also, in the cost born by every great lover, deep pain.

The *Los Angeles Times* threatened to run a story that Wendi was in a relationship with Chris DeWolfe, then the head of MySpace, which Murdoch acquired, in part at Wendi's urging, in 2005. Company lawyers and communication people debriefed them both. It was a humiliating inquisition (designed to produce consistent stories) that quickly filtered throughout the company.

And yet admitting defeat in his marriage would be worse for him still. It became a terrible struggle, if not a war, between each party in his and her designated camp. Several times, during the period I was interviewing Murdoch, he would seem to have shown up at his house just minutes before I got there, clutching his overnight bag. Wendi, eager to be well represented in Murdoch's story, was adamant that I interview her close confidant the former prime minister Tony Blair, who, for the better part of a day in his London office, described for me Wendi's vital position in the Murdoch family drama.

* * *

If the media was surprised by the dissolution of the Murdoch marriage in 2013, insiders were surprised only by the Murdoch wrath and resolve. The Wendi situation—the various people with whom she was linked and her geographical distance from her husband (her appearance at the parliamentary hearing in London during the hacking investigation, where she blocked a pie thrown at her husband, was carefully negotiated)— became an "I-see-nothing-I-hear-nothing" theme of executive life at News Corp.

His break from Wendi came a few months after reports of a new relationship. More eye-rolling, but events were in motion. He dispatched Wendi in a sudden divorce filing, catching her entirely unawares. For good measure, and closing the Murdoch iron door, his side leaked reports that she was having an affair with Blair. He had once again blown up his family life—his two young daughters learned of the divorce when paparazzi showed up in front of Brearley, the school they were attending on East Eighty-Third Street in New York—and at eighty-two he was single, with his older children competing to influence his life's new turn, and, as it happens, nixing the new relationship.

It was quite a restless wilderness, marked by a succession of feel-good real-estate deals. He bought an estate and vineyard, in Bel Air, California. He bought the penthouse triplex in a new cool modernist billionaire development in the unenticing Madison Square neighborhood in Manhattan—and then sold it before moving in. Then he bought a romantic town house with bohemian and arty airs in the West Village. But it has five stories of steps for a now eighty-four-year-old man and, opening onto the street, offers virtually no security—and he put it back on the market almost straightaway.

Meanwhile, the wife of every man of clout and wealth in Manhattan of a certain age is trying to fix Rupert up. He tells people he's lonely and depressed. His children tell people he's lonely and depressed.

A worry among his children and various of his close executives is the young woman Natalie Ravitz, who was installed as his chief of staff during the hacking crisis (his secretary of more than forty years, Dot Wyndoe, was forced into retirement) by Joel Klein, a close lieutenant. Ravitz curates a Tumblr account—"Murdoch Here" after his phone greeting—that seems, even for a Murdoch employee, alarmingly adoring. She left the job last spring, reportedly at the urging of his son James.

Rupert *Agonistes* is a figure who shuttles between action, method, calculation, control and yearning, fantasy and passion. Perhaps that is the secret chemistry for successfully gambling and winning. Likewise when it comes to women, he is awkward, buttoned-down, baffled (during the nine months I interviewed Murdoch on a weekly basis for my 2009 biography of the mogul, I was often accompanied by my research assistant, Leela de Kretser, a young and attractive Australian, who had previously worked for the *New York Post* and for Murdoch's paper in Melbourne, with Murdoch never acknowledging her presence), and aggressively retro (I once asked him why he had no women on his board; he replied, "They talk too much"). And yet he develops obvious crushes (Rebekah Brooks, the red-haired editor of his biggest paper, the *Sun*, being one of the most flagrant and long-term), is a goner when it comes to female attention and flattery, and has taken some of his biggest risks, in a life of risks, when it comes to women.

All reports put him over the top when it comes to Jerry Hall, whom he apparently met in Australia over the summer, introduced by his sister Janet Calvert-Jones at a benefit. And she is on board with him. Visiting the set of a movie in London, she was overheard explaining her new shorter hairstyle as something Rupert wanted, and that she likes "a man with strong opinions." At fifty-nine, Hall is almost age appropriate, or, at least, not going to have more Murdoch children, which makes her an ideal companion from the point of view of his sons and daughters. What's more, if Wendi Deng, a Yale management school graduate, often intruded in Murdoch business affairs, Hall, a former model, seems to be a much safer business bet. Indeed, each of Murdoch's sons has married a former model.

For Hall, quite a collector of cultural icons, Murdoch may be one of the few men with enough standing to rival Jagger's. If your romantic inclinations tend to take you to the center of attention and immediacy, the soon-to-be-eighty-five-year-old Murdoch, still striding the earth with full purpose and faculties, might yet be quite a satisfying date.

For Murdoch, it is another worthy chapter in his unlikely quest for love and beauty.

Rupert Alone

O ne of the distinctive and sometimes even poignant ways that Rupert Murdoch's intimates describe him involves his isolation. He's on his own path. His isn't a shared world. It's a dogged one, rising early, fetching his own porridge. "A horse," he says, with more resignation than humor, "needs its chaff." His mumble often suggests that he's talking to himself and you're just faintly overhearing the interior monologue.

Which perhaps helps explain his strategic, as well as eccentric, adoption of Twitter: it's his way of expressing his inner conversation. Twitter is to Murdoch as voice software is to Stephen Hawking.

Murdoch's almost seventeen hundred tweets as of this writing are a subject of concern, eye-rolling, and sometimes stupefaction among his family and closest business associates. They are a cautionary tale in other C-suites the world over. For CEOs tempted to start using Twitter, their PR handlers have an easy response: "You don't want to be like Murdoch, do you?" It is something of a sign, in fact, of Murdoch's unique position among public company executives that he can, without too much public opprobrium and shareholder panic, regularly, and often absently, type out terse—even by Twitter standards—koan-like asides about the nature of race ("Moses film attacked on Twitter for all white cast. Since when are Egyptians not white? All I know are"), climate change ("Wild winter in U.S., U.K., etc. no respectable evidence any of this man made climate change in spite of blindly ignorant politicians"), technology ("NSA privacy invasion bad, but nothing compared to Google"), the pope ("Watch Democrats politicise Pope Francis visit, who has no understanding of free markets and their role in lifting billions out of poverty"), sharks ("Shark population and attacks increase as greenies stop culling, claim sharks are also 'human'. What next?"), with the occasional ad hominem attack, even against people he considers friends ("Piers Morgan seems unemployed after failing to attract any audience in U.S. Seemed out of place. Once talented, now safe to ignore").

And it is not just that everybody is merely shrugging off the screwball bons mots of an eighty-four-year-old. Rather, within his company and the larger Murdoch-dependent universe, his Tweets have the impact that cryptic comments from the Federal Reserve chairman might have on the world's economy. His tweets are messages and policy.

His Twitter knifings of Donald Trump ("When is Donald Trump going to stop embarrassing his friends, let alone the whole country?" the first in a steady stream of anti-Trump tweets) have shaken and confused many of the very people in his company who have helped elevate Trump—and indeed who are responsible, presumably to Murdoch's satisfaction, for making unprecedented money from the Trump surge. (Does he really want Trump, the golden goose of political television, to be slaughtered?) At the highest levels of the *Wall Street Journal* there is often considerable deciphering of his slurs, dismissals, and occasional compliments and how they ought to be reflected in editorial positioning, with News Corp chief executive Robert Thomson the ultimate arbiter of what is a suggestion, order, or jest.

Murdoch began tweeting on December 31, 2011, at just about the time, intimates note, that his marriage to Wendi Murdoch started to seriously unravel. For all of Murdoch's sense of aloneness, he doesn't actually like to be alone. When his marriage to his second wife, Anna, started to fray in the mid-nineties—when the couple was mostly living in Los Angeles—it became a tactical issue for senior Fox executives not to be the last to leave the Fox lot for the day, otherwise you'd be stuck for the whole evening with Rupert. Twitter helped fill his time after Wendi's banishment. What's more, it was a way for Murdoch to reclaim a bit of pride. Wendi, often to the consternation of Murdoch's staff, had largely run his personal technology. If you wanted to reach Rupert by e-mail, it went through Wendi. She often was the one who carried and dialed his mobile phone.

Indeed, in the beginning, many assumed it was Wendi who was tweeting for him. But by tweeting himself he was rather sending a message to her: "I'll show you." (Rupert as a technological rube has long been a favorite joke in his company, one he's been happy to have Twitter help him disabuse.)

He was encouraged here by another controversial office presence. Murdoch's longtime retinue of official guards, including communications chief Gary Ginsberg, general counsel Lon Jacobs, CFO Dave DeVoe, and his longtime secretary of fifty years, Dot Wyndoe—each of whom has helped restrain the famously off-the-reservation Murdoch—had been disbanded at the peak of the phone-hacking crisis, in part in a power grab by James Murdoch, and then by the introduction of the new executive and sudden favorite Joel Klein. It was Klein who—stirring more consternation among Murdoch lieutenants—installed Natalie Ravitz, who had previously worked for Klein, in the new role of Murdoch's chief of staff and primary gatekeeper. As so often happens in Murdoch-land, an odd, uncomfortable, and, to many, infuriating corporate quirk was quickly institutionalized. As strange as Ravitz's presence in Murdoch's traditionally all-male world (except for his secretary Dot) was—together with her even more uncharacteristic fan-girl tone—overnight she became the new normal. Many held her responsible for his uncontrolled tweeting—that the tweets were to impress her. Still, in equally characteristic Murdoch fashion, what is in favor invariably goes out of favor, and Ravitz fell from grace in June, a victim, many say, of the new clout of Rupert's sons, James and Lachlan, and their long game against her.

And yet the tweets go on . . .

He's a natural. He writes in headlines. He enlivens dry stuff with signature pithiness. He can do lifestyle, too: "Vegans wake up! Bill Clinton looks incredibly healthy after giving up this nonsense. We all need a little red meat." They are a vivid and tight narration of his invariably off-center political take, his current and still active travels, and curmudgeonly if not dyspeptic views. He's a gifted diarist, offering the kind of quirky asides Twitter seems made for.

Curiously, Murdoch's tweets suggest some of the aspects of the form that seem to increasingly make Twitter the laggard of social media. Twitter is best suited to journalists, maybe even old journalists. With its hard space restrictions, it's expressly not suited for the gassy self-expression of social media oversharers. Rather, it soars on the wire-service succinctness on which Murdoch grew up. Twitter might feel to Murdoch like coming home.

The divided Murdoch personality—the two sides that have arguably formed his success—splits between ruthless, bottom-line proprietor and newspaper acolyte and obsessive. If the fates had been different, and if the job had paid more, he might have been a journalist himself rather than a proprietor.

One of Murdoch's earliest properties in the United States was the *Star*, a weekly, supermarket checkout counter showbiz tabloid that *Rolling Stone* publisher Jann Wenner, meeting Murdoch in the late seventies, noted had a very good, if unlikely, political column. Murdoch proudly admitted that he himself was writing the column under a pseudonym.

At the same time, Murdoch's proximity to and power over the means of expression—even for all the decades he has been accused of unremitting interference with his papers—has also been inhibiting for him. Standing at the very center of verbal quickness, he himself was often, and to his own shame, incredibly inarticulate.

One aspect of his famous battle with Harold Evans at the *Sunday Times* in the early eighties was his anger that Evans always talked over him, even, and most annoying to Murdoch (something his current handlers counsel visitors never to do), sometimes helping Murdoch finish his ever-faltering sentences.

The joke among almost all outsiders who find themselves dealing with Murdoch is that he can seem, with his mumble, unfinished sentences, and sometimes violent gesturing (waving and pounding the table), quite incomprehensible.

Once, when I was with Murdoch going down in the elevator from his apartment in a building, a Trump building, where his neighbors were Jared Kushner and Ivanka Trump, the elevator stopped and Donald Trump got on. Murdoch offered some passing and mumbled greeting. Whereupon, Trump turned to me and asked, "Do you ever understand what he's saying?" (Trump is reported to have been impressed by or even envious of Murdoch's tweets.)

It is, not implausibly, the struggle and dominating theme of his life—to be able to say something.

His father, Sir Keith, had a stutter so paralyzing that he was tutored by Lionel Logue, the same therapist who attended to King George VI and was memorialized in the movie *The King's Speech*.

Rupert's mother, Elizabeth, and two sisters, he believed—and they readily agree—were vastly more articulate than he was. His mother, at age ninety-nine in 2008, speculated that her son, the owner of the world's largest publishing empire, was probably quite dyslexic.

That might, then, be the foundation of one of the great ironies of the postwar era. The modern media business exists in its present form—a set of colossi almost all of them in some way formed to imitate or defend against Murdoch—all because Murdoch, insecure about his ability to put words together, was somehow trying to ensure that his voice might be heard.

But perhaps it is Twitter, rather than Murdoch's own empire, that is his ultimate facilitator. If his inarticulateness can frustrate him, the layers of insulation inside his company that are designed to keep him from talking often frustrate him to the same effect. For one thing, everybody who works with him knows what he is capable of saying and is terrified that he might say it. A key part of their jobs is to distract him enough so that his verbal impulses pass uneventfully. (Indeed, Twitter is something of a demonstration to the panicky people around him that he actually does have some sense and some filters. As piquant as his tweets might get, they really never rise to the actually colloquial Rupert Murdoch.)

For another, there is a great competition within the Murdoch executive suites to have him only talk to you—that competition may be the fundamental shaping mechanism of the company. To be able to say, "He said . . . ," "He thinks . . . ," "He told me . . . ," "He's concerned that . . . ," "He's not happy about . . . ," "He's really focused on . . ." is the motor that drives the operations of Fox and News Corp. And it is the driver of a career to be the one who can relay those words.

The periodic reorganizations of the company all revolve around who jumps to the head of the line of who talks to him first (and last). Hence, the basic mechanism of power within the company is to keep him from widely talking—not least of all because, even mumbling, he is a promiscuous talker, a man of spontaneous desires, pronouncements, and sudden tactical redirections and strategic overhauls.

Twitter is, therefore, quite an annoying, if not incomprehensible, new element in the ecosystem of Murdoch power. He can jump over everybody's head. He escapes the minders.

Within the company it's now a potent variable and vital question. Has he tweeted that? Do you think he will tweet that? Can you keep him from tweeting that? It is similar to questions about how much he's had to drink, another significant corporate variable. Indeed, how much he's had to drink is a question related to how likely he is to tweet (and how problematic the ensuing tweeting might be).

It is, too, an uncomfortably humanizing aspect of the often not-very-human-seeming man—and not a little disconcerting for that. If there is one constant and overriding issue in the Murdoch empire it is about signs of his possible slippage. His tweets are the new tea leaves here. They are read as the measure of his mental state. Is he? Isn't he? Curiously, the more open and convivial he seems—and in large measure the tweets are jaunty and transparent—the more people worry. Is this a new Murdoch, an expressive one, even an approachable one? And what does that mean? And where does all this end? This indefatigable, querulous, sly, and crafty heartbeat.

Fox News

The Death of Roger Ailes

I made a mental note last night to call Roger in the morning and get his take on the Trump events of the last few days. There are few conversations more entertaining and insightful than Roger Ailes on Republican politics, where he's known all the players, their strengths and particularly their weaknesses. Liberals might despise and fear him, but some of his most scathing and hilarious critiques have often been reserved for conservatives. His fifty years among the kahunas of GOP politics—as one of the creators of modern Republican politics—made him, in addition to his other political claims to fame, among his party's sharpest observers. On his friend Donald Trump, and the unthinkable developments that put him in the White House, no one has been keener—or crueler. But at 8:30 Thursday morning, his wife Beth texted me that he had died a few minutes earlier. Days before, on ever-weakening legs, he had fallen, not for the first time, and hit his head.

It was a particular cruelty of the anti-Ailes press that it often focused on Beth, with rumors of a breakdown in their marriage and impending divorce. In fact, she was fierce in her devotion to him, and his most implacable defender. In the ten months since he had been forced out as chairman of Fox News Channel, the network—arguably, the most significant political force in American life for a generation—that he launched, built, and ran for twenty years, she carried him. This past autumn, after their hard summer of accusations and media conviction, she had flown down to Palm Beach and bought for themselves a waterfront mansion, where she hoped he would retire and where living well would at least be some revenge.

Retirement was more Beth's idea than his. Roger and I spoke a week ago, just after the last ouster at Fox—Bill Shine, his lieutenant who had taken over his job, following by a week the ouster of Bill O'Reilly—and, invariably, the subject was Fox's increasing disarray and the possibilities for a new conservative network. Yet proscribed by the noncompete provisions of his separation agreement, Roger nevertheless had a plan in his head and was taking calls. "I can't call. But I can't stop people from calling me," he said. As we spoke, Beth texted pictures of their view and of a newly svelte Roger lying lazily in the sun.

All things considered, it was a happy winter. Or, anyway, he was certainly weighing the benefits of being out of the office and out of the fray. Still, clearly, both he and Beth could only get so far from the bitterness they felt about his end at Fox. Worse still, the terms of his departure from Fox put draconian limits on what he could say and how he might defend himself. The payout that he believed he had earned—having created a $30 billion asset and Twenty-First Century Fox's most profitable business— was the price of his silence. The most voluble and pugnacious man in American media was forced to keep still.

But privately, angrily, he couldn't wait to settle scores.

In his view, the political showdown at Fox News that was always bound to happen—which, to me, he had predicted several years before—had finally taken place, albeit uglier, and with more finality, than he had ever expected. "They got the memo," he said, with some forbearance. "If you strike the king, you better kill him."

By "they," he meant Rupert Murdoch's sons. And most particularly James Murdoch, who, two years ago, was elevated to CEO of his father's company, and whom Ailes regarded as an impetuous, grandiose, self-satisfied rich kid. Wryly, he admitted bringing this feud on himself: "I made the money those kids spent. So, no, I wasn't going to suck up to them."

Not long before his ouster, Ailes had enraged James by going behind his back and helping to convince his father to squelch a plan for a new, temple-like Twenty-First Century Fox headquarters that James wanted to build.

The relationship of Ailes to Murdoch senior, often his loyal patron but frequently just a boss stuck having to indulge his highest earner, was also always a fraught one. When I wrote my Murdoch biography in 2009, one of the few stipulations of my access to Murdoch was that I not interview Ailes, who Murdoch felt got too much credit for the company's success.

In July, over a two-week period of press leaks after former Fox anchor Gretchen Carlson filed a sexual harassment lawsuit, Ailes was ousted without opportunity to defend himself. James hired the law firm Paul, Weiss to investigate the charges against Ailes, but Ailes himself wasn't called. In effect, in order to get his payout, he had to accept his disgrace—$40 million in press accounts, in reality closer to $100 million.

Surely, less is true than what the various lawsuits allege, because that is the nature of lawsuits. As surely, his political enemies, the legions of them, were concerned much less for the truth than that he be gone. But there would be no argument that Ailes lived in a world of retrograde vividness, politically and sexually. He embodied what he was accused of, guilty in spirit if not in the details.

In the end, the larger story is, or ought to be, about someone who, from Nixon's "silent majority" to Reagan's "Reagan Democrats" to Fox News, understood the intensity of the unhappiness and anger in another America that Ailes sometimes described as existing in a perpetual 1965 and that we liberal media people are now so confused by.

The Rise of Fox

1

Some people think Fox News is on the verge of creating the kind of revolution that CNN made ten years ago—altering the basic habits and assumptions of why and how we watch news.

It's certainly been killing the competition. On a series of big events, Fox—with its narrowcast approach—has taken larger ratings than its nonsectarian brothers. Starting with the Republican Convention in July, building with each debate, then with notable peaks during the Florida phase of the election, and followed by Inauguration Day, Fox trumped both MSNBC and CNN. Now, it's true that these events are all Republican-focused, but that's the fear. In a Republican era, the Republicans will have a monopoly on such events—and so will Fox.

Or, really, what happens is that the Republicans will have enthusiasm for the news and will be eager to tune in to play-by-play coverage and postgame analysis, while the larger but less engaged (or more dispirited) Democratic and agnostic audience will forsake the news.

This is already a big transformation in the way we see the news: Republican news versus Democratic news. News, in other words, becomes not so much about the event itself but about how we identify with the event.

It's the European way—every newspaper, every news outlet, has its proud bias. There's left-of-center news; there's reconstructed-Communist news; there's hardline-Communist news; there's Christian Democrat news; there's neofascist news. It's the nineteenth-century way—every paper a party paper.

Or you can look at it in exactly the opposite fashion. The larger trend is a systemic erosion of the audience for Washington-government-policy-politician-oriented news. But while CNN, MSNBC, and the networks are casualties of the militant disinterest in formal political news, Fox is the beneficiary. Except rather than Fox's success representing some new ideological trend in America, it suggests that the only audience left for political news is one with an almost autistic attachment to politics.

Ideological purity, in other words, meets media purity. In a highly competitive market, you want to focus on a core interest group, which, by the nature of its obsession, is an audience that is easy to attract, easy to hold, easy to service.

The networks, along with CNN and MSNBC, continue to represent the dispassionate tradition. This fifties-sixties-seventies-eighties objective norm came about because in a three-network world, the idea of broadcasting as a public trust had great currency (and the force of government regulation), and because the accusation of a liberal bias in the media was as dogged and widespread as it was true—hence the news was buttoned-down in tone and blurred in point of view.

But in a fragmented media world, that tradition can be a commercial disadvantage. What it means is that without a pointed bias, a single-minded reason for existing, a clear and persuasive shtick, you're left to court a general-interest audience. This is an audience that demands wide variety and constant new forms of stimulation (*expensive* stimulation), is fickle in its interests, and, because it lacks any sort of emotional attachment to what you have to offer, is easily attracted by somebody else's clearer sell.

CNN, in its early incarnation, grabbed the easy-to-grab news-focused audience. But the thing about the notion of targeted media is that someone can always target you finer. The success of an all-news network invites an all-sports-news network (and then an all-golf network), an all-entertainment-news network (and then an all-hip-hop network), and, obviously, an all-conservative-news network.

I doubt, though, that this is what Murdoch had in mind. I think he thought he'd create a head-to-head, competitive twenty-four-hour news broadcast organization. If Turner could do it, he could do it; if GE and Microsoft were going to go for it, he was, too; plus, Murdoch just wasn't going to cede the market to Time Warner after it bought Turner.

So when chairman Roger Ailes, at the launch of the Fox News Channel in 1996, said, "We'll have more live news and produced programming than either CNN or MSNBC," and that Fox would be more "balanced" in its reporting than the other networks, that opinion programming would be clearly distinguished from straight news reporting, he may have meant it (sort of, anyway).

But from the beginning, there was something embattled about Fox (indeed, it had to fight Time Warner for space on its cable systems). It was almost a class thing. Fox was trailer-camp life on Sixth Avenue. Moldy food in the greenroom, and, even in the world of television, women with way too much eye makeup. For a period last year, Fox, alone among news stations, refused to send cars for its guests (the Fox guests tend to be far enough down the guest pecking order to be willing to get there on their own). And, for on-air talent, you didn't go to Fox—at least until recently—if you had alternatives. (Court TV was better than Fox.) Not only was Fox on the tail end of talent, but it was on the tail end of news. One Fox producer recounts having to carry his footage from satellite truck to satellite truck at the site of a European terrorist attack, begging for an upload to New York.

So on the one hand, you had a deep lack of resources and clout; on the other hand, you had the standard television imperative—mimic the competition, be as broad as possible. But then you had Roger Ailes—the purest melding of media and politics. He's one of the few political consultants to actually come out of television. He meets Nixon in 1967 on the set of *The Mike Douglas Show*, which he is producing. After Nixon (Ailes is the most vivid character in Joe McGinniss's book *The Selling of the President 1968*, about the Nixon campaign), he closely counsels Reagan and Bush. Then, out of power in the Clinton years, he runs CNBC and launches America's Talking, the precursor to MSNBC, before joining Fox.

Media professionals and political consultants have a fundamentally contrary view. The media professional—the writer, reporter, producer, anchor—believes that politics is of large concern to a broad number of people, or if it isn't, then it should be; that our job is to force-feed the public. The political consultant, on the other hand, recognizes the uniquely specialized nature of politics. That people are almost never interested in politics in general, but in their own self-interest and bias; that, in fact, fewer and fewer people are interested in politics in any shape or form; that it's a shrinking market. Nonvoters, non-newspaper readers, nonparticipants are the growth industry. Still, you have a core group of enthusiasts that remains loyal and strong—reaching it is the job.

While this is as true on the Left (from anti-WTO-ists to the free-Mumia crowd) as on the Right, in pure media terms, the Right is a much easier audience to reach and to hold. Conservatives are older and more settled in their political views and media habits; they are more rural and hence less restless in their pursuit of diversion; they are more anchored to their families and to their homes and to their televisions; they are more homogeneous in their interests—it's easier to speak to them as one. Plus, and this should not be underestimated, they feel, largely because it's true, that the world is against them. That what they believe in is going away. That they are endangered. Tap that and you've forged a bond.

Fox, having successfully made this bond, is flush with success. And success has made it trumpet ever more confidently its view of the world.

In that view, Bill Clinton is the twentieth century's most preposterous joke (one thing that distinguishes Fox from other news channels is that it's actually funny—they have a good time on Fox); Ronald Reagan is the century's paramount leader (at the moment, Fox seems to be conducting an ongoing living funeral for the former president); and, most important, it's the other networks that are biased—liberal-biased—rather than Fox (what bias Fox has is merely a counterweight—hence George Bush's cousin's key role on Election Night in the Fox newsroom).

In the Fox world, you'll find Newt Gingrich, Dick Morris, Pat Robertson—who, however discredited or marginalized in the larger world, are still bigger than life on Fox. You'll find a ragtag bunch of Democrats who have come out for tax cuts, or recanted one or another liberal orthodoxy, all with hairpieces askew and, clearly, alcohol on their breath (the Fox vision of Democrats). And you'll meet the world's most tongue-tied liberals and neo-socialists (none of whom you've ever heard of), the straw men for O'Reilly to knock down. It's a chip-on-the-shoulder, love-of-mother, red-in-the-face, *Reader's Digest*, Irish Catholic world (although, in fact, its audience tends toward southern and western Protestants).

The logical view is that the Bush victory will make it more difficult for Fox, that it takes away its reason for being, that it's the Clinton thing that fueled the channel's good fortune. But then the inauguration numbers killed.

Now, the counterview is that it's the fickle, general-interest public that tunes out first.

The core Republican audience holds.

* * *

Of course, the most sophisticated media view—which in some sense goes to the heart of Republican resentment—is to question what exactly the Fox audience, this older, downwardly mobile, less acquisitive demographic, is worth. From an advertisers' point of view, you're talking Preparation H and Mylanta. You're not talking mobile telephony and a wide array of entertainment products.

In other words, we are at the fundamental schism in American cultural, political, and economic life. There's the quicker-growing, economically vibrant, but also more fractious and more difficult to manage, morally relativist, urban-oriented, culturally adventuresome, sexually polymorphous, and ethnically diverse nation (Bill Clinton's America, if you will). And there's the small-town, nuclear-family, religiously oriented, white-centric other America, which makes up for its diminishing cultural and economic force with its predictability and stability (the GWB-ies).

This is not by any means a new schism. There have always been two countries—we just haven't had the bandwidth to create parallel media nations.

The Rise of Fox

2

Here's the biggest problem politics has today: all but an exceptional few politicians suck at making, or understanding, media. This is a surprise, because the only thing politicians want to do is get on TV. That's their basic job. But they're talentless. They're zeros. The media consultants they hire to help them are mostly hacks and rejects, too.

Political ads? Sheesh. It's a form that has not advanced in twenty years.

Of course, professional Republicans and right-wing people are usually no more capable than the Democrats and sappy liberals of creating a compelling and credible story line.

But then there's Roger Ailes.

There's something incredibly creepy about Ailes. He looks the way you imagine the man behind the curtain looking. That is, he doesn't care about how he looks (which is, as it happens, gray and corpulent). He understands it's all manipulation. When he got found out giving the president ex parte advice on handling the war, he didn't for a second whinge or show remorse. Let others pretend—he's too old and too good at his job to start making believe the world works any other way than the way it works.

The rap on Ailes is, of course, that he's a hopeless partisan, a true believer, a Republican agent. But that deeply misses the point. Ailes is a television guy. He's been doing television practically as long as anyone. His digressions into politics (for Nixon and for Reagan) have always been more about television craft than about Republican craft. His is the singular obsession of any television guy: to stay on the air.

Fox really isn't in the service of the Republicans. Ailes can say this baldly and confidently. (The Republicans, more and more, follow the Fox line.) Fox isn't in any conventional sense ideological media. It's just that being anti-Democrat, anti-Clinton, anti-yuppie, anti-wonk turns out to be great television. Great ratings make for convenient ideology.

Now, professional political people, while surely corrupt and cynical, are also sentimentalists. They believe everybody else is as interested in politics as they are. A good television guy, who has to command the attention of the public, would never make that mistake.

The West Wing, in its original, surprising incarnation, was not at all about politics. It was a show about an office that happened to be the White House. It was the basic joke, even—working in the White House was not really different from working any other place. Then, in an unconscious shift, it became not only about the White House but about some schmaltzy, patently phony version of the White House.

Similarly, Fox is not really about politics (CNN, with its antiseptic beltway POV, is arguably more about politics than Fox). It certainly isn't arguing a consistent right-wing case. Rather, it's about having a chip on your shoulder; it's about us versus them, insiders versus outsiders, phonies versus non-phonies, and, in a clever piece of postmodernism, established media against insurgent media.

Perhaps most interesting, it's about language, or expressiveness—which politics has not been about in a long time (modern politics is the opposite of expressiveness). Fox has cultivated a fast-talking garrulousness. Traditional news is rendered slowly, at a deadly, fatherly pace. Fox gunned the engine.

This was a *West Wing* signature, too, before it got gummy—automatic-fire patois. Cable talk. Fox, too, is about arguing—rather than the argument. It's a Jesuit thing. Thesis. Antithesis.

In the conventional-wisdom swamp of television, this passes for serious counterprogramming. It's the tweak. This is really the Fox narrative device. The entire presentation is about tweaking Democrats and boomer culture. The Fox message is not about proving its own virtue, or the virtue of aging Republicans (except, of course, for Ronald Reagan), or even of the Bushes, but about ridiculing the virtues of Democrats and their yuppie partisans. Pull their strings. Push their buttons. Build the straw man, knock it down. Night after night.

Here's the way not to get labeled a phony: accuse the other guy of being one. Always attack, never defend. And have fun doing it. A media nation demands great media showmanship. What's more, in a media nation, it's logical to make the media the main issue.

The most audacious part of the Fox story line—the point that drives liberals the craziest—is that Fox is the antidote to massive media bias. And that the Fox people resolutely stick to this story. The wink is very important in television.

Which brings us to what may be the central political conundrum of the era. Why do conservatives make better media than liberals? Fox is, after all, just the further incarnation of a successful generation of conservative radio provocateurs. There aren't really even any liberal contenders.

No, nobody who's seriously interested in ratings and buzz wants liberals on television or even near an op-ed page. Part of the explanation of the conservative-media success is that in a liberal nation, they have had to develop a more compelling and subversive story line. They've fully capitalized on the outsider, tough-talking, Cassandra thing.

A part of this is the dancing-dog advantage. Conservatives have been hired by the heretofore liberal media to be, precisely, conservatives—hyperconservatives, even; eager exaggerations (wink). Whereas, when liberalish people are hired by liberalish media organizations, the issue is to be neutral, unliberal. The main challenge for George Stephanopoulos on ABC's *This Week* is never to let on that he once worked for the Democrats.

It's an understanding-the-media-game point, which, if you're building a media career—exactly what all the conservatives tend to be doing—you get. But which if, like many liberals, you see yourself as having a higher calling than just a media career, you may not get.

We can talk about politics as a metaphor for something else, as Fox does, for being left out, and as *The West Wing* was doing, politics as a metaphor for working too hard, living in your office, being too involved with your coworkers. Likewise, there's Ann Coulter, who really uses politics to talk about some S&M thing. But what we can't do is talk about politics for its own sake. It's way too boring. It's too disconnected—it's too Al Gore.

And you can't say, as almost all liberals do, "It's boring, but it's important." That would be bad writing, as opposed to the Fox writing style, which is to thrust and parry and dump on Clinton and thump a liberal snob or egghead when things get dull.

The Rise of Fox

3

JANUARY 2012

For more than a decade, the traditional media business in America—print, television, movies, music—has been contracting and losing value along with influence, as advertisers and audiences have fled to newer forms of delivery, interaction, and entertainment. Except for one notable exception: Fox News.

The Rupert Murdoch–owned 24/7 cable news station has just reached its fifteenth anniversary and is the bone in the throat of liberals everywhere—nothing less, really, than the dark heart of everything that is unenlightened in politics and culture. It has had a rocket trajectory of ratings growth, financial success (it is now the most profitable division of the Murdoch empire), political clout, and its ability to infuriate its adversaries.

On a business basis—with growth over fifteen years from zero to profits climbing to as much as $1 billion this year—it is, on its own, the single most successful media company in America, and perhaps the world. On a zeitgeist basis, it has helped transform American culture into a two-state nation. The Tea Party is its child.

In America, what Murdoch is best known for is Fox News. For better or worse, it is his legacy to the media business and to journalism: brilliant, in terms of business, his admirers would argue; lower, meaner, coarser, and propagandist in terms of journalism—arguably, more so than any of his other enterprises (including the *News of the World*)—his critics would say.

But, in fact, Murdoch himself has had little to do with Fox News. He is often as confounded by it as any liberal. He is frequently castigated for its rude excesses by his large circle of liberal friends (or, rather, his wife's circle of Hollywood liberal friends). His family fulminates about it behind and in front of his back. It is, to them, their company's biggest embarrassment—more than the hacking scandal, even. And the man who runs it, Roger Ailes, is—more than hacking—the damnedest problem for the Murdochs at News Corp. Indeed, one of the unintended and, for the Murdochs, infuriating consequences of hacking-gate is that it has made Ailes even more powerful and indispensable to the company.

I'm not sure what Ailes might consider his biggest accomplishment: to have changed the nature of American news, to have changed the nature of American politics, or, to do what no man has done before, to have reduced Murdoch within his own company; to have, in many ways, become bigger (and much more fearsome) than Rupert.

* * *

I first met Ailes about nine years ago when, after I had called him the new American Antichrist (quite an understatement in many ways), he asked me to lunch. This is not to say that Ailes is thick-skinned or ironically amused by his critics. Quite the opposite—he tends to be easily riled. But he had somehow decided that my diss in his direction was lesser than my disses of his enemies, and so, in that, we were kinsmen of a sort. And, indeed, it was a salubrious lunch in which together we surveyed the landscape of the self-serious, the pompous, and the smug. "The Establishment," as Ailes said.

More lunches were to follow—all of them marked by brilliant and counterintuitive analysis of the media business, sharp slurs against the elite, and utterances that, taken on face value, might spark a liberal counterrevolution but that, in person, were quite hilarious. I came to be in possession of this curious information: while all of my fellow liberals believed Ailes to be a brute and a bully, I knew him to be whip-smart, witty, flirtatious, companionable, and, as it happens, generous, too. When my college-age daughter needed an internship, all it took was a call to Ailes. When I filled in for the hapless Alan Colmes, the liberal foil to the hard-charging, right-wing Sean Hannity on the talk show *Hannity & Colmes*, Ailes took pains to tell me how to look less hapless.

Once, he offered to hire me as a Fox commentator, if that's what I wanted, but counseled that, if I worked for Fox News, I was never likely to be hired by the liberal outlets to which I was more naturally suited.

And then we fell out. Or, in a sense, suddenly engaged in News Corp politics, I sold him out. But more of that in a bit.

* * *

The secret history of Rupert Murdoch is not so much hacking's skulduggery but that, as the empire expanded, Murdoch himself got older. Murdoch, at some turning point, began to represent the past, and Ailes, I would argue, the future.

Ailes is certainly an unlikely representative of modernity. At seventy-one, he's just nine years younger than Murdoch. He's a rotund-ish, pants-high, mopping-sweat-from-the-brow, W. C. Fields type. His career was launched as Richard Nixon's television adviser in 1968. He did the same for Ronald Reagan in the eighties. He then exited politics for television, and went to work for NBC in its effort to compete with CNN, the dominant force in the nineties in cable news. In 1996, enter Murdoch, the inveterate newspaperman who perceived the power and money in cable news and who had tried to buy CNN and been bitterly rebuffed. If he couldn't buy it, he'd start his own cable news network—for this he solicited Ailes. Largely because each man can talk politics with gossipy granularity, they hit it off and Murdoch offered Ailes the job.

Ailes extracted two key transformational concessions from Murdoch. Cable carriers traditionally pay content providers for "carriage," which means a long and slow process of convincing carriers to put new networks on their dial; Ailes's requirement was that Murdoch reverse this, offering to pay the carriers, changing the cable business model overnight, and getting Fox News a national audience. Then, too, Ailes insisted that this be his show. While Murdoch has always had the last word in his newspapers, he agreed that Ailes's word would be final—that Murdoch, the great meddler, wouldn't meddle.

It was a pivotal moment. Murdoch, a man who has run governments on the basis of his control of the press, leveled enemies, and been a kingmaker to political careers, had passed that privilege to someone else in the form of cable television, a medium that, other than its cash flow, he had little interest in.

As it happens, Ailes achieved what Murdoch himself has never managed. All Murdoch's efforts at building a profitable and influential tabloid press in America have never amounted to much. His papers in Boston, Chicago, and Texas, and his experiment with a supermarket tabloid, had never really taken off and had all been sold. After years of trying, he had only one news outlet in America, the perpetually money-losing *New York Post*. And, suddenly, Fox. (He later had the money-losing *Wall Street Journal*, too.)

Ailes's confection is, in a way, what one might have imagined Murdoch himself might have created at the most aggressive and hungry point of his career—that is, if he knew anything about television. But he doesn't. And, indeed, as it grows more powerful, more vivid, more louche, more an even greater demonstration of the Murdochian press than even Murdoch has ever achieved, a kind of ultimate *Sun*, but more profitable, the deal of non-interference between Ailes and Murdoch becomes more secure—because nobody else could do what Ailes has done. Indeed, Ailes's control is total.

Murdoch is a sideshow. Ailes is central.

Curiously, the rise of Fox News started just as Murdoch himself was becoming less, well . . . Foxified. The anti-Fox factions in his life and company began to surround him, for lack of a more official moment, when he met and fell in love with Wendi Deng, his future wife, in 1997. Wendi, the Chinese émigrée to America and Yale School of Management graduate, nearly thirty-nine years his junior, was not the only young liberal voice around him. All of his children, an increasingly voluble and insistent bunch (and all the more so because they were mad at him for breaking up his marriage and running off with Wendi), are more or less yuppies and Ivy League liberals (only his eldest daughter, Prudence, famous in the family for ridiculing her father's old-man conservative ways, did not go to an elite American university). What's more, the executive team that has, of late, emerged around him is from the company's big profit center—Hollywood and entertainment. In other words, they, too, are liberals. Peter Chernin, the former head of Twentieth Century Fox and ex–News Corp COO, is a prominent Democratic Party contributor. Gary Ginsberg, Murdoch's PR lieutenant—almost always at his side—was an aide in the Clinton White House (and John F. Kennedy Jr.'s best friend).

What they all have in common is an increasing antipathy to Fox News and abhorrence of Roger Ailes.

But Fox News is so successful, and Ailes too wily, for anybody in the company to effectively challenge him. When Murdoch's son Lachlan had the temerity to try to cross Ailes, Ailes arranged his ouster (effectively forcing Rupert to choose between his son and the increasing profits of Fox News—he chose the profits).

Fox is not only a ratings juggernaut—within a few years of its launch taking the top cable-TV news spot and relegating the once-dominant CNN to something like irrelevance—but, after 9/11, the single most important force in American politics.

Fox set the tone for the voice, persona, and theatrical style of American conservatism. The media presence that Ailes had helped develop for Richard Nixon and Ronald Reagan reached its fruition in Fox News—all the more so because the media had become stronger than any candidate. Indeed, conservative hopeful after conservative hopeful turned up on the payroll of Fox News.

Murdoch's fundamentally buttoned-down, backroom, fiscal-and-regulatory, elite sort of conservatism was turned into a carnival of self-dramatizing, exaggerated, simplistic, lumpen, family-value political caricatures.

He was gobsmacked—and all the more confused about his options, because he was also beholden to the Fox News money (as his newspapers fall, Fox News rises). His wife, children, and closest executives were apoplectic when it came to Fox and Ailes.

Fox and the Murdochs reached a critical disjuncture during the Barack Obama election, with all the Murdochs, including Rupert, supporting Obama, and Fox News portraying the future president as a Muslim and a terrorist.

Which is just about where I came in and sold out Ailes. One of the reasons I was invited in 2007—shortly after Murdoch's takeover of the *Wall Street Journal* (an enterprise supported by the profits of Fox News)—to write a biography of the mogul with his full cooperation was, in part, I came to understand, because I was a useful weapon in the increasing war against Ailes.

Among the sponsors of my biography were Murdoch's PR aide Ginsberg, who, being so close to Murdoch's ear, was fighting an almost constant rearguard action against Ailes.

My arrangement to do this book involved no deals or agreements or limitations on access—save for one. In return for all the access to Murdoch I might have wanted, I made a devil's bargain not to talk to Ailes.

I believed that steering me away from Ailes was partly out of spite: Murdoch loyalists wanted to diminish Ailes's ever-larger part in the Murdoch story. And it was partly fear: Ailes is nobody's fool; he briefs with the best of them; unlike Murdoch, he is a great storyteller; if Murdoch's people were trying to undermine Ailes, given the opportunity, he might easily have jujitsued them. And it was partly a political move of the most delicate sort. It seemed clear to me that a set of forces was being arrayed against Ailes. Murdoch was being encouraged to get rid of him. Murdoch had, certainly, soured on him.

"He's crazy," Murdoch told me at one point. Indeed, I was offered a cornucopia of damaging anti-Ailes anecdotes. One choice leak to me involved how Murdoch took Ailes into a meeting with Obama, whereupon Obama, with Murdoch's permission, lectured and humiliated Ailes. (Not long after this was published in the biography, Ailes, to the family's fury, confronted Murdoch and forced him to back down and have the *New York Post* endorse Republican presidential candidate John McCain instead of Obama.)

And then, in early 2010, Matthew Freud, Murdoch's son-in-law, delivered what was clearly supposed to be a coup de grâce. He gave his now-famous interview to the *New York Times*, saying: "I am by no means alone within the family or the company in being ashamed and sickened by Roger Ailes' horrendous and sustained disregard of the journalistic standards that News Corporation, its founder and every other global media business aspires to."

In other words, Rupert Murdoch's aversion to confrontation and his love, ultimately above all else, of free cash flow may have offered Ailes an amount of reliable protection. But none of that was going to protect him against James Murdoch. It was not only that the Murdoch children are ashamed of the Fox vulgarity, but, even more, they were unforgiving about Ailes's part in the exile of Lachlan Murdoch: revenge was obviously required there.

It was a simple corporate fact: as the Murdoch children advanced within the company, Ailes necessarily declined. At the inevitable inflection point, they would be in, and Ailes out. No matter what profits he was producing, News Corp would move into the next generation without him and with a new sense of pedigree and professionalism.

But I think Ailes knew whom he was dealing with. As Rupert faded and James rose as the would-be head of the family, James not only successfully lobbied to oust any executive, including the liberals Chernin and Ginsberg, who might have independent power bases within the company (and the ability to challenge not just James, but Ailes, too), but he blundered into hacking-gate, squandering his own reputation and future.

The children are further from the throne than ever, and Murdoch himself is increasingly fragile. But Fox News, fifteen years on, is one of the mighty forces on earth and Roger Ailes is, pretty much, king of the world.

Defeat

Bloomberg

In a journalistic nevermind of quite some proportions, *New York* magazine's cover story profile of Michael Bloomberg and his extraordinary, virtually overnight emergence as a transformative candidate in the race for the Democratic presidential nomination hit newsstands on Monday, March 2, 2020. The next day, Super Tuesday, after fifteen new primaries, he was dead, a joke. Having spent more of his own money than any politician ever in history, he won just one, American Samoa.

Bloomberg had long been a reliable guilty pleasure for *New York*, the conscience of the city's consumer, arriviste, and aspirational culture. Sometimes more guilt; sometimes more pleasure. As much as Donald Trump, Bloomberg emerged from 1980s New York as a comic-book figure of CEO status, billionaire moxie, and media power. These were attributes *New York* often extolled and admired, except when, in its frequent spasms of self-abnegation and political virtue, it felt the opposite. At one point in the 1990s, it all but banished Donald Trump, a figure it had helped create, from its pages for his surfeit of self-promotion. In 2001, during the race to succeed Rudy Giuliani, who had reached his two-term limit as mayor, *New York* turned indignantly on the upstart mayoral contender Michael Bloomberg, a wannabe trying to buy himself a political identity—indeed, the magazine assigned him to me for a ritual disemboweling.

At the time, Bloomberg, a former Wall Street executive, had a fortune of some single-digit billions. This came from his 1980s brainstorm to systematize disorderly bond prices and supply them directly to Wall Street traders over a desk-top terminal—a Bloomberg Terminal. "Bloomberg" became a master-of-the-universe brand. If you weren't important enough to have a Bloomberg Terminal on your desk (subscriptions currently cost upward of $20,000 a year), you weren't important.

Bloomberg himself, artless, awkward, underappreciated (in his view), joined the legions of the city's desperate social climbers. On the advice of the many consultants he hired, he bought himself into the Manhattan social world with outsize philanthropic gifts. He was said to admire Trump for his gall in putting his name on everything; Bloomberg, with his terminal and his own building, followed suit. Trump had a book, *The Art of the Deal*, and Bloomberg had one, too, *Bloomberg by Bloomberg* (where Trump's was a bestseller, Bloomberg's book was not).

With the stupendous profits from his financial information company, he retrofitted a more glamorous consumer media arm onto his business. He built a state-of-the-art newsroom to supply a radio station, a television studio, and a magazine. No matter that his media outlets reached an audience of pretty near zilch, the very promotion of his effort and the scale of his hiring spree made his Potemkin media company—$500 million, by some estimates, spent to create a $50 million media company—seem sort of real.

He assembled a personal staff of former political operatives to promote him—a new sort of branding strategy. That is, Trumpian. If he, Bloomberg, was promoted, the company also was promoted. In an ultimate branding exercise, his new handlers convinced this Democrat to run for mayor of New York City as a Republican in 2001. Here was not a plan, mind you, to actually be the mayor of New York, because Republican mayors were strictly a black swan event in the city. But if you had sufficient financial muscle, the Republicans, without hope of electing anyone (Giuliani, a Republican black swan, was by 2001 a widely derided figure), would gladly give you the nomination. Bloomberg would run, as Trump would run for president in 2016, as a quixotic leap of personal identity.

It is difficult from this vantage to truly express what a nonevent Bloomberg's candidacy was or what an odd duck he was thought to be. Indeed, *New York* was one of the few outlets to give his race serious attention—and this only because he was such a tempting target. As the designated hitter, I flogged him with merry cruelty. It would be hard to find someone, beyond Trump himself, so easy to mock. And then I found a smoking gun of ridicule.

A friend of mine, a former high-ranking Bloomberg executive, ousted a few years before in a war with one of Bloomberg's new personal branding tsars and abidingly bitter for it, had been supplying me with choice and unflattering details about her former boss. And then she remembered she had something else. In 1990, for Bloomberg's birthday, the company had prepared a booklet called *Portable Bloomberg: The Wit & Wisdom of Michael Bloomberg*, a Chairman Mao–style anthology, purportedly of Bloomberg's Wall Street–type abuse-as-hilarity witticisms, broadly denigrating almost all the key New York political constituencies: women, African Americans, Hispanics, gays, and anyone from any other borough than Manhattan. I wrote this story, quoting gleefully from the booklet, and minutes after the magazine appeared on its Monday publication date, Bloomberg's campaign, such as it was, went into terminal meltdown. Other media outlets began gleefully quoting from *Wit & Wisdom* (that is, repeating what I had quoted) and a lineup of New York politicians immediately began to demand he exit the race.

That, however, was Monday, September 10, 2001. The next day, the world was transformed. My scoop was forgotten. Giuliani became America's most heroic figure and, with his support and the implicit suggestion that he would be acting in Giuliani's stead, Bloomberg, despite his wit and wisdom, became the mayor of New York.

As New York mayors go, this unintended one took quite a break from what is traditionally a chaotic management approach in city hall, ever beset by warfare among New York's fractious interest groups. Bloomberg brought to the job a focused, goal- and message-specific management method; a deliberate personal style in contrast to the mercurial Giuliani; and, with strategic deployment of his own fortune, a measure of peace among competing groups—everyone was on his payroll. Crime continued to go down and prosperity continued to rise.

After eight enervating years of Giuliani governing the city with no small amount of hysteria and conflict, Bloomberg had the trains running with significantly less drama and more predictability.

A year or so into his term, I found myself at a cocktail party facing the glowering mayor from barely two feet away. "This is a first for me," I said, "but I apologize."

"You should," he said and turned away.

If the oligarch mayor could not escape the contempt of New York's not inconsiderable to-the-barricades left wing, he certainly managed to court, soothe, and reward the moderate liberal majority. (*New York* magazine became a reliable booster.) After the financial collapse in 2008, he somehow, with an oligarch's sleight of heavy hand, managed to arrange a runaround of the mayoral term limits and get himself another four years in office.

By the end of his three terms he was his own kind of New York monument. Not lovable, not even particularly liked, but reliable—what you saw is what you got. And he had helped advance, if you considered this an advancement, New York as the world's super city.

As a corollary to this, while working his $195,000-a-year mayor's job (for which he took only $1), his own fortune increased nearly sevenfold. The Bloomberg business grew exponentially; his add-on consumer news business became a mainstay of New York media and one of its biggest employers; and his philanthropy arm became a national power, reaching into city governments around the country. Bloomberg himself rose to a business status near Bill Gates and Steve Jobs. He became a personal brand name rivaled only perhaps by Trump himself.

But in some sense this made him not like Trump and, in fact, in the minds of many, the anti-Trump. Trump became the president of the United States by pretending to be a self-made businessman and billionaire. Bloomberg was, indubitably, a self-made businessman and billionaire. If you liked Trump (and were not a hopeless bigot), how could you not like Bloomberg? And if you hated Trump, how could you not like Bloomberg? Even if, actually, no one liked Bloomberg.

He saw himself as a rebuke to Trump and Trump as an insult to billionaires everywhere. Trump, after all, had built nothing, despite having his name on many buildings; he had no money beyond the money his father left him; and he had hardly managed any organization at all, other than that of his own family. Trump merely played Bloomberg on television.

At the Democratic Convention in the summer of 2016, a gathering dominated by the party's left-wing faithful, Bloomberg, the billionaire businessman, delivered in his address to the convention one of the most searing and passionate attacks on his doppelgänger.

Bloomberg had toyed with running for president in 2008, when he would have been sixty-six, then again after Barack Obama's term in 2016, at seventy-four. Out of office, he had held together his political brain trust. Where other sidelined politicians wanting back in the game might have to begin again and rebuild their operations, Bloomberg kept his payroll going. His political operatives were not paid like political operatives; they were paid like successful executives. And he got two of the best.

His number one, Kevin Sheekey, a movie-style political operative, canny, funny, knowing, everyone's friend and no one's friend, had been Bloomberg's political alter ego since shortly before his first run for mayor. Sheekey had become one of the key city hall powers and, after that, a Bloomberg minister without portfolio. The number two, Howard Wolfson, was a central player in Hillary Clinton's primary race against Obama in 2008. A take-no-prisoners, us-against-them type, seemingly so preternaturally grim and resigned to liberal failure you could hardly help having a feeling of great relief when he joined the safety of the Bloomberg entourage after Clinton's first bitter defeat, a captive talent for Bloomberg's theoretical political future.

Sheekey and Wolfson both became rich as the barons of the billionaire king. Still, while life was salubrious, neither Sheekey nor Wolfson was doing what they each believed they were destined to do: elect a president.

After November 2016, the overriding question for Democrats was who could beat Trump in 2020—that is, if he couldn't be gotten rid of before that.

Bloomberg's position was straightforward: he combined demonstrably able administrative skill and largely middle-of-the-road views with the ability and willingness to spend quite literally whatever it might cost to be the president of the United States.

If this sounded desultory in any true liberal sense, if not completely suspect, it was, for some, an enlightened proposition: elect someone because of his managerial competence and freedom from the conflicts of political financing.

In a system now virtually indistinguishable from the demands of how you raised the money to succeed in it, here was a candidate who could not just bypass those demands but outspend anybody beholden to them. It was purity on a novel, albeit counterintuitive, level.

On the other hand, he was, at the same time, more obviously, an unlovable technocrat and despised plutocrat.

What's more, as much as he might have given half his fortune to be president (though certainly not all of it), he was ambivalent about almost everything else involved with running for president. Already being Michael Bloomberg, why risk the eminence he already had on the very good chance of losing, he reasonably assessed. He understood the inherent political hitches of being cold, tetchy, soulless, short, old, Jewish, and filthy rich—and would make no great effort to moderate those disadvantages. Publicly partnered to a longtime companion, he was still an unmarried man and did not want to have to explain the variables of that status. On top of that, he had a longtime friendship with the other older, middle-of-the-road establishment figure in the race, Joe Biden, and had given assurances that he wouldn't run against his friend.

But Sheekey and Wolfson worked hard on him—with Bloomberg now seventy-eight, the 2020 race would be their last chance, too. The Sheekey-Wolfson pitch was not to run a campaign against Biden but, if Biden faltered, against the socialist Bernie Sanders and become the one true candidate who could, in a match of money, business credentials, and sensible politics, beat Trump. Plus, the 2020 campaign calendar was closing.

On November 24, 2019, with Biden still on top of national polls, but precariously in all estimations, Bloomberg, facing a key filing deadline, declared.

Rather than a long slog, with some candidates having entered the race nearly a year before, Bloomberg would leapfrog the first individual primaries and blitzkrieg the super contests with a blanket of advertising so much greater than any campaign had ever attempted (or been able to attempt) that every other candidate would be but a shadow to his vivid presence. Sheekey and Wolfson had designed the perfect campaign for a hopeless campaigner—one without any time for him to do much personal campaigning.

Bloomberg would simply be an idea, a brand, rather than a struggling, emoting, walking-the-walk, talking-the-talk politician.

Here was a candidate without personal appeal, but with a set of old-fashioned business virtues and a vast fortune to prove them. He was a post-ideology figure who differed from most other technocratic types, with their varied governance theories, by the fact that he actually had managerial accomplishments. He was, for better or worse, a businessman-turned-politician distinguished by his lack of interest in demonstrating that he was a capable politician—you could hardly get a smile out of him. This earned him a particular, if circumscribed, base of admirers, mostly consisting of other successful businessmen and the fast-dwindling group of people who admire successful businessmen. Even among these admirers there might not be many who found Bloomberg personally pleasing or engaging or exciting or inspiring.

There were many stories involving the dinners at his town house on East Seventy-Ninth Street, organized by the staff of people dedicated to organizing dinners for him—dinners that often resulted in anecdotes about his coldness, brusqueness, and dismissiveness.

This necessarily became part of the theory of the case. Charm was the enemy of good government—the distraction, the false promise, the cover-up, the way to avoid the hard choices. The likability that he lacked could be compensated for with his fortune—now at $55 billion.

Money was necessary, but, according to the standard political view, it only went so far. But slowly the political world began to wake up to an altered equation. Fifty-five billion dollars would generate more yearly income than all other presidential aspirants would spend on their campaigns—indeed, that would be spent on all other races for all other offices in the country. Bloomberg, in other words, could outspend his opponents by a factor of twenty or thirty times without even decreasing the size of his fortune.

While Bloomberg might be a hard sell, in truth they weren't selling; they were buying. That was the true premise of the campaign.

Many wealthy men and women had used their fortunes to finance political campaigns before, some successfully, some not. In this, the formula was usually to spend what a given race might cost or to spend a margin more than your opponent might raise, but, almost always, to function within the basic political market. From December until March, Bloomberg broke the market. He bought so much television time that other campaigns found little left to buy. The goal seemed to be to create the perfect test case for the theory that there was some heretofore untried threshold amount that could win any election—and to now establish what that amount was. Entering the race well after any date that was reasonably practical and competitive, and beginning with negligible polls, he had reached contender status in thirty days. A curious side commentary was that he had proven the ever-in-doubt efficacy of television advertising: enough TV ads could make you admire even Michael Bloomberg. By the middle of January, the almost octogenarian Bloomberg, who seemed as likely to dismiss the voters he met on the campaign trail as embrace them, had become the new great moderate hope and a grave threat to the Democratic Party's left wing.

It should be said about Sheekey and Wolfson that to the degree they were running a custom-designed campaign for Bloomberg, they were also running one for themselves—a virtual campaign featuring media rather than the candidate. Both men, however respected they might be as operatives, had personally been out of the street-level game for a long time. They had become corporate executives rather than political guns.

And, indeed, they handled their first challenge like flacks instead of hacks. Bloomberg had been trailed by controversy from his mayoral term involving his stop-and-frisk policies. Empowered to detain young men in troubled neighborhoods and search them for guns, the police disproportionately targeted minorities. Crime might have continued to decline at impressive rates (largely, the Bloomberg people often argued, to the benefit of minority neighborhoods), but this became a left-wing flash point. There was, plausibly, a law-and-order advantage here for Bloomberg (what campaign has ever suffered from embracing law and order?), and given his record he might as well have owned it. But in a corporate-like effort to run from controversy, Sheekey and Wolfson decided to try to bury the story with an apology—that is, to have the unapologetic Bloomberg apologize. A new corporate position is one thing—the company stands above any one person—but, in this instance, here was one man, who, with evident exasperation, apparently continued to believe in the rewards of stop-and-frisk. It worked. Crime went down. What else did anyone want? Cue Bloomberg's sour and uncomprehending face as he tried to now explain why he was wrong.

And, then, alas, there was Bloomberg's indelible wit and wisdom.

Here was a demonstration on two levels of Bloomberg's political disregard and hubris. It was not just that he was believed to have said unfortunate things. He had left himself wholly exposed to the one person who could pin these things on him.

The former Bloomberg executive and antagonist who had supplied the *Wit & Wisdom* booklet to me so many years ago had risen to further prominence in the financial information industry, while continuing to nurture her love-hate feelings toward her old boss. At the same time, because Bloomberg and Sheekey knew she was the source of the leak of *Wit & Wisdom*, they nurtured their antipathy toward her. Bloomberg holds a grudge, even an unnecessary one, and prosecutes it. When the antagonist reached out to the then mayor's office to see if a city hall tour might be arranged for her daughter's high school class, she was rebuffed. When, in a family health emergency, she reached out again, hoping for Bloomberg's help over a bureaucratic hurdle, she was once more spurned.

And here, now, in 2020, she still had, as payback, if she wanted to use it, *Wit & Wisdom*.

There were two copies known to exist: mine and hers. Mine in a storage locker and hers on the hard drive of an Apple IIe computer in her summer home.

As the Bloomberg campaign advanced, I got more and more calls from other reporters and colleagues hoping to get their hands on my copy of the booklet. Along with not wanting to dig through my storage locker, my heart wasn't in the game. If there were only two known copies in existence—it certainly hadn't been widely distributed—it appeared likely to have been no more than a novelty party favor. It seemed to me, too, that, after thirty years, the context of what had surely been an inside joke was unrecoverable now. Bloomberg was undoubtedly a man of the Wall Street 1980s, but were these bons mots a hopeless expression of that or a mark of self-awareness? Of course, it didn't matter, because any expression that might seem to be a deviation of new liberal norms was a gun pointed back at you. I now questioned my jolly use of this material from nearly twenty years ago and called Sheekey.

"They are coming for you on this stuff," I said, "but won't get it from me."

Which left one other source.

Bloomberg's antagonist called me. I said, "Don't do it. What's the point? Really, is it fair? You know what will happen."

But love-hate, without adroit political handling, is strong. In short order, a *Washington Post* reporter was driving with the antagonist to her summer home.

The *Post* published the thirty-year-old artifact in its entirety. Hence,

Bloomberg, in the middle of the Democratic primary race, with its premium on the soft skills of inclusion, identity, and the nuanced particulars of modern political language, now had a supposed record of utterances marking him as fatally retrograde: anti-woman, racially insensitive, contemptuous of minorities, and tolerant of sexual violence. There it was, written down.

To the degree that the view of the left wing of the Democratic Party had coalesced into a single issue, it was against old, rich, white men, of which Bloomberg, next only to Trump, appeared to be the oldest, richest, and whitest.

Still, it remained a viable proposition that $1 billion might well buy you out of this perception problem. Because, in truth, there was no Bloomberg to really take the measure of. Yes, in person, he did seem seriously out of touch, but the in-person Bloomberg was rescued by the cavalry of an advertising campaign revising, reimagining, and reconstructing him. Simply, Michael Bloomberg was a plausible, enlightened (comparatively), and unstoppable alternative to Donald Trump. A good guy (relatively speaking)—and rich. That idea became a powerful one.

There are two basic approaches to modern American campaigning: paid media and earned media. That is, the power of advertising, with a campaign's full control of the message versus the attention the media might provide you, with its ungovernable and unpredictable coverage. Advertising is of course expensive and news coverage free—hence, dark-horse campaigns can rise on the basis of free media notice. But the problem with advertising is not just its cost; it's that most front-runner campaigns are marked by their ability to raise the maximum amounts, therefore canceling out the advertising strategy of others in the front-runner rank. News coverage, in competitive races, is therefore as important to those at the head of the pack as to the dark horses. That's why there are now so many debates; they are beauty contests for free media coverage.

The Bloomberg paradigm was different. It was that he could afford so much paid media, at such a profound and unprecedented magnitude, that he could not only bury anyone else's paid efforts, but use it to effectively compete with any other candidate's earned media coverage. Indeed, this was the singular strategy of his campaign: paid media at a never-before-experienced disruptive level.

But politics is a series of bets. And while one audacious bet might win

(Trump, likely inadvertently, made a singular bet in 2016—he would forgo traditional organizing, fundraising, and ground game in favor of his pre-ternatural ability to generate nonstop cable coverage), most politicians try to hedge their bets.

Bloomberg's initial numbers did not qualify him for the early debates in the campaign, and so he sat them out. But his numbers rose fast enough and significantly enough, together with lots of lobbying from his side with the Democratic National Committee, to qualify him for the debate in Las Vegas on February 19. One logical view (and, in hindsight, the obviously correct view) was that if his numbers had improved so dramatically without appearing in any of the debates, why debate? Don't change the strategy now. But it is hard to forgo that sense of official arrival. Major contenders get on the debate stage, don't they? Being part of a presidential debate is nearly the same as running for president—you can't be president if you don't do it. Can you? Bloomberg's candidacy, no matter its paid media success, wasn't real—likely in Sheekey's and Wolfson's minds, perhaps in his own mind—until he was on a debate stage.

So what if he wasn't a natural? Merely being on the debate stage would compensate for the fact that he can't debate, didn't want to debate, wouldn't prepare to debate, and couldn't imagine what a debate would prove about him more than his $55 billion proved.

Of course, it was a hopelessly unfair fight. Everyone else on the stage—Bernie Sanders, Elizabeth Warren, Amy Klobuchar, Pete Buttigieg, even that most hapless of debaters Joe Biden—had been doing this for years. Bloomberg was just led to slaughter.

Out of the gate, he died on the stop-and-frisk question, could not seem to understand why he was being asked it, could not summon what lines must have been rehearsed to answer it. He was more naked under its glare than if he had just snarled and said, "So what of it? The city is safer because of it," as he truly seemed to feel.

And then he was utterly obliterated on the issue of his "wit and wisdom." Warren, in her effort to make news and earn more media, delivered a succinct, practiced, unsparing, and malevolent broadside, painting him in her prepared bite as the temperamental and philosophic enemy of every new and good impulse in the Democratic Party. Under the barrage, he came apart before the eyes of the nation, as if his flesh peeled back to reveal his true nature, his body dissolving in its own toxicity ("I'm melting! I'm melting!").

It was simply as bad as it could be.

The billionaire campaign, which might have succeeded if Bloomberg himself had not shown up for it, was over.

Super Tuesday, on March 3, completed the story of the most expensive crash and burn in the history of politics. But *New York*'s cover—a grumpy-looking Michael Bloomberg, dwarfed by his own suit and custom-made shoes—had two weeks more to linger on newsstands, a living reminder not just of Bloomberg's failure, as foregone a conclusion as that now seemed, but of the fragility and delusions and deep ambivalences at the heart of many liberal hopes and dreams.

Hillary

Hillary Clinton is, as polls regularly remind us, one of the most disliked and distrusted people in the United States, her name curdling good humor and milk everywhere. The U.S. electorate, quite pointedly, did not elect her in 2008 when the election seemed hers for the taking. If she is electable, she is, too, rejectable.

It is one of the things that makes people recoil from her: she can't take the hint. It's stomach-turning to witness someone who is so constantly vilified. Certainly Clinton is not one of those people who carries enmity with a jaunty joie de guerre (one of the decidedly Trump virtues, thriving on ill-will).

To look at her is to have a pretty good idea of her pain. Enduring a public life of humiliation and hatred has rather become her calling card and leitmotif: I can take anything you can dish out. Or, really, I can survive anything you can dish out—as one might survive the cruelest torture, marked forever. It is, in the end, part of what we who admire her admire her for, however begrudgingly.

She has been crucified and risen from the dead many times. For all the Republicans who curse her for not being brought down by what surely would have brought more ordinary politicians down—and who assume that she could only have survived on the strength of dastardly conspiracies and Faustian deals—there will be more Democrats who understand that by the mere fact of not being brought down, she deserves to win, or if not deserves, at least defaults to the win. You have to give it to her. She's just unkillable.

Her band of retainers and loyalists, like her, reflect a survivor's view, roughly translating as, "We have been sorely tried and tested and, with the greatest fortitude, have proven that we are different from other mere political mortals, so fuck you."

There is another thing that so infuriates Clinton opponents as well as the political culture in general: the Clintons function as a world apart. You are a member of the Clinton club, for which you have to prove yourself and, in some sense, be born into, or you are not.

The Clintons are a closed political organization. It is a kind of secret society. It's a strict, if often dysfunctional, extended family: our experience as Clinton loyalists, the most existential and embattled folk in American political life, is unlike any other, so don't ever try to pull rank on us or to assume you can ever truly be one of us. One of the frustrations of the Republicans is that they have been mostly unsuccessful in equating the word *Clinton* with *Mafia*, which, to them, seems so head-smackingly obvious.

The historical point can hardly be missed (although it often is) that the age of killer politics, of take-no-prisoner politics, of politics being war instead of professional calling, begins with the us-against-them fatalism of the Clintons. The fact that Hillary's election might be a restitution of the Clinton White House, wholly subsuming impeachment, shame, excess, and, to boot, vindicating Hillary Clinton's own personal mortification and victimization, adds further psycho-political drama to the long-running revenge opera. More prosaically, it is always payback time with the Clintons.

The Hillary inner circle, notable not just for its loyalty to her, but hers to its members, certainly comprises a frightening list of resentments, grudges, bitter memories, sycophantic loyalty, personal survival stories—that is, Clinton business as usual.

There is Huma Abedin, whose professional-personal relationship with Clinton is so complex—crossing over State Department, campaign, and Clinton Foundation lines—that no org chart could accurately describe the nature of the relationship or Abedin's actual job function at any point in their long history. Perhaps most notably, Hillary and Huma are united in the weird shaming ritual of modern politics. Abedin is the wife of Anthony Weiner, the former congressman run out of office for sending penis pictures across social media.

Then Cheryl Mills, whose promising career as a young lawyer began with the Clintons, and might reasonably, over the almost twenty years since she came to prominent notice, have turned her into a leading legal or business figure. Instead she has remained a Clinton functionary. Her forays into the wider professional world, in media and education, seem only to have served to draw her back to the Clinton flame. The Clintons are her one and only real client.

And Sidney Blumenthal, the political journalist who found his way into the first Clinton administration, and became central to it through his access to Hillary, in particular. For more than twenty-five years, he's been hatchet man, whisperer, and courtier, often making almost Zelig-like appearances in the various Clinton legal messes. Christopher Hitchens accused him of perjuring himself over press leaks about Monica Lewinsky, getting him hauled before Congress. Last year, hauled before Congress again, his e-mails and testimony became a prime evidentiary point in both the 2012 Benghazi attacks on U.S. diplomats in Libya and the Clinton e-mail scandals. Notably, when Hillary Clinton became secretary of state, the Obama administration specifically forbade her to bring Blumenthal with her. Hence, he went on the Clinton Foundation payroll, from where he continued to advise her.

Her campaign is the closed society of Clinton professionals: Mandy Grunwald, John Podesta, Jennifer Palmieri, Neera Tanden, and several dozen more have not so much made their careers in politics, as made their careers as Clinton people. (On the other hand, having spent time either in the White House or in the long-term shadow administration, they are professionals, quite a unique condition among the many White House staffs of recent years.)

As much as Clinton offers neither inspiration nor excitement, there is, for many, something of a secret hope that maybe, immersed in a life of political intrigue and deadly power games, she has actually learned something. We've made an investment in Clinton, so we might as well reap the rewards. Clintonism represents a body of experience, however low and grubby, that reflects the cold reality of American politics. There cannot be, for the Clintons, many illusions left.

Indeed, as the larger political parties have increasingly broken into distinctive subsets, the Clintons have come to represent a separate party

within the Democratic Party. The virtue, to some, is that the Clinton sub-
set, quite different from most others, is not ideologically driven. That's
another point of critical frustration for a good part of the political world:
as ideology has become the modern political driver, it is the Clintons,
believing practically speaking in nothing but themselves, who prevail. Or
at least keep going—and going. That view of politics as a tawdry, cynical
affair, designed entirely to perpetuate itself, which has in part resulted in
the counteroffensive of ideological purity, is perhaps most specifically a
view of the Clintons.

That's what the Clintons are hated for, and yet, the possibility that what
you see is what you get is in many ways a good alternative to Obama's what
you got was not necessarily what you hoped for.

Curiously, many Democrats have acceded to Clintonism not because
of their cold practicality and political professionalism, but because the
Clintons are the sworn enemy of the Right. The Clintons, in other words,
while hardly being left, have been defined as the opposite of being right—
the enemy of my enemy being my friend.

That's largely been true up until now—but this is where we enter the
territory of the unknowable. The most characteristic aspects of the Clintons, a political couple who might otherwise largely see themselves as
practical-minded centrist consensus builders, is, of course, how much
personal hatred they inspire. While that has seemed to be most virulently
a right-wing phenomenon, heretofore uniting the Democrats around
them, Clinton-hate has now emerged as a powerful emotion on the left.

It's almost a binary break—this sizable part of the Democratic Party, as
much in some polls as 30 percent, that cannot abide her. What is the Left
to do? Bend or bolt. So far during this election, the Left, first in its flirtation
with Massachusetts senator and anti–Wall Streeter Elizabeth Warren, and
then with socialist candidate Bernie Sanders, has headed ever more left. It
almost seems that the more efforts Clinton makes to move left, the farther
the Left moves—just to get away from her. Hence, the Left becomes more
polarized in its anti-Clintonism, leaving Hillary, herself having moved
with some desperation significantly left, more vulnerable.

The unspeakable, and, up until now, practically unimaginable, is that
Donald Trump will be the Republican candidate. While the continuing
assumption is that the out-of-control Republican train will be brought to

a safe stop, the train-wreck scenario is more and more plausible. Trump as the candidate, with his uncanny powers of embodying whatever most represents anger and negativity, becomes the ultimate Clinton hater, the anti-Hillary embodiment.

If, on the other side, the Left continues to find its raison d'être in Clinton hatred, then, in an extraordinary demonstration of democracy's weakness, Hillary's intolerable inevitability could actually make Donald Trump president.

And therefore make Hillary pure again.

Weiner

The evidence mounts that virtually everyone is engaged in some socially unacceptable form of sexual expression. But at the same time, there are ever-fewer people who seem to have a good word for sex. In New York, this has been the summer of Anthony Weiner, the congressman from Brooklyn who was found tweeting tumescent pictures to interest women who weren't his wife (he would have been in only marginally better stead, and looked only slightly less foolish, if it had been his wife). His scandal was the result of two pieces of bad luck: meaning to send a private tweet, he sent a public one; his name is Weiner.

In some sense, these two pieces of terrible fortune made him not just the poster child for sexual ridicule but the stand-in for everyone else's fears about their unruly and shameful sexual lives. That is, rather than identify with the person with whom you have most in common, the fear of being seen to be like him means this is exactly the person who most needs to be ostracized.

What we know from untold numbers of more or less objective studies of online behavior, from domestic court cases around the wired world, from the evidence available from the simplest Google search, to the confessions of our friends and coworkers, is that anybody with any sort of sexual itch (i.e., almost everybody) has pushed its barriers online.

In fact, the most elemental motor of the digital revolution, I hardly think it's necessary to argue, has been pursuit of this itch. It began on remote bulletin boards in the eighties and early nineties (the first issue of *Wired* magazine contained the revelations of a woman with the then breathtaking handle of "nakedwoman"). It spread to the AOL chat rooms, an underbelly of extraordinarily segmented deviance, which supported AOL's family face. It expanded geometrically when AOL shifted to a flat fee in 1994. It jumped to the Web in visual form—the GIF and JPEG phase of the new sexual revolution. E-mail, with its ease, privacy, speed, and lack of formality, became the most natural means of flirtation in the history of courtship. Then, instant messaging, first a teen novelty, outdid even e-mail as a tool of seduction. SMS made IMs mobile and ubiquitous. Then high-speed access arrived and with it the video-porn explosion. Everybody became a casual porn consumer, if not connoisseur or addict. And Skype: that dreamed-of futuristic sexual connection became a reality. Then smartphones and sexting. And social networks and Twitter.

We are all connected to a vastly efficient system of titillation, sexual availability and experimentation, and erotic gratification. And an irresistible one.

It doesn't seem unreasonable to see the involvement in wild-side digital sex as on the level of involvement with illicit drugs. Who hasn't done it?

And it's as easy to be caught. The more you do it—and the more you do it the more you do it—the more likely it is that you are going to get caught. The very nature of the medium, that it saves, catalogs, and recalls, that it demands a certain technical dexterity, orderliness, and attention (remembering to close, to save, to wipe, to password-protect), seals everybody's fate.

Including Anthony Weiner's.

I can remember all the Weiners I have ever known—a surprising number—and my pity for them. Penis, Anthony Penis, would have been a better name, at least it would be clinical (and perhaps it could be pronounced *Penee*). But Weiner is the broadside comic form. It's the punch line. And it's always funny. One of the Weiners I have known is now formally called Wine. Another is Wilder. In other words, the teasing was so great, with the constant knowledge that even if you weren't being teased, anybody might at any second get one in, so anxiety-producing—the seeing of yourself as the butt of the joke, the penis in the room—so isolating, that the neediness and humiliation of actually changing your name was worth it.

My nineteen-year-old son, home from college, and preternaturally capable of avoiding almost all awareness of anything in the news, fell on the floor laughing when I told him this story. It was so perfect and satisfying that my son went out and bought a newspaper the next day on his own.

It's a heavy-handed point: the Weiners of this world represent the shame and mortification we all feel about everybody else knowing we are peculiar sexual beings.

And now we all know so much more about what everybody else is up to.

We are all pervs, hence eager to pin it on someone else.

You don't get a better foil than Anthony Weiner. Millions, hell, hundreds of millions of people, are sending dirty pictures every day, but nobody was rising to Anthony Weiner's defense and saying I do it, too.

Instead, what they're saying is . . . Weiner, Weiner, Weiner.

* * *

There have been two sexual revolutions in my lifetime. That first social and media embrace of libidinous expression that began in the fifties had an ever-growing population of supporters. The message of sex was largely positive, repression-free, libertine-ish lives (the playboy), the impulses that led to multiple partners (the explorer), the explicit chroniclers of the subject (the artists), even the new and heretofore outré sexual behaviors (blow jobs among them), were all at the heroic vanguard of the culture.

This next sexual revolution, the internet sexual revolution, has been received in a vastly more equivocal fashion.

There is a continuing reactionary basis to the opprobrium. The first sexual revolution contributed to the disruption of marriages and families—with ensuing blowback. Many women, who in the first revolution began to exert their own sexual rights, also found that their sexual freedom was not necessarily aligned with the interests of men's sexual freedom—and a power struggle commenced.

A political movement grew up representing and coalescing the conservative sensibility that had been eclipsed by the first sexual revolution—sexual censoriousness became good politics. There were STDs, including AIDS. Even the liberal media—one of the primary agents of the first sexual revolution—with its current aging readers and viewers, has been much more circumspect in its outlook during this second time around.

And yet who doubts that many more people, a quantum increase, are having ever more profligate and baroque sex? The political-media-values superstructure takes one view while everybody else does the opposite.

Indeed, there has been a kind of democratization of sex that may be part of the problem. The first sexual revolution was really sex from afar. It was idealized sex. It was reflected in magazines, movies, and music. Someone else, more beautiful than you, was actually having it. People more articulate than you described it. Sex was glamorous. Sex was a club most of us had not yet been admitted to.

The internet really changed that. Suddenly everybody had access. Suddenly everybody had access to what everybody else was doing. The disintermediation of writers, editors, photographers, directors, replaced now with ordinary sexual civilians creating the narrative and the visual package, has been perhaps the most profound part of this second sexual revolution and its user-generated sweet-nothings and porn.

Sex, one of the most idealized, fantasized, scripted, posed, airbrushed forms of expression, had become shockingly real.

And that—real people documenting their courtship and coupling— makes for a confounding and rather appalling condition.

We are beyond the messiness of desire, and even the anarchy of desire, and face-to-face with the cheesiness of it. It is not that we are all perverts. It is that we are all silly, dopey, ridiculous, puerile, moronic pervs.

Sex is mortifying.

Sex turns out to be named Anthony Weiner.

Sex, for anyone but the people having it, is now a big joke.

Being caught in the act is not being found in flagrante delicto but in hapless stupidity.

Here's Anthony Weiner in a now widely published exchange with a political volunteer, Lisa Weiss, in Nevada.

"Ridiculous bulge in my shorts now. Wanna see?"

"Yeah! Can u send a pic? I want to sit on your cock so bad right now."

"Jeez, im rushing. Let me take a quick pic."

"Awesome . . . how do I get it? Right on here? . . . how r u gonna to work with a raging hard on?"

"It won't go away. and now im taking pics of it, making me harder still."

"So hot! u are making me wet again."

"Jeez, i have to go. ill hit you later . . . off to the shower. this thing is bobbing up and down."

"Aahhh . . . wish I was in the shower with you to help."

"You give good head?"

"Ive been told really good . . . and love doing it."

"Wow a jewish girl who sucks cock. this thing is ready to do damage."

We know from vast and mounting documentary evidence that this is the language not just of cheeseball politicians but of sports figures, starlets, moguls, high school kids, and, as well, everybody else.

This is how we talk when we talk sex.

So it may not be sex itself that so many people are getting hoisted for, but the pathetic expression of it. Actually, with poor Anthony Weiner, it's not even sex—he doesn't meet any of the women he's messaging—it's just desire.

That's a hell of a disconnect. We feel but we can't express.

Or, worse, the way we express some of our most vivid and urgent needs is, in everyone else's eyes, a public joke—even though everyone else's expression is as ridiculous.

Could that mean that there is a next phase of this second sexual revolution that is bound to occur? An inevitable embrace of our fundamental cheesiness?

In the first sexual revolution there was Woody Allen making original and empathetic, if not heroic, comedy out of sexual foibles and absurdities, and Philip Roth turning Alexander Portnoy (like Anthony Weiner, a New York politico) into the greatest tragicomic sexual figure of all time.

True, it is unlikely that novels or movies, superseded by precisely the new forms of expression currently causing all the problems, are now going to rise to this new sexual challenge (books and movies seem strangely to have lost their sexual mojo). That means the new form itself, speaking to a new generation, has to reunite feelings and expression, and create the condition in which we are not laughing at the Weiners in the room—all the millions of secret Weiners—but laughing together in shared sexual sympathy and good cheer.

Cuomo

1

The real thing is a mythological species searched for by political reporters and campaign operatives. It's a kind of great horse, or beautiful athlete, or incredible crush. There are, of course, not too many sightings of the real thing anymore. In this day and age, the real thing doesn't become a politician. And if one did, would we be able to recognize him or her anyway, or is that just so over with?

Still, if only for anthropological reasons, the search goes on. I'm in a parked car on the corner of Water and Whitehall. I'm with Peter Ragone, the same political op I was with at this time a year ago when he was working for Al Gore. In significantly reduced circumstances (stripped of his earpiece and in a rented Taurus instead of a caravan of Suburbans), he is back, at the dawn of the Andrew Cuomo campaign for governor. Peter, who worked for Cuomo at HUD for nine months before taking off to join the Hillary senatorial campaign and then the Gore presidential campaign, is, naturally, trying to convince me that Cuomo is the real thing. No doubt, trying to convince himself, too.

I'm open. It's spring in New York. And there's something about this point in a campaign—no real organization, not too many handlers, few speeches (at least you haven't heard the speech a million times)—that puts reporters and candidates in a flirtatious mood.

I was formally introduced to Cuomo a few weeks before. Early in a campaign, or before one even starts, candidates visit media offices for off-the-record meetings. There's a catered lunch at a conference table, and then the candidate gives a pitch and takes questions. It's hard to say what you're grading a candidate on in such a situation—part policy (always a small part), part look and feel, and part patter. At any rate, my mind didn't wander too much during Cuomo's pitch over the salmon and wheat-berry salad. He told a good story. He was funny. He seemed eager to prove himself in a not-too-ham-handed way. In fact, he had the part down so well—an intelligent, good-looking, wry, hardworking, liberal sort of guy—that you necessarily became suspicious. Where's the body?

Even the Mario thing is subtle and effective, I was surprised to see. Andrew has the rubbery face and the cadence, but not the imperiousness, of his father. And despite my better democratic and meritocratic judgment, I can start to see why the generation thing works in politics—the brand recognition and, too, a sense of getting an upgrade.

On the other hand, I can't imagine why, if he's smart and funny and ambitious, he's a politician.

* * *

So I got into the car. The car is the natural element for a politician. Politicians are not creatures of offices or restaurants so much as of vehicles. It's an intimate act for a reporter to strap in beside a politician ("I'll get you in the car" are the words you wait to hear from a candidate's people).

Cuomo, who seems to have a more or less permanent look of coming from the gym, meets us curbside at the concrete esplanade in front of Fried, Frank, Harris, Shriver & Jacobson, the Wall Street law firm that is accommodating him while he gets his campaign off the ground (that is, while he works the phones—a New York race costs at least $20 million).

Ragone jumps into the back seat, and Cuomo, shedding top coat and stowing his bag, takes the wheel (only he knows the way). Then we head to Brooklyn.

He's been a public figure in New York since he was seventeen: constantly at his father's side during the first quixotic campaign against Koch for mayor, then, at twenty-three, running Mario's winning gubernatorial campaign, then getting his housing-project business off the ground, then marrying a Kennedy, then getting close with Clinton (a memorable scene in *Primary Colors* is when the impressive son of New York's Governor Ozio comes to meet with the unimpressive southern governor), then a cabinet post. This familiarity makes him seem a little like someone you

knew in high school. Except now, pumped on success steroids, he's better dressed, more comfortable with himself, and more interesting than you remember.

We start in immediately on the housing problems of the former secretary of Housing and Urban Development. His wife and three kids are still in their home in Washington; he's staying at a friend's apartment in Manhattan. (On a friend's couch? In a celebrity friend's pied-à-terre? He doesn't say.) They'll settle in New York when the kids finish school in June. His wife, Kerry, wants a house in Westchester, but he doesn't want the commute (nor does he seem like a suburban guy—he's not going to make that Clinton mistake). Which means, he says, he needs three and a half bedrooms in Manhattan.

"A classic seven," I tell him.

And that means, his wife says, private schools, which he seems rather unfamiliar with and vaguely irritated at or possibly intimidated by.

In fact, I can tell him what private schools Kennedy kids go to.

It occurs to me it might have been more interesting to hang with him looking for an apartment on the Upper East Side, rather than going where we're going—down Atlantic Avenue, passing the Bed-Stuy Restoration Corporation started by Robert Kennedy, the father-in-law he never knew, by the refrigerator-equipment plant on the corner of Utica and Atlantic once owned by Cuomo's mother's father, and then deeper into Brooklyn to East New York.

* * *

I'm curious about Cuomo and the class thing—the divide between Manhattan and the boroughs, between the Cuomos and the Kennedys. Mario always made class an interesting and confusing subtext of the Cuomo message. He was at once a Queens pol and yet the most patrician figure in American politics. In some sense, way too patrician for American politics. But obviously not enough—in any discussion about Mario and the presidency, somebody always brings up the Mafia thing ("Well, you know why he didn't run . . .").

For his part, Andrew segues artfully between Italian-from-Queens-ness and purebred-yuppie-ness. It's unclear which Cuomo is realer.

"Why did you go to the schools you went to?"—Fordham and then Albany Law School—I ask him, because it seems enough out of place on his résumé—and because we're pretty much the same age, and our backgrounds aren't that different, and why pretend it isn't a curious thing.

He defends the schools but understands what I'm asking: Why would the son of Mario Cuomo go to local, commuter schools? Why would an ambitious guy not have been more ambitious (Bill Clinton from Arkansas made it to Yale)?

He pulls on his rubber face. He doesn't seem defensive (certainly not in the sense of Lyndon Johnson among the Kennedy Ivy Leaguers). "I went to a boys' parochial school in Queens. I don't think anybody went to an Ivy League school from my high school," he says, and shrugs. "We went to St. John's. Mario went to St. John's. Fordham was a step up. Then there's affording an Ivy League school. I don't know how we would have done that."

"Like everyone else," I say, "you'd get loans."

"You know, Mario was a rebel. Even if he could have gone to those schools—he was turning his back on these people. The Wall Street–lawyer crowd. He was a Brooklyn lawyer."

So when did the striving begin?

The whole family has traded up. He's married a Kennedy, his sister has married Kenneth Cole, the shoe brand designer, and another sister married the millionaire video producer of *Buns of Steel*; his brother is a television personality who hangs with Hamptons socialites. Even Mario and Matilda live on Sutton Place now.

"Your kids won't go to Fordham and Albany Law School."

"I know that," he says, with some fatefulness. He talks about their earning their own money, and his not buying them cars, and getting them to work real jobs over the summer.

"Right," I say, laughing.

But I know what he's saying. It's a lot harder nowadays to preserve than to escape your roots. In a sense, Andrew is the last of a kind (he may well have the last Queens accent—in the future it will have a much different, polyglot sound). Despite top-flight yuppie accomplishments, he's also uniquely old-fashioned: apprenticed to the father; made, effectively, a political runner; then graduating to ward heeler and promoted to consigliere at an early age. I don't know how you save that.

On the other hand, the last thing Andrew Cuomo wants to be is a Queens pol—even a princely one.

* * *

We reach the site. Politicians need a backdrop. Hands to shake, backs to clasp. A photo op even without photographs.

We've come out to the first help project. This is the thing that Cuomo did as a twenty-seven-year-old: *he built housing for the homeless.*

That, however, is an abstract or bureaucratic concept—which is, no doubt, why he's hustled me out here to see what he's built. As he tells it, he visited the notorious Hotel Martinique, where, given the rules of federal-assistance laws, the city was housing homeless people in squalor and degradation for a near-luxury price tag during the seventies and eighties. Andrew, who had left working for his dad and spent two years with the Manhattan DA, and who was then restlessly practicing law, figured you could take that federal money and, within federal rules, do a lot better. In addition, he had a Clintonesque third-way point of view, which is that the homeless are homeless for reasons other than the fact that they have no homes—you had to rehab the whole family unit.

Because he's the governor's son, and because he is, supposedly, a son of a bitch (he was, and perhaps still is, relatively unpopular in New York political circles, unlike, say, Hugh Carey's kids in the seventies, who ran restaurants and were very popular), he gets his building built.

One big test of public housing must be how it looks a generation or so after it's been in use. This place opened, with Cuomo as landlord and night manager, in 1988. Thirteen years later, it's a liberal proof of something (unless somebody went running ahead to round up the crackheads and clean the graffiti and fix the windows). It's a clean, sunny, orderly place. GED classes are in progress as we wander the halls, peeking into windows, with Andrew shaking the occasional hand; so is computer training, day care, exercise for pregnant women. The premise is: families move in here from shelters; with social support, the families get themselves together; then they move into a permanent place.

Across the street is the permanent housing that Cuomo built. It's a four-story rectangular building overlooking a large, landscaped interior courtyard. Cuomo, who I imagined can talk about public housing as knowledgeably as anyone in America, has many points to make (if you like this sort of stuff, and I do, it's a good talk—why there's always an el train in such neighborhoods; why cities always dump facilities in poor neighborhoods, which then contributes to keeping the neighborhood poor). One of his most obvious points is about architecture. Because this is a well-designed building, it sends none of the messages that public housing usually sends (i.e., to the people who live here: *You're prisoners*; to the taxpayers who pay for them to live here: *They're criminals*).

Andrew has created St. Mark's Square in East New York. A staircase at the corner forms the campanile; the common rooms and community space (they've held weddings here) form the basilica-like structure; the apartments, looking into the courtyard, the *procuratie*.

This is his pitch. Liberal solutions can work (forgetting the fact that, here in East New York, we're also surrounded by former generations of public housing, like sedimentary layers, that didn't work). Government, or, in middle-of-the-road speak, a public-private partnership, can make something functional, economical, uplifting, and dignified; indeed, there are thirty-five hundred people in help housing—in Brooklyn, the Bronx, Manhattan, Westchester, Philadelphia. The other part of his pitch, which I find hard to resist, is that he's the only modern-American politician who's actually put a roof over someone's head.

It's very movielike. The young, idealistic politician against this background of accomplishment and hope. It's almost eerie in its foreboding—where's the body?

* * *

He courted his wife out here. On their first date, he took her, on his Harley, to see her father's Bed-Stuy project, and then he took her to see his own deal.

He shoehorns his wife into almost every conversation in a way that suggests that either he thinks the Kennedy thing is the biggest political asset he's got going for him or she's been after him to get some credit for herself (*It's not all about you!*).

Or it may be that, like many liberal Democrats of a certain era, he has a Kennedy fixation—he's just taken his a little further than most.

Peter Ragone tells me that Andrew was giving a talk the other day to which he'd brought his family, and, in the middle of his speech, his young daughter walked out onto the floor. "Upstaged by a Kennedy," Andrew said proudly. (I ask him if he thinks of his children as Kennedys. He says, with some amazement, that they have Kennedy mannerisms and gestures.)

I think it's part of the class thing.

You can make the case that there's a lost generation of pols. If you were a hotshot in the eighties and nineties, you didn't go into politics—you became a finance guy, or technology guy, or media mogul. But Andrew, because he had to help his father, or because he was an underachiever, or because it was the way out of Queens, did go into politics, and he really doesn't want to be thought the less of for it. In addition, even putting aside the doing-good part, housing the poor seems, as he talks about it, at least as interesting as being a finance guy or technology entrepreneur.

Still, I don't think he has any illusions about politics or people in politics. He knows it's largely low-grade work. A politico is not high up on the doing-big-things ladder. When he talks about George Pataki, you feel that's what he objects to most—Pataki is small-time (he seems embarrassed that this is his opponent, that they would be in any way comparable); Carl McCall, too. These are just political-class guys.

Whereas he's pitching himself on a higher level. So even though he is a vastly more accomplished politician with a brighter future than anyone currently named Kennedy, I think he thinks the Kennedy thing helps dignify his endeavors (there are rumors, though, of dissatisfaction among the Kennedy men about a non-Kennedy using the brand). He's in the Kennedy political class and everyone else is in another political class.

* * *

You get a powerful sense that it is Andrew who is searching as hard as anyone for the real thing. He has forged a filial bond not only with the Kennedys but with Bill Clinton—he's one of the few Clintonites to have lasted the entire term.

Then, too, he's among the most loyal and dedicated Gore-ites (if Gore had won the presidential race, in all likelihood Cuomo would not be running now but would have ascended to some higher, executive-branch place).

And while I don't see any trace at all of reluctance about running—after all, he's been doing this for more than twenty years; in some sense, there has never been anyone, at least since Bobby Kennedy, as well prepared to run for public office as Andrew Cuomo—I wonder if knowing what he knows must not engender a certain painful self-consciousness. What is your chance of not disappointing yourself and everyone else?

Indeed, the one liberal giant with whom oddly, or not so oddly, he doesn't seem to identify is Mario. Mario's ambivalence is something to steer clear of.

We're sitting back on Water Street, the car idling. I'm starving, but politicians never go out to eat (they scarf something down and go on to the next event). Peter Ragone is scrunched up in the back seat, paying rapt attention to Cuomo. I wonder if he's worried about Cuomo's motormouth—Cuomo is, for a politician, unusually aware of the process of being a politician, and oddly willing to talk about it. (Most politicians are absent people— there but not there. Whatever they say, they've said innumerable times. You never have a real conversation.)

He's demonstrating for me the Clinton touch: holding my shoulder, taking my hand, stroking my knee. It's perfect mimicry. He seems to understand both the humor of it and the power of it.

"He knew every nuance of what he was doing," he says, with some awe, about Clinton. "The effect of touching you there, or touching you here."

The real thing, Andrew seems to be saying, is, of course, always partly a phony.

He goes on to a brief deconstruction of Mario—that he could accept an intellectual relationship with the voters but was not at all interested in an emotional one. So, equally, the real thing may fail because it's not phony enough.

He keeps chewing. What does it take to be the kind of person who voters or the media want you to be, or think they want you to be—and do you want to be that person (Gore, he believes, in the end did not)? And what does it take to be a politician who is not tainted by being a politician?

The question he seems to be trying to answer, at the beginning of his first campaign for office, is: How far is it possible to distance yourself from the pack of hacks, seducers, wonks, special-interest-group guys, and fathers' sons?

"What do you think?" asks Ragone, after Cuomo has gone back to his office, and we go looking for a sandwich.

Not to jinx it, and because you always end up paying for a political crush, I say, "He looks good, but there's a long way to go."

Cuomo

2

I first met Andrew Cuomo a little more than two years ago when I started to write about his incipient gubernatorial campaign. He'd drive his rental car to meetings with New York State Democrats, expounding on most anything that came into his head while I sat in the front seat taking notes on what he said. He seemed to me then—as he still does now—a smart, funny, engaged liberal politician.

The intensity was the thing. He drew you in. It was all personal appeal. One-on-one (often hours of it). Unlike most professional politicians, he was a great, expressive, unguarded talker. And of course, in the age of Bush, he had the legacy thing going, too—Cuomo and Kennedy. More intensity.

As it happened, all of these promising political traits had something to do with why his campaign ended so ignominiously late last summer. His great drive came to seem like a personality problem. His unguardedness resulted in extraordinary gaffes (notably his after-9/11 Pataki-was-just-the-coat-holder gaffe). And the legacy began to look like rank opportunism—almost feral opportunism. He resigned from the race even before the primary election.

Now these same qualities—his overheatedness, the operatic political heritage he's been selling, and his need to talk to everybody constantly—provide the background for what is shaping up to be a super star-studded and extremely naked political domestic drama.

The need for self-dramatization here is evidently greater than even the desire for self-preservation and the calculation of how to run again another day. The window that's been opened into this marriage and this political life has been flung wide by people who appear to have lost all sense—certainly media sense.

The Cuomo-Kennedy marriage exploded just before the long, zero-news Fourth of July weekend, guaranteeing full-blown, uninterrupted attention to the details of this virtually real-time breakup.

You could turn up your nose at the tabloid smell of it all. Or enjoy the summer sport of watching well-known people behaving badly—the he-said/she-said, the in flagrante, the polo player, the appearance of the family eminences, the awkward housing arrangements. Or you could read it deeper, as American realism, Theodore Dreiser, or John P. Marquand—promising people caught in traps of their own making, struggling against conventions and expectations.

At any rate, Andrew Cuomo was once again the country's most unmanaged and unmanageable politician.

* * *

Andrew's ambition is of the manic type—he's obsessive, and a perfectionist. If he's not winning, he's losing. And blaming himself.

Since he dropped out of the gubernatorial race, he's been caught in a deep, distracted funk ("I'm not sure it's a clinical depression, but it's pretty bad," diagnosed a political consultant earlier this year when we sat down to rehash Andrew—a popular New York State political pastime), unable to get beyond his failed campaign, or to see his next move, wandering around the house in Bedford. (Andrew had wanted to live in the city when they moved back from Washington; Kerry had insisted on the suburbs.) It is against this backdrop that his wife takes up with the polo player.

The story of political failure in American life is a mostly unwritten one (shortly after Andrew withdrew from the gubernatorial race, when I knew he was looking for a book to write, I suggested, idiotically, that a book about being a loser would be interesting). Politicians surely don't want to talk about the misery of losing, nor are most self-aware enough to face having lost. Suck it up. You're just supposed to go back to your real life—or to making big money off your past political associations.

But not only does Andrew not have another real career and not much evident interest in making money, his personal life is his political organization. It's two organizations, actually—the Cuomo one and the Kennedy one—comprising just about the most competitive people who have ever lived. And you can bet both organizations judge you only as a winner or as a loser.

Surely Andrew and his father have one of the most complex and competitive father-son relationships in politics. (As a politician, Mario Cuomo was controlling and ambivalent, and so as a father . . . ?) It's long been a sideshow among political reporters in New York State: the Mario-and-Andrew act. They talk about each other—Andrew always calls his father Mario—with remarkable and weird dispassion, as though each were an analyst, most often a disappointed analyst, of the other. They're not the Bushes.

Andrew is twenty-four years old when he runs his father's upset campaign for governor and becomes one of the most powerful people in the state. But his next imperative is to achieve power independent of his father—to escape his father and to escape being his father's hatchet man. He quickly distances himself from Mario by launching his Robert Kennedy–style public-private-housing initiative.

Further executing on his grand plan, his first date with Kerry Kennedy is a tour of one of his low-income complexes not far from the housing project (less successful than Andrew's own) started by her father in Bedford-Stuyvesant twenty years before.

Now, marrying a Kennedy not only plunges him, he must feel, into the slipstream of destiny but gains him further independence from Mario.

As does his embrace of Bill Clinton.

In the early nineties, the two opposing poles of the Democratic Party— stylistically and philosophically—are Bill Clinton and Mario Cuomo. The presidency is not Clinton's only victory over Cuomo (who, in 1992, is the presumptive Democratic front-runner until, in a pique of ambivalence, he withdraws)—he takes his son, too.

Andrew goes to Washington as HUD assistant secretary and then, inevitably, secretary and becomes in personal affect and in political lineage more Clinton-esque than Cuomo-descended (and Cuomo-dependent).

By the time he returns to New York, he's carrying the Clinton and Kennedy connections much more proudly than the Cuomo mantle. The rap on Andrew is that he's running against George Pataki (who defeated

Mario in 1994) to avenge his father. But just as true, he's running against Pataki to beat his father.

Well, he doesn't beat Pataki—doesn't even make it to the primary. And doesn't beat his father. And doesn't do what he told his wife (who didn't want to move from Washington to New York anyway) and her brothers (who spent political capital on him) he would do. Political defeat must be as hard on political spouses as on politicians. Add such defeat to marriage to a Kennedy, whose issues with regard to winning and losing none of us can imagine. Also, the governor's race was not just a defeat—not a good loss. It was a colossal blunder—precariously close to political death. So Andrew is left without a job, without a career, without clear prospects, exiled in Westchester County (not far from his former colleague Bill Clinton).

At this point, at something near the nadir of his professional life, his marriage breaks up, and with a kind of unerring instinct for the politically unsayable that marked his campaign, in a pure moment of reflexive aggression (while he has tried to make the transition from operative to candidate, he still hasn't lost the cold heart of the political hatchet man), he sends his lawyer out to accuse his wife of "betrayal."

* * *

It is, in fact, the Kennedy marriage—more than even the entitlement of the Cuomo legacy—that in many ways most attached the stain of opportunism to Andrew (while all politicians are opportunists, some are credited with a special walk-over-your-mother status).

There isn't a voter in the land who wouldn't draw the obvious inference: on some level, it's got to be a marriage of crass utility. There was hardly any pretense. Putting these two dynasties together was supposed to be a two-plus-two-equals-five proposition. Everybody got the point.

But in this regard, Andrew has been amazingly tone-deaf. So tone-deaf that only love, perhaps, could explain it. Love of something.

Indeed, it sometimes seemed that Andrew Cuomo was the last believer in an unrevised Kennedy myth. Even the Kennedys themselves seemed more sheepish and circumspect about Kennedyism than Andrew. Only Andrew seemed to miss the point that the Kennedy dynasty had a fast-degrading half-life. The Kennedys had become the sideshow to the main political event (even the sideshow to the sideshow: as Andrew and Kerry's marriage fell apart, JFK Jr.'s dreadful marriage was back in the news).

Still, every Cuomo stump speech included a paean to the Kennedy family, a vivid evocation of his father-in-law (who'd been dead for a couple of decades before Andrew made his move), and a picking up of the torch. Of course, he always pushed Kerry out front to give an official Kennedy imprimatur, although Kerry, with the clenched, uncomfortable look of her mother's family, the Skakels, was mostly devoid of anything that said Kennedy.

It was all a little cringeworthy.

The Kennedys themselves helped attach the label of opportunism to Andrew. His brother-in-law Robert Kennedy Jr., a presumptive heir to power in New York State—and now, along with Mario, the family emi-nence called in to broker a marital cease-fire—often expressed irritation about Andrew's muscling in on the Kennedy turf (for his part, Andrew seemed in awe of Bobby Jr.—crediting him with a political stature greater than he realistically possessed). It was not just an issue of political terri-tory but also a primal issue of political identity. A brand issue. Indeed, to the extent that there were a lot of Kennedy girls floating around, if all of their husbands started to run—Arnold Schwarzenegger, married to Maria Shriver, was another major problem—what brand consistency would be left?

And, of course, Kennedy brothers-in-law had a very specific place in the traditional Kennedy hierarchy—lower down.

Stylistically, too, Andrew wasn't a Kennedy. He was some more natural cross between Lyndon Johnson and Bill Clinton. He was hot, not cool.

And there was the money thing, with the Kennedys complaining that Andrew's campaign was taxing the Kennedy-family donor lists.

In fact, though, the finer irony, and the one that might have been the more complex worm in the marriage, is that, actually, Kerry Kennedy rose on her husband's coattails. There are, after all, lots of children of Robert Kennedy—this doesn't necessarily give you a full-time career, or that dis-tinct an identity (or even that much money). But Andrew's status elevated Kerry, with whatever resentments and reverse resentments that entailed. He put her into the spotlight. He was the one who made her into a Ken-nedy symbol and allowed her to be promoted to the odd job description she seemed to favor, "human-rights activist," whatever that is (possibly a person with good intentions who doesn't have to work for a living and who likes to travel). She held the spotlight, too—often, oddly, dominating events.

At campaign appearances, you could see the workings of the modern political marriage. Something deeply impersonal. Parallel orbits. Even within their own suburban house, they often spoke through campaign staff and other interlocutors (as Bill and Hillary did in a much larger house). They arrived at events separately and left separately. (Shortly after I wrote what was the first long profile about Andrew during the campaign—a mostly flattering *New York* magazine cover story—he introduced me to Kerry, who appeared unaware of the article.) She was running for whatever she was running for, and he was running for what he was running for, without there necessarily being a mutuality of interests.

* * *

And then there's the sex thing. It hovered everywhere.

As soon as I started to write about Andrew's campaign, the question everybody asked was, *Is he a womanizer?* Or, *How much of a womanizer is he?* And, *What about so-and-so—are the rumors true?*

And, indeed, this now is the subtext of the present mess. If she is guilty, how innocent could he be? If he's accused her of infidelities, could that possibly mean he didn't live in a glass house himself? Or was this a preemptive strike? She was going after him, so, in Andrew Cuomo fashion, he leveled her first.

A friend of mine (a woman) writes me, speculatively and unprompted.
What I think happened was this:
Kerry has been having an affair with one person.
Andrew has had a series of dopey, Clinton-style flings with many people over the years.
Andrew does not consider these equal transgressions. In fact, at some point, Kerry probably told him to quit tomcatting, and he did, sort of, or at least became more discreet about it. But then Kerry had the nerve to fall in love with someone. Probably someone he knew fairly well. He was chumped. Humiliated. She destroyed the marriage, destroyed the family. And after he cleaned up his act, too. How dare she?

Let's admit it. This is not just gossip, not just tabloid stuff, but among the most significant political issues of the age. A politician's sexual background is as meaningful to a political career as the subtleties of his anti-communism would have been in the fifties.

There is no politician of whom this measure is not now taken by the opposition and the press (and even by admirers). How *flagrant* is he? Are there partners who will talk? And what's his opponent's zipper status?

This is what people talk about. This is what people really want to know. A consensus develops (we believe the consensus to be more truthful than the public statements). We are imagining lives here, imputing character. Sexuality is part of the postmodern political analysis. And indeed—Clinton, Giuliani, Gingrich, etc.—we tolerate wide extremes. It is no longer a moral issue—we are well beyond that—but an issue of who you are. How real are you, how arrogant, how shifty, how crass, how human?

It may be that the single greatest Bush political achievement is that he was able to cordon off his sexual life. He admitted to having one in the *past*—that was the stroke of genius.

Now, I have no idea of the reality of Andrew Cuomo's sex life. I do know that the wide assumption is that he has a sex life at least commensurate with his status as a good-looking, powerful, aggressive man.

"I would not find it intensely believable that a guy like that could go his whole life without some slippage," remarked a friend of mine when I argued that Andrew might have been faithful to his wife.

"His eyes drink you in like straws," said a young woman I know who has been around Andrew.

Certainly this sense of Andrew's being too hot to handle became a factor in the campaign. The Clintonian aura attached to him. The flirtatiousness was real. In any given room, he was a serious serial flirter. The intensity—physical, sexual—was ever present. Nobody looks at this uncritically anymore. Everybody has well-developed radar.

Including the wife—who we know now, courtesy of the *New York Post* and a photographer's long lens, has been spending lots of time in the gym.

It has the feel of irony and payback: she cheated on him.

And this now has revealed him, in a further irony, as not a cynical politician but a naked, cuckolded husband with real hurt and rage. The political world may be less postmodern than it sometimes seems.

* * *

And then the comedy.

It is not just that your wife is having an affair but whom she's having an affair with.

This really becomes the illusion-shattering thing. And your illusions not just about your wife but about yourself.

A long time ago, almost fifteen years, I had some dealings with Bruce Colley. It was one of those being-involved-with-people-you-shouldn't-be-involved-with things (Andrew may be feeling something similar now). But I was trying to raise money for a business venture, and that led from one more-or-less-questionable rich person to another.

Colley's father was among the largest McDonald's franchisees in the country (possibly the largest), meaning the Colleys were worth hundreds of millions. The father ran the business and the son didn't—it seemed that simple. But the son didn't appear to do anything else, either. He was pompous and ridiculous. Disengaged and superficial in a way that made you think it really is damaging to be rich. And not so bright. That was in fact his calling card—"He's not so bright," said my friend who was his friend—so, in other words, there was some chance he might invest in what I was doing.

You could hardly imagine two more opposite people than the fatuous and self-satisfied Bruce Colley and the intense and hungry Andrew Cuomo. At least on the face of it.

But if the human-rights activist was once interested in the liberal politician but now madly in love with the Republican polo-playing McDonald's franchisee (human-rights activism and polo playing are, in the end, both leisure-time activities), well, there it is.

* * *

The point remains: it really isn't all that hard to follow the standard playbook here. You issue a statement. You leave town for a little while. You appear amicably together in public once or twice. You quietly sort out your real-estate issues.

Political or economic self-interest, or just the desire not to be publicly and vastly humiliated, should win out. You put on a game face.

What's more, Cuomo is advised by his longtime chum Dan Klores, one of the city's consummate PR crisis managers. And certainly, the Kennedys know a thing or two about managing personal disasters.

Perhaps it's simple. You have two organizations—the Cuomos and the Kennedys—that, when their interests are not aligned, can be counted on to turn against each other, resulting here in tabloid tit-for-tat (because they are both so often the focus of tabloid interest, they are both wired into the tabloids).

And so commences the fanzine melodrama: the charges of betrayal . . . then the revelations of the polo player . . . then Andrew waving his finger at the polo player: "Stay away from my kids" . . . and the polo player threatening legal action . . . and Kerry pronouncing her love . . . and then how distraught she is that the polo player might not be in love back . . . and Andrew, in a moment of gallantry, announcing that he still loves his wife.

And, of course, Andrew just can't stop talking.

The rap that he went negative on her—went public with her affair before she could go public with anything about him—suggests he is more in control than he really ever has been.

Indeed, Klores was denying all over town that any of the affair stuff came from him or from Andrew. And technically, that may be true. But—imagine—Andrew is on the phone night and day. He's not consciously talking to the press, but he's talking to anybody who will listen to him. He isn't different from any other wounded husband—except that he can talk longer, can explain further, can analyze better. Indeed, he can't stand for anybody else to tell the story. He is his own narrator—that's his need.

How many people did he call? No doubt, a good portion of the biggest gossips in the state.

Likewise, to counter Andrew's gossip, the Kennedys have to deploy their own gossipers in the field.

And then, after the hardy band of tabloid reporters wring the gossip out of everyone who has talked to anybody who has had any contact, Andrew is on the phone with reporters (or at the end of his driveway going on and on), pleading with them not to call everyone he has called.

The rap on Andrew may be dead wrong—he's not a lover; he's a talker. As promiscuous and indiscreet a talker as there has ever been. It's his mouth he can't keep zipped. He wants you to know what he thinks and feels.

Now, this is obviously a political liability of some magnitude. Andrew's inability to shut up now holds him up to vast torment and ridicule—not to mention meaning, in any conventional sense, the end of his political life (betrayal, unlike with Hillary Clinton, has not lent him stature).

But let me return, before he is hopelessly cast aside, to the idea of Andrew as a political figure.

The interesting thing is that people are always trying to shut Andrew up, trying to manage what he says, trying to get him on the straight and narrow.

But what if you gave Andrew free rein? Let politics again become what it has not been for a long, long time—an expressive art.

After all, there's hardly anything left to hide. He's devastated, destroyed, finished, report people who have spoken to him, just like all left-behind husbands. But this is the subject, the real-life political subject, that people want to hear about. This isn't a phony issue.

Let him talk.

Gore

The call for the press pool is at five-thirty on a cold February morning in the Sheraton lobby.

"Let's snuggle!" says Nathan Naylor, Al Gore's tall, thirtysomething, defiantly blasé, perfect *West Wing*–type press aide. He wears a Secret Service earpiece, flesh-tone corkscrew wires going down his neck, and talks into his sleeve. "Roger, copy," he says.

"Spread your bags for the canine," commands a genuine Secret Service agent. The bomb-sniffing German shepherd noses through the luggage. This is what's called the sweep, and it occurs before every vice presidential departure.

It's been some time since I was last on the campaign trail—the worst, if most mythic, job in journalism. Chronic physical discomfort is combined with an almost total absence of real information.

I'm here because I've been promised virtually cheek-to-cheek access to Gore for the day. I've pitched Gore's staff that Gore is going to have to show himself in a way that he hasn't before and that I would be an ideal agent for this new Gore. Of course, his only real opposition, New Jersey senator and former NBA star Bill Bradley, is also quite a stiff—and Bradley is already fading. And George W. Bush, the strongest Republican, is hardly more expressive than Gore.

I offered, too, that I liked the guy (or wanted to). After all, it seemed fairly obvious that he was in the top-top percentile of intelligence for politicians (if he didn't invent the internet, as he is so often ridiculed for claiming, he at least propounded the metaphor—the information superhighway—that helped make it possible). And while we might not be able to count on his vision (and whose could we count on?), I thought we could trust his attention to detail, which is no small thing.

"You're in the pool van in the motorcade," says Nathan, voice lowered. "We'll keep you close to him."

"I'm getting time with him, though, right?" I try to clarify.

"Hey!" says Nathan with the greatest authority and good-guy-ness. "Nobody will get more than you."

The motorcade, a few vans, some black Suburbans, police cars, and two funeral-type Cadillacs strong, is moving by six (best case, Gore arrived at his hotel at one forty-five a.m. from a one a.m. rally at LaGuardia, maybe he slept till five a.m.) down predawn Park Avenue, all of the side streets blocked by police details, to a six-fifteen arrival at Grand Central Terminal. It is a pride of the campaign that Gore is one of the few candidates (possibly one of the few candidates ever) to mostly keep to his schedule. No doubt this is because a vice president is a sort of event-and-appearance machine. But perhaps it's also a reaction to the Clinton inability or unwillingness to stay on schedule. (I wonder how much this has bugged Gore?)

At Grand Central, the pool reporters are "diverted" to a "holding area" on one side of Michael Jordan's restaurant while the vice president is brought to the far side of the balcony for morning-show interviews. Bus reporters complain that Gore as vice president prefers to deal with upper-echelon national shows rather than with campaign reporters. He's a media snob.

"Peace Corps position, guys," says one of the photographers, crossing his legs on the floor.

"My news director calls," says one of the drive-time-radio reporters to no one in particular, "and wants to get a few minutes live with Gore. I said, 'Ha ha ha ha.'"

"McCain would give you a few minutes," puts in another of the reporters. John McCain is the surprise of the primary season—an animated candidate, willing to talk to anybody.

Chris Lehane, the Gore-campaign press secretary, a slicked-back-hair, wiseguy-looking fellow, is busy deflecting a series of requests and protests from the press pool. Lehane and Nathan Naylor and many of the other Gore staff have spent their entire careers in the Clinton-Gore administration; they are less campaign cowboys than employees taking the next step up the corporate ladder. They don't talk about Gore much. When they do, it's as an entity, the vice president, the VP, seldom Gore, never Al, no personal or anecdotal stuff. There aren't any real insiders. There isn't a Gore mafia.

I'm watching Gore across the station floor. He's silhouetted by the television lights, doing a chop-chop motion, one hand into the other. It's a tight-shoulder, Kennedy sort of posture. Patrician. Harvard. Cold War. He looks good from afar. He's doing one morning show after the other. Between interviews, a makeup person powders him and fusses with his hard-coiffed hair as he reads his press clips from the day before and sips bottled water.

The assumption I'm working on is that Gore can't be Gore. Nobody is wooden—people are just described as wooden by people with poor descriptive powers. The media can't see past seven years of familiarity—Gore as wallpaper, Gore as potted plant—and all its various Clinton resentments. We can't let Gore be something other than a guy with egg on his face, a semi-guilty party.

Gore is certainly no help to himself. He is a literalist (in the recent abortion flap, he was unable to articulate the surely sympathetic fact that he'd had a doubt or two). He has no evident irony—irony would be helpful when you've been Clinton's vice president. And he works too hard. He's a grind. The minutiae of government are what he excels at. In many ways, he is the opposite of an empty suit—he's stuffed so full of facts and work product, he can hardly move. Can I animate such a figure?

"He can balance anything on his nose," says one of the press-pool people. "In the '92 campaign, he'd come back into the bus balancing stuff. He was a pole-vaulter in high school and practiced balancing the pole."

"On his nose?"

"Hey, guys, pep talk," says Nathan. "He's going to do a walk-through. So let's not do the Cuban-grandmother thing. I know you want to get close, but getting close all depends on if we can move as a cohesive unit and not spaz out."

Almost everyone is saying, "Nathan . . ." in a beseeching, pleading, desperate-ingratiating sort of way.

Gore is positioned on the steps up to Michael Jordan's. He's perfectly creased. Precise. In his CEO or catalog-model pose. Frozen eyes. Turn-on-turn-off smile. Is it so bad that he's learned to shut people out?

Commuters are fed up the steps in gauntlet fashion to press his flesh. Political handlers say a good candidate "feeds" off the crowd. A sort of frenzy rises. The candidate wants to be touched. The crowd wants to touch. Everybody goes a little crazy. It's all sex.

Not with Gore.

He does what he has to do—concentrating.

There is the idea of the good Clinton: Clinton the artful centrist, Clinton the powerful analytic mind, Clinton the workaholic, Clinton the genuinely compassionate guy. Clinton without the cravings, without the neediness, without the sex. In other words, Al Gore. (But do we really want the good Clinton?)

I annoy myself by helplessly thinking about *The West Wing* (a show recasting the liberal view of politics in a similar way to the first *Making of the President* book). I can't keep from comparing Gore and his people with that pleasant and energetic cast. The fictional people on television are smart, good-looking, professional, liberal, Ivy League. Top-drawer. They're not hacks, bumpkins, ideologues, tax cutters. They are, almost convincingly (courtesy of fabulous set design), the kind of government, or style of government, we people who once dreamed of being president dreamed of. Gore and his crew probably come as close to that—that is, reasonable, educated, intelligent, liberal people (Maureen Dowd recently described Gore as a "phony, smarmy, sniveling, preppy sneak," which would also describe the characters we like on *The West Wing*)—as any possible presidential team in my memory. Of course, you have to look hard to see that, partly because Gore is disinclined (and probably unable) to romanticize the above traits. You need writers for that.

* * *

"The game is afoot, gentlemen," says Nathan as we saddle up into the vans, bound for what is described on the schedule as only a "private residence," and then, after that, on to an event at a hospital in Brooklyn. Then on to Ohio and California.

Even in tough-guy campaign terms, today's schedule is a bitch—even on a full night's sleep. Gore himself has ramped everything up; three-event days are now five-event days. This new determination is probably not just from seeing the winning light in the distance but also from having come so close to blowing everything. He's running against surprises and uncertainties. If he pushes as hard as he can to March 7, he no doubt thinks, the last seven years will not have been a waste.

There's speculation that the private residence is the home of a donor, a fat cat, a Park Avenue pit stop. But then the consensus shifts. We're headed up a blockaded Park Avenue, Imus on the radio, to Gore's daughter's home, where he will spend a quality half hour with his new grandson, we come to believe (although that destination is neither confirmed nor denied).

"Ahem, guys," says Nathan, riding shotgun in the press van. "Just want you to know that today is going to be, ahem, fucked up."

"Are we scratching the private residence or the hospital event?" asks one of the pool.

"All will become clear," says Nathan.

"We're obviously not going to his daughter's house, unless she lives in the Bronx," observes someone else in the pool.

"We're heading to the airport."

"Okay, listen up," Nathan says, "but swear—everybody put your cell phones down—that you won't call your desks. Okay? All right, he's returning to Washington."

"What do you mean, he's going to Washington?" several people demand at once.

"How is he going?" Someone asks the more basic question.

"He's going by commercial carrier," Nathan announces.

Separation anxiety starts to roll through the van. Maintaining contact, knowing the exact whereabouts, the minute-by-minute relationship of him to us, is the overriding job.

There's a vote, a potential tie vote, an abortion vote, we learn, that Gore will have to break. Nathan takes a few seconds to pump the abortion thing—Gore will do anything to support abortion, etc.

There's intense speculation now about who might go where, under what means of transportation, under whose auspices. There's Air Force Two, which is still being serviced; the press plane, which is a less secure appendage to the vice president; and now, novelistically, the shuttle, a commercial

232 • **Too Famous**

carrier, which, apparently breaking some taboo—the president and vice president do not fly commercial—will take Gore to Washington.

The mounting anxiety could not be more acute if some national emergency were taking place. It is the panic of the head being severed. It is the panic of people who have no access anyway being given even less.

But Nathan, after talking into his sleeve, has something for us—a photo op, a historic photo op: the vice president buying a ticket on a commercial carrier.

It occurs to somebody that if it's the shuttle, we can all just buy a ticket. Why not? And tail the vice president on our own steam.

Nathan is getting marching orders piped into his ear. Yes, the vice president will continue on with the day's schedule, heading out from Washington to Columbus, Ohio, and then on to Los Angeles. Air Force Two will head down to D.C. to pick him up. The press plane will fly directly to Columbus.

I lean forward to remind Nathan that I am supposed to be with the vice president. "You are with the vice president," he says.

Then something happens. It is not clear what—a wrong turn perhaps, a misinterpreted signal. The press pool is diverted from the motorcade. We're suddenly in a sort of access free fall. "We're diverted, we're diverted," Nathan is yelling into his sleeve.

"Come on!" he says, as panicked as everyone else, jumping from the van, curbside at LaGuardia.

In movie fashion, then, a dozen middle-aged men from the press pool, several with awkward, outsize dangling cameras, are running through the terminal (cell phones flying out of their pockets). We are following, to a wholly unclear destination, the vice president's boyish and determined staff member, who barrels down the concourse and, with little thought or fare-thee-well, suddenly charges through the metal detectors amid the hysterical protests of the Hispanic ladies working the machines. "We're with the vice president," Nathan shouts.

That, clearly, does not impress the metal-detector ladies.

"So arrest me!" Nathan proclaims with the greatest *West Wing*–ish misguided enthusiasm. "Call the police! We're coming through. We have to maintain contact with the vice president."

After a moment of uncertainty, the press people, who seem unaccustomed to breaking rules, are running down the US Airways gate area—suddenly being hotly pursued by various security forces of the airline, airport, and FAA.

In short order, as the vice president is peaceably boarding his commercial flight, the press pool is, in fact, corralled and detained.

"Oh, fuck," says Nathan.

"This is really serious," says one of the poolers. "This is really, really serious. You could get five years for this."

"Shit, we're really going to have to kiss some butt," Nathan says.

A long while later, after we are identified by the metal-detector ladies and have surrendered identifications and Social Security numbers, we are released. ("I've made a call and believe me this will be handled at a very high level and will all go away," says the *Daily News*'s Harry Hamburg.)

"I never asked anyone to follow me," Nathan keeps saying.

* * *

I'm sitting at a table in the luncheonette in back of the Marine Air Terminal—one of the few eating establishments at a major airport that's not a chain; rather, it could be a small-town diner—with Tony Coelho, the campaign chairman, waiting for Air Force Two to get gassed up.

Coelho may or may not be the genius of the revived Gore campaign (there is divided opinion on this), but he is certainly its most interesting figure. In leather jacket and jeans and dark glasses, he's some unexpected aging hipster. A cool and mysterious operator. He's not *West Wing*. He's an old-fashioned pol.

When I bring up the character issue, that Gore remains a blurry figure, that our sense of his motivation remains unclear, that the basic details with which you draw a character have not been supplied, that, in fact, the character traits that we have are actually the absence of traits, his woodenness, his robotic quality, because we haven't been let in, Coelho looks at me with something just this side of lack of interest.

"No, he's energized," Coelho says. "He used to be freaked out by the crowd, but now he's okay."

I wonder if Coelho really thinks this is true, or if he thinks the wooden issue, the failure-to-connect issue, isn't all that important anymore. Gore is obviously playing better in the personality department than Bradley is (if he had to run against someone, think how lucky he was to get Bradley). And more and more, they're confident that whatever Gore is or isn't will play just as well against Bush. Gore's virtues are clear. He's intelligent, he's experienced, he performs under pressure. Likewise, Bush's failings have become clear: not too smart, not too experienced, unimpressive in the clutch.

Everyone around Gore is pleased with his new ferocity—the debating Gore, Gore as litigator. He really, it seems, wants the job, which has come as something of a surprise to a lot of people. He's been pacing the hotel halls at night urging aides to add more stuff to his schedule. He gets an A for effort; Bush is strictly a gentleman's C.

But what, I say, if it's McCain? (*Hello?*) Don't you think that what McCain is doing is fundamentally changing the terms of this business? A redefinition of political personality. He talks to anybody. There are no barriers. There's no resistance. It's all just here-I-am. He's deconstructing the whole campaign artifice. As a Gore partisan, however mild, I suggest that Gore has got to start hanging out, or something.

"Bush is where we were in August, when we had to fix the campaign," says Coelho, meaning Bush will get his campaign up and running again. That's their thinking: Bush wins the Republican nomination, and they'll be in good shape. Gore is the clear contrast gainer. Bush is a gift.

"We've gotten through the persona issue," Coelho adds.

* * *

I am bumped up from the press plane to Air Force Two with the handful of pool reporters. The schedule is that the press plane will fly directly to Columbus, for the rally at Ohio State, and Air Force Two will swing down to Washington and pick up Gore and then head to Columbus. Even stuck sitting on the tarmac in line with every other plane ("Without the VP aboard, we're just like any other Cessna," says Marty Kasindorf, the pool reporter from *USA Today*), we're able to make up the time and get back close to the published schedule.

I've been promised face time on the Washington-to-Columbus leg (and I don't think I'm the only one), but Gore stays shut in his compartment, a sort of handicapped-bathroom-type arrangement on Air Force Two.

The other pool reporters spend the flight trying to reconstruct what might have happened on Gore's commercial airline flight.

"Sleepless from a post-midnight flight from New Hampshire and a pre-dawn wake-up call . . ." the AP reporter Sandra Sobieraj dictates into her cell phone. Later, working the phone, she comes up with the fact that Gore himself stowed his tray and returned his seat to an upright position.

* * *

The Columbus stop is billed as a three-thousand-person rally, but really there aren't more than five hundred or six hundred people—the room couldn't have held too many more. Lots of kids from different Ohio schools have been bused in—I see some Kenyon and Dennison sweatshirts; on the stage, there's an Up with People–type group of kids in Gore regalia.

A plump girl steps to the microphone: "Welcome to Ohio State, where the vice president of the United States will talk to our student body."

Then the Columbus mayor introduces Gore.

The loud music has a heavy bass line, and Gore, coming through the crowd and onto the stage, is trying to move to it. It's awful—or endearing.

He is wearing cowboy boots. It's hard to figure the message of this look, the boots with the Italian no-vent suit (must be inside-the-Beltway fashion; on the bus, they're still talking about last week's too-tight jeans).

He hugs the plump girl. It's a curdling hug, painful for him and for the girl and for the audience. He hugs the mayor, and this is horrible, too. He can't wait to let go (as opposed to Coelho, who is working the edges of the room, getting the local pols into no-escape headlocks). He doesn't know where to put his hands. He knows he's in someone else's space.

You can make a case for Gore's lack of seductiveness—that it might be good to get the nation off its sex-appeal binge. But it's pretty terrible to watch.

"Thank you," he says into the microphone to the mayor, using some exaggerated kind of syllabification (*tha-ank* gets two syllables, for instance), "for your support, your enthusiasm, and for the leadership of this great city—and hello, Buckeyes!"

He could obviously give a great PowerPoint presentation. It's just that he's not good at being everybody's friend. I don't think he gets much from the adulation (and, accordingly, doesn't get much adulation). The problem is, he's trying to be Clinton. This is Clinton shtick, down to the boots, I suddenly realize. The hugging, the beat, the coming through the crowd.

Is that what being vice president is all about? You just lose yourself in the other guy? Or is it that Clinton has reinvented how politicians have to behave—and everybody in this campaign is doing Clinton (McCain most successfully)?

Now, there is an argument here, if you're a sucker for subtlety, that the more sincere you truly are, the harder it is to mask your insincerity.

Gore speaks for about twenty minutes and says nothing remotely of any interest. It's disconcerting how hard he works at it, too, as though the job is to make it even more vacant. Undoubtedly, he thinks this cornball stuff is communication. You'd hate him for his condescension if he didn't seem so exposed by it.

He does five local TV interviews after the speech.

I'm staring at Gore (intently, rudely actually), and he winks at me. Yes. There it is: an ounce of irony. I'll take it.

His demeanor in front of the cameras for these little local interviews is all fifties TV dad—good guy, tolerant, not a lot of fun (no sex). The practiced calm and bedside-manner voice are a little frightening.

"I want to fight for . . ."

"Prosperity means we have a responsibility . . ."

"I have always supported . . ."

"I want to make available resources at the local level . . ."

Then, between camera setups, he looks at me again, and grimaces. A gargoyle grimace. For a half-second, his tongue is out, hangdog, or retch-like, to the side.

I think, *There's someone in there.*

In the only vaguely human question of the five interviews, a reporter asks, "What pets do you have?"

He misses a beat—it becomes nearly a blush. "I'm only thinking," he says, "about winning." But then, realizing that's no answer, he says he has two dogs and Tipper's mother has a cat, and she lives with them, so, he says, he has a cat.

More telling, I note, is that he lives with his mother-in-law.

He's slept and changed clothes before the nine p.m. arrival at Burbank

Airport. He's gone casual—although it's Nordstrom rather than L.A. casual. There's a crowd of a few hundred mustered from various unions (SEIU 660!) standing in the hangar, and a line of minor dignitaries waiting to receive him on the tarmac.

Jay Leno in jeans and Harley jacket, carrying a gym bag and talking on a cell phone, wanders out near Air Force Two and over to the head of the receiving line.

Gore is a Leno kind of guy.

After greeting the dignitaries, Gore, followed by photo scrum and a boom mike, works his way down then back along the rope line. He gives high fives aggressively, hitting hard.

I have a brief talk with Lehane, the press secretary, pointing out that I've yet to exchange a direct word with Gore.

"But it's been a good day, right?" he prompts. "You've gotten close to him. Tonight's town meeting," he says, "will be cool."

Motorcycle cops part the way for us across L.A. to Los Angeles City College.

These *Oprah*-style town meetings, first used by Clinton to powerful political effect, are now credited with the revival of the Gore campaign over the past few months. But where Clinton used them to do his I-share-your-pain thing, Gore uses them to demonstrate his stubborn, determined, immovable, even stoic presence. In Lebanon, New Hampshire, a few nights before, he conducted a town meeting that went on for three hours and thirty-five minutes (a personal best).

* * *

You're voting for pure stamina here. His absolute determination to do what does not come naturally. A fat boy who won't be shamed.

"I will stay here," he says to the crowd of a few hundred (I cannot get a ready answer as to where these demographically correct people, willing to sit into the early-morning hours, come from), "as long as anyone has a question. I'll stay here until March 7 if that's what it takes." And no doubt he would.

He begins with a moment of silence for the Alaska Airlines crash victims, then goes into a thirty-minute rendition of the Albert Gore story. It's rote, memorized, one-man-show stuff. "Tipper and I have been married for twenty-nine and a half years. . . . How many other grandparents here? . . . Give the grandchild anything he wants, and if that doesn't work, give him back to his parents. . . . Can I ask all the teachers to stand? You are heroes. . . ." Then there's the story of his parents, both poor, both striving; his mother becomes a lawyer, his father a school superintendent, then a fabled southern senator. Al grows up in Washington. He tells his sixties biography: "The civil rights moment lifted and inspired me—and then Martin Luther King was assassinated."

He says then: "I became the most disillusioned young person you'd ever meet."

This is a wholly improbable notion.

Still, you strongly feel the presence of the achieving parents. You get a sense of the intensity of the pressure and the expectations—perhaps that's what he means about his disillusionment. You can imagine he had nowhere to turn. This might explain the enlisting-and-going-to-Vietnam business—which does seem like either a remarkably calculated career move or an ass-backward order of rebellion.

If I ever get the chance, I'd surely like to ask how he might imagine his life without a political career. I'll bet he's imagined it, too (in a way that Clinton obviously hasn't).

I'm sure he would have been a terrific business guy. A modern CEO dealing with an intellectually challenging, technologically complex world. But he's here, instead, in some way, you even suspect, not living up to his full potential.

The questions begin—the first one from a Lyndon LaRouche cult person, which he dispatches with alacrity (and without meanness). The most interesting and telling thing is that he doesn't really answer the questions, even the easy ones. He seems intent on making the questions, no matter how simple and soft, larger than they are. He's looking for grand themes and substantial meaning. He's looking to impart all the information he possesses.

This is much more of a conversation with himself than it is with anybody here.

The worldview he seems to be trying to project is about reasonableness. There is no reason for extremes, for polarization, for bad things to happen to good people, he seems to think. Hence his constant effort to navigate between interest groups and his tendency to reduce issues to a question of semantic blurring, with the result that he appears to be a hairsplitter and dissembler—not to mention a gasbag.

"Do you profess to be a born-again Christian?" he is asked.

"The answer to your question," he replies, "is yes. But what I want to say hard on the heels of that answer is that there is a tendency to hear that phrase and to associate it with Jerry Falwell and Pat Robertson . . ."

Indeed, five or ten minutes later, he has reduced and redefined being a born-again Christian into being, well, a Protestant.

Again and again, whether the question is about the internet or reparations for slavery or his position on abortion, he manages to return to some bedrock, fundamentally bland, infinitely uninteresting middle ground—and stay there, and win his point (mind you, no one else is competing for the point) because he can talk longer, even on virtually no sleep, than anyone can listen.

It is a sort of torture.

* * *

AFSCME District Council 37—that is the American Federation of State, County and Municipal Employees—on Barclay Street near city hall is roiling in the turmoil of union members, New York politicos, and press, a scene vainly orchestrated by inept union officials, inept campaign officials, and resentful Secret Service agents.

"Okay," Nathan says, grabbing me and doing an elegant maneuver through the crowd and down a corridor, pushing me into one of District 37's large executive offices.

There are two aides in the room, and Gore behind the desk on the phone. He looks like a successful midwest business executive. His aides are silent. Gore does not look happy. He seems to be absorbing bad news. He closes his eyes, appears almost to be near tears. But then he responds—in Spanish. So that's it: he's concentrating. Not only is he trying to understand Spanish, but he's getting his ear chewed off in Spanish.

He's doing phoners, remote radio interviews. After the Spanish interview, his aide dials another call, but the station isn't ready yet. The two aides and I, and Gore, sit there in dead, breathless silence. Gore is a wax figure behind the desk. Red tie, power blue shirt, mouth slightly open, thin-lipped. Waiting . . . frozen . . . no one breathing . . . finally Gore's eyes glance at the laptop in front of him.

Does the absence of charm, the inability or unwillingness to take responsibility for other people's social well-being, the inclination to retreat from people rather than advance on them, say something about your presidential abilities?

Or is it just that we feel we're paying for well-developed presentation skills? Though one more schmoozer is precisely what we don't need in this marketing age.

Gore is actually authentic—he is an authentic political professional. A hardworking, earnest guy in government. A reasonable idealist. A plausibly honest elected official. He is the prince of a southern political family, but without unusual arrogance or over-the-top airs of entitlement. What's more, he's studiously, assiduously prepared for the job.

Still, we begrudge him it.

It comes back, I think, to my *West Wing* feelings. Al Gore in many ways is a kind of fantasy president—with the qualifications and the preparation, and looking the part as well. But the fantasy, his as much as ours, has taken a bit of the life out of him. Or the fantasy, realized, is, of course, a disappointment.

What's more, being the president—the notion of the presidency (which we people who still vote largely carry from another era)—is and has been for some time a disappointment.

It's my turn.

He moves to the couch, holding a copy of *New York*. He is wearing his black cowboy boots.

"What if McCain wins the Republican nomination?" I ask. "How do you match him for openness, humor, accessibility, joie de vivre?"

"I'm not very good at tactics and political analysis," he says in his slow cadence—a patent falsehood that I'm sure seems harmless enough to him (a southern white lie, an I'm-just-a-country-boy sort of thing). "And you know we're in the semifinals now—we haven't made it to the finals yet. I'm concentrating on March 7." He doesn't, in other words, believe he'll ever be facing McCain.

"What's your sense of the meaning of a personality-driven campaign?

Good? Bad? Is it something that we're evolving to because of our enormous prosperity and because there's no risk of war?"

In other words, it's a party, and McCain is the guy having the best time.

"The kind of person a candidate would be as president is always a central issue for voters," he says, trying to rationalize the issue. "As the campaign continues, people learn how a candidate reacts to pressure, how they react to the issues that arise in a campaign."

"Is there a line that you draw in your head where you think, *I'm not going to go beyond that—I don't owe voters everything*?"

"I have a line I won't cross in my refusal to make a negative personal attack," he says, offering one of his stock answers to a question that hasn't been asked—which he realizes. "Or do you mean about privacy?"

"Really, I mean about how much of yourself you'll give. McCain, for instance, seems to be saying, 'Take all of me—'"

"Oh, I see. I see what you're getting at now. And your theory is that's changing the nature of the campaign? Okay. Ahhh—I mean, I think openness is a good thing. I think each candidate has to decide what approach he's going to take for the desire of the media for all news all the time. I prefer to be in a relationship that's all voters all the time"—he laughs, pleased with his formulation—"and try to communicate directly with them as much as possible. But there are some common features between my campaign and his. I've relied on what I call open meetings. Did you go to the Los Angeles open meeting? Did you stay?"

"I certainly did," I lied.

"Bare-bones, open format, so you never know—but I don't plan to go to extremes."

"In thinking about this whole campaign process," I ask, pressing slightly (his formality keeps you from pressing more), "at what point do you feel, *I'm just freaking out*—the exposure, the emotional cost . . ."

"I don't experience that. I'm motivated by the mission. I want to make our country a better place. Education—we're in an information age. Health care. The environment. I'm driven by that, and I'm driven right past any concern about daily Q&A with the press and shouted questions. I don't mind that at all. I used to be a journalist. But I don't think a campaign for president has to be *The Truman Show*—all campaign all the time. McCain is as close as it comes to that."

He sees McCain, I suspect, as some kind of fool—a clown. McCain doesn't get it. He's become a national entertainment. In fact, he's the only one who doesn't know the whole process is fake, scripted. On the other hand, you could argue, it's Gore who seems like the *Truman Show* character, at war with the dawning understanding that people are looking at him all of the time—wanting him to entertain them.

"Well, who," I ask, "Bush or McCain, would you rather run against?"

He easily avoids the question, chuckling.

"If you couldn't have been a politician—"

"A writer." Then he says: "David Halberstam."

At that moment, maybe for the first time, I see Gore clearly. I see him as a Halberstam figure, from an era when politics and governing were intellectual, social, professional disciplines, more than pure media plays. Then, you could weave your own personality with the great issues of the day instead of having to go it alone, inventing yourself out of whole cloth. Indeed, his personality traits, personal reserve, Ivy League classiness, mild southern corn are the stuff of Washington in the fifties and sixties.

He is undoubtedly the best and the brightest of this campaign, but he is also a man out of place.

Can we get comfortable with that?

Boris

The Future PM

SEPTEMBER 2004

When I show up at the home of the possible prime minister at eight a.m., the door is opened after a long delay by an eleven- or twelve-year-old girl with clear anxiety on her face. After an embarrassed apology, she races up the staircase of the semidetached house.

"What are you doing?" I hear her demand.

"Is the chap here?" a sleepy voice asks.

"Yes!"

"Could you tell the chap I'm in the shower?" says the possible PM, Boris Johnson, who, at thirty-nine (he turns forty the next day), is the most charismatic Tory politician of the day.

The house, in Islington, in North London, a sort of liberalish Upper West Side and not at all a natural neighborhood for a wellborn conservative—Tony Blair is famously from Islington, and the Johnson house abuts the home of Ian Katz, a top editor of the *Guardian* newspaper, the antithesis of all things conservative—is a vast shambles. Piles of newspapers, jumbles of coats, a very old bicycle (Boris is a well-known London cyclist—but his is no yuppie piece of equipment), and, in the small living room adjacent to the small foyer, more piles and an unplotted area of mismatching chairs and a haphazardly slipcovered sofa. The house is surely worth an impressive upper-middle-class-homeowner sum, but there is no equity in the furniture.

A child of four or five—though not necessarily the youngest of Boris's four children—with angel-blond hair shortly appears. She, too, offers to try to fetch her father.

It is thirty minutes before the possible PM—due to catch a train at nine—appears, apologetically but not abashedly, in dress shirt and boxer shorts. He has the same uncanny, unkempt, ethereal, angelic hair as his four- or five-year-old. "Can't seem to find my trousers." The pants turn up, undoubtedly where he dropped them, on the living room floor. The possible PM, I can report, puts his pants on one leg at a time. "A very hard night," he offers.

I follow him—his state of dishevelment is as great as any I've seen in an employed person and has achieved near mythic status in the U.K.—down to the kitchen, where he pours some cereal for himself, sweeping it into his mouth as he paces the room.

He remains unmindful of the time and supremely confident that we will make the train, which, in fact, we miss. Not only are we late, but we proceed with blithe certainty—Boris's certainty: "I'm sure I would have been told if I needed to be told otherwise, wouldn't you think?"—to the wrong train station, King's Cross, instead of Liverpool Street station, on our way to a day of campaigning in the countryside.

* * *

I begin in the disarray of Boris Johnson's home because his is to some degree an artful presentation. He quite clearly invites underestimation. (And because I will now forever feel better about my own house.) And because this is the way pundits—critics and commentators and columnists—if not prime ministers naturally live (when we're not living beyond our station). And Boris is, arguably, the English language's most successful pundit.

Along with being the member of Parliament from Henley-on-Thames and the vice-chairman of the Tory Party, Boris is the editor of the *Spectator* magazine—the world's most literate, funny, snobby, bitchy, and readable journal of opinion—a weekly columnist for the near-million-circulation *Daily Telegraph*, a U.K. television personality of eccentric verve, the author of three books, including an upcoming thriller, and the automotive columnist for British *GQ*. While he is a subject of constant controversy and gossip, he is also a practically beloved, nearly Queen Mum-ish national figure.

His status is in dramatic contrast to that of most pundits in America, where the role of the public commentator is an embattled and wearisome profession—lethally partisan, personally ruinous, consumed with envy, and pretty nearly humorless. (A roundup of the usual U.S. pundits might include the conservative moralizer Bill Bennett, the Clinton loyalist Sidney Blumenthal, the conservative gay-themed columnist Andrew Sullivan, the doctrinaire liberal Paul Krugman, the doctrinaire conservative Bill Kristol, the formerly witty, now priggish op-ed writer David Brooks, and the obviously enervated Michael Kinsley.) Indeed, pundits in the United States have lately been replaced by entertainers—hence the rise of Michael Moore and Al Franken.

Boris Johnson prompts something of a sense memory: to match his sort of pundit charm, bite, influence, self-confidence (and self-regard), you'd have to go back, in the United States, to William F. Buckley Jr.

So I've come here, in part, for a lesson.

How, in a toxic opinion environment, do you continue to float like a butterfly and sting like a bee? How, in this virulent age, when all opinions are hateful opinions, does an opinionist have a good time, a really fabulous time, like Boris Johnson obviously is having?

* * *

His strategy (as well as his natural countenance) is to not be very serious about his opinions or intentions (American pundits are among the most deadly serious people to have ever lived). While he may more and more often be mentioned as a future prime minister, it is always with incredulity. Indeed, Boris is—and not just to the left-leaning and right-thinking but also to many of his friends—quite preposterous. (A. A. Gill in the *Sunday Times* described Boris on the campaign trail as eyeing a voter's baby as if it were "Sunday lunch." IT'S BORIS, THE WORST POLITICIAN IN THE WORLD, declared the headline on Gill's story.) He is a self-styled stumble-bum and semi-incompetent.

After many cell phone consultations and running between platforms and schedule boards in King's Cross station, we get on an alternative train, where I press the obvious question: "How far, *really*, do you mean to take your political career?"

"Yes, well . . . as far as I possibly can. I suppose. Why not?" His voice, with plummy stutter, is orotund.

"But don't you think that, in the end, being a writer, a political pundit, limits you in politics? How could it not?" He has provided a record of detailed views and eccentric stances, witticisms, and hyperbole (during the recent German-French-English contretemps about who should be the next head of the European Commission, Boris argued for Bill Clinton) that could be the knife of a thousand cuts.

"Ahh. Yes. Something of a problem. B-but surmountable. I think surmountable. Churchill and Disraeli surmounted it. There aren't any rules, are there, that writers can't be politicians? *Are there?*"

We turn to the subject of the disgraced Conrad Black, for whom Boris has spent much of his career working, and whose media empire is, imminently, being auctioned off. Along with the *Telegraph*, the *Spectator*—among opinion magazines, the 63,000-circulation *Spectator* has the unlikely distinction of being profitable, making $2 million a year—is on the block.

It is no secret that Boris, as well as wanting to be prime minister, would also like to be his magazine's proprietor—and has assembled a group to help him buy it.

"B-but possibly you have been sent by greater forces to instruct me in the harsh realities of this sort of thing," he says, aware that I was recently part of a group that tried and failed to buy *New York* magazine, where I had worked. "Or possibly you've been sent by your present employer to terminate me with prejudice?" (Condé Nast, the parent company of *Vanity Fair*, has been rumored to be a possible *Spectator* buyer.) "Still if the owner is someone other than myself, I am ready to be Vichy-like. I am prepared to praise and flatter shamelessly."

Now, Boris's ambition—his power grabs and his hyper-overachievement (however clownish)—is quite un-British. Its nakedness is the kind of thing that ambitious Brits have long envied and, especially in the media business, emigrated to America for. But, in a cultural turn, Boris's overtness and showboating and perilous exposure would now likely be just the type to invite instant backlash and takedown in the United States (not least of all by fellow pundits—or by a thousand bloggers), while in the U.K. he has become some kind of icon of personal promotion. The Martha Stewart of toffishness.

It could be that there is a British class allowance going on here. Boris is after all a Tory, with the entitlement that implies. (In trying to arrange an interview with him, I have had to go through his sister, Rachel, who, on my behalf, e-mailed Boris's formidable secretary: "Please be nice when someone called Michael Woolf [sic] rings to fix a *Vanity Fair* flatter-a-thon of Boris. . . . I have warned Al by leaving msg on his mobile but forgot to mention it to you which I know was probably a mistake given how everyone wants a piece of the Living God at the moment.") He is Eton and Oxford (president of the Oxford Union, which is like an even more exalted *Harvard Crimson*) and, on top of that ruling-class stuff, a Thatcherite—he's the toff as new entrepreneurial Brit. Oh yes, and he is also an American, born in New York to English parents—his father was with the United Nations and the World Bank—and raised in Norwalk, Connecticut, until the age of five. Oh, and the "Al" in the above e-mail is what his family calls him. He was born Alexander Boris de Pfeffel Johnson, changing his first name in some more or less calculated effort at public branding.

* * *

Unlike American opinionists who, when in ideological exile, hone their rancor, Boris, as an out-in-the-cold conservative, has made conservatism rather more facile and self-deprecating. Certainly, his quick ascent—from columnist to MP to Tory vice-chair to a member of party leader Michael Howard's shadow cabinet—has lots to do with the otherwise charmless and starless Blair-whipped Conservative Party.

His mission today is to bring some star power and charm to the conservative sticks and gin up local press and support for the conservative slate, which is how we find ourselves at a truck stop (lorry depot) waiting for the local Tory candidate—who because of our missed train in London has to drive a hundred miles or so across England—to pick us up.

There are a series of press events—at a radio station, with a reporter crammed up against Boris in the back seat of the car, and a photo op at a glassblowing factory—where Boris propounds his breezy, libertarian, quasi-nationalistic views.

"Do people continue to trust the conservative image?" asks the young woman from the *Sheringham Independent* in the back seat with Boris as we pass through the strawberry fields of East Anglia.

"Well, yes, hmm, the stodginess question. Hmm . . . I certainly don't think we have to start to break-dance or wear an earring in our navels . . . although possibly you have an earring in your navel . . . if so . . . I mean no . . ."

"Do we still have a great Britain?"

"Yes. Very great. The greatest. It's amazing when you fly around the world and see how really great Britain is," he affirms, but then digresses to observe how "Africa is now sending us missionaries, traffic wardens, nurses—quite an irony."

England, in late June, is rising in the 2004 Euro championship—a soccer tournament as hotly followed in Europe as the World Cup—which means that almost everywhere there are English flags flying. This is not the Union Jack but a revivified Cross of Saint George, once the symbol only of hooligans and racists, now meant to distinguish England from Scotland and Wales (which field their own teams) and, as well, to suggest some anti-immigrant, anti-Europe primal Englishness. Boris, who first came to prominence as the *Daily Telegraph*'s correspondent in Brussels, covering the workings of the European Commission (migrating from "a position of moderate idealism to one of fairly vinegarish skepticism"), is riding this new nationalism.

"I grew up," he says, "with the constant story of national decline. Peter Jenkins was a journalist who said he wanted to be the poet of decline. That's what intellectuals thought. Imagine that. Indeed, who'd have thought twenty years ago that Great Britain would be a bigger military player than Russia?" After a beat, ". . . albeit as America's loyal lieutenant."

"Do you think there's been a collapse of the British gentleman's code of conduct?" continues the reporter.

"Yes. Appalling."

"And do you see a moral decline among young people? *Big Brother* on telly . . ."

"I think there is far too much trash on the telly, far, far too much smut. Although I'm in favor of smut in many ways."

The politician's and pundit's vice of wonkishness (or of consistency) is not Boris's. Boris is politics as affect. More than being conservative, he seems, in something of a great oxymoron, flamboyantly English—just down from Brideshead.

* * *

We arrive—late—at a luncheon for a hundred or so aging North Norfolk Tories. Boris struggles into his coat and tie—the tie front is down to his fly, and his shirttail hangs below the bottom of his jacket. The room yields to him. If there is not exactly a frenzy, there is, nearly, a shiver that passes through the desiccated.

I'm put at a table with various ninety-year-olds, several of their daughters, and one twenty-three-year-old, whose mother rushes to seat her, sacrificially, next to me. Mother and daughter want urgently to explain Boris.

"He's like someone out of Jane Austen," says the daughter.

"An English gentleman," says the mother.

"He's a fop," analyzes the daughter, "which is sort of a girlie man, but in a good way. Sweet. He's a teddy bear. And look at him—such an unmade bed. And those sleepy eyes. Kind of 'Ooh, ooh, what happened? I've just woken up.' That complete obliviousness. It's sexy, really. He's Hugh Grant."

". . . who plays the PM in that recent movie—what was it?"

"*Love, Actually*," supplies the daughter.

Boris's luncheon speech violates every convention of political speechmaking. It's all riff—anti–political correctness, anti–personal regulation, pro the verities of English life (hunting and smoking and smacking). It is not just without notes but without evident structure. It contains all manner of amusing digressions far from the primary subject, helpless wittiness, and unexpected afterthoughts. ("You may want your children to sit on plastic banquettes," he rails at a new European Commission–mandated car-seat regulation, adding, "even hulking eleven-year-olds . . .") He advances and retreats. Equivocates madly ("My trumpet is uncertain"). Apologizes and reverses himself as a constant motif (he opposed the Kosovo war, which he now regrets, causing him to support the Iraq war, which, alas, he admits, has turned out to be wrong). And manages to hit some intimate groove that holds these elderly people's absolute attention.

* * *

What you see with Boris—of no small point is his hair, so blond it casts a light on his face, so askew the manliest want to mother him—is an exaggerated version of what you get. It's reverse slickness, overdramatized fallibility. Which may be how he has so easily sidestepped the scandals and bad-boy stuff that have brought derision to so many politicians and pundits (in the United States, Bill Bennett was discovered to have large gambling losses, Andrew Sullivan was found to have placed a personal ad for unsafe sex, and Sidney Blumenthal was accused of perjury in the Clinton-Lewinsky investigation).

He's been married twice—the first time, youthfully and briefly, to socialite Allegra Mostyn-Owen, the second and present marriage to Marina Wheeler, a liberal lawyer. London gossip columnists and newspaper diarists have often discussed his "mentoring" of a younger female *Spectator* staffer.

He got fired from his first journalism job—at the *Times*—for making up a quote.

He was subsequently embroiled in a scandal referred to by everyone, including Boris himself, as Guppygate, in which he was caught on tape seeming to be aiding a former school chum and convicted insurance scammer, one Darius Guppy, in a plan to beat up a reporter on the scandal sheet *News of the World*.

He speaks openly of his drinking ("Two are all right, but after three you rather lose the thread of what you are saying").

And yet he manages to somehow make this all a kind of human-stain homily—a comfort zone, even, of waywardness. There is no evident guilt or mortification here, in the Clinton sense, or effort at righteous indignation, in the Bill Bennett sense, but rather a greater human context—the expectation that things will, at some point, always get dodgy. Indeed, this is, in some ways, the focus of his conservatism. Not the anti-abortion, religion, family-values U.S. version but just the opposite: a live-and-let-live, don't-hold-us-to-impossible-standards, you-have-to-accept-some-level-of-mess-if-you-want-some-higher-level-of-freedom conservatism.

It's the politics of letting Boris be Boris that the old conservatives in North Norfolk are so enthusiastic about.

* * *

And he's very funny. This is his real political and polemical breakthrough. There may not be any other political writer as loose, playful, smart, and wise-guyish as Boris. He is always being lectured by more seasoned politicians about having to make a choice between politics and comedy. But obviously they don't understand humor: his is confessional, ingratiating, seductive, and, even when he turns the screw, winning.

He is not a conservative writer, as pundits, left or right, mostly are—literal, formal, constipated, pickle-up-the-assish. He's a free-form narrator. A raconteur. A storyteller constantly refining the story ("that amazing, Latin American carnival of grief," he recently wrote, reflecting on the events that followed Diana's death). His politics is really the process of telling the story of his own political experience. ("I first stood in the physical presence of Margaret Thatcher when she swept past me in her twinset, at the Madrid summit in 1989. Not only was she really rather beautiful, with a sort of glow about her. She was also very cross. Perhaps she looks beautiful when she is cross.") His 2001 campaign memoir, *Friends, Voters, Countrymen*, about the ludicrousness and exasperations and low farce of campaigning—a gentle and instructive comedy—is surely the best campaign book ever written by a politician.

It's a surprising advantage, it turns out, to be a politician who can write. (Imagine how Bill Clinton might have moved the world if he could write.)

* * *

We arrive in Great Yarmouth, a depressed, or at least depressing, seaside town, to have tea with another forty or so biddies waiting (patiently) at a Fawlty Towers–style hotel.

He is, it occurs to me, as he woos and charms and radiates good humor, Ronald Reagan. And Arnold Schwarzenegger. Like them, Boris comes to politics with a national audience and a cultivated persona.

While American pundits are marginalized by niche publications and ever smaller cable audiences (there's a kind of desperation that infects cable pundits), the U.K. is still a mass-audience nation. The *Telegraph*'s near-million readers make it vastly bigger than any paper in America. Even the erudite *Spectator* is proportionately many times larger than any U.S. political publication. And then there is the BBC show *Have I Got News for You*. This is an amazingly popular prime-time quiz show (think *What's My Line?*, if you are old enough—Boris as Bennett Cerf) that uses the news as an excuse for a game in which contestants—comedians, journalists, politicians, and other clever people—wildly insult one another.

Boris has been one of the show's most successful participants (he famously endured a tsunami of insult about the Darius Guppy affair, for which, in retaliation, he blithely revealed that much of the theoretically ad-libbed show is scripted), a largely good-natured (indeed, often bumbling) target for all manner of jokes related to toffs and Oxbridge graduates—making him, at the very least, the best-known twit in the nation.

Boris is, like his fellow conservatives Reagan and Schwarzenegger, an act—like them, but unlike most politicians who are acts, an authentic act. And a cheerful one.

Like Reagan and Schwarzenegger, he seems also to appreciate that there is a great population of voters who might prefer almost anyone to a politician. That if you have an interest in politics (which most nonpoliticians don't) but are not, by profession or temperament, a politician, and, indeed, if you are someone who has some true sense of language and style and humor, you can probably go to the political moon.

One difference between Boris and American pundits is that American pundits are closer to actual politicians than Boris is. American punditry, indeed, is dying over the issues killing politics—sanctimony, witless partisanship, and bad prose.

Boris, I notice from the audience at the Fawlty Towers hotel, has gotten progressively more disheveled throughout the day. The middle buttons of his shirt have come undone, and, it seems, the top button has been mysteriously transposed with the next button. There is a large stain on his pants, and his fly is halfway down. His loose speech has become even looser. His eyes are shining. His hair is wildly, ridiculously, at odds with itself. And he is telling a long story about fixing windows and the European Commission and the Kyoto Protocol ("if you break your window in your home as you are entitled to do, say in a violent fray with a loved one . . ."), which does seem to have a political point, but far from a clear one.

The Sextator

L ondon is the gossip capital of the world—people don't seem to be able to help themselves; discretion is nonexistent; to tell, to confide, to speculate, often to make up out of whole cloth, is joy.

Lots of the people breathlessly eager to talk to me about the sex scandal that is consuming England—and which, in column inches anyway, may rank alongside the one that, forty years ago, brought John Profumo down—think it's about the fixation English men of a certain generation have on American women. Certainly, the scandal has created a towering figure of man-hungry American feminine guile. Others think it's principally about, as all things in England are principally about, class. Still others, about the abuse of high office.

But I think the scandal—which has brought down the home secretary as well as one of the rising stars of the Tory Party—is really about the nature of the magazine business. Of the fantasy world of status and attainment and sensibility and clubbiness, of the in crowd and the out, that a good magazine constructs—and its creators can so easily come to believe in.

The fallen woman at the center of the mess is the publisher of the *Spectator* magazine. Before that she worked in London as a public relations representative for *Vanity Fair*. Her husband, with whom she began an adulterous affair (ahhh . . . the language of sexual scandal . . . it rolls so easily off the tongue) while working for *Vanity Fair*, is an executive in the London offices of Condé Nast, *Vanity Fair*'s parent company. I work for *Vanity Fair*. If this represents a conflict . . . well, truly, there is hardly anyone, in the miles of British print so far devoted to telling this tale, who does not have some personal, professional, or intimate relationship with one or more of the parties. Everybody's in bed with everybody.

The scandal—dubbed Sextator, because so many of the protagonists are connected to the *Spectator*, or "the year of sexual intercourse," by Rod Liddle, one of the *Spectator*'s leading writers and a scandal principal himself—formally begins last August. But it's worthwhile to flash back to the previous autumn to find all of the protagonists gathered in celebration of the magazine's 175th Anniversary. This longevity itself is an important backdrop.

Perhaps no magazine has for so long and so successfully created such a fantastic, exclusive, sought-after, and illusory world as the *Spectator*. It is a world not just of snob appeal but of snob identity, of snob ideology, snob militancy, snob brilliance.

Andrew Roberts, the British historian, social figure, and *Spectator* writer, who says he began to read the magazine at age fourteen, describes it, lovingly, as coming from a time "before the middle class was enfranchised." Charles Moore, *Spectator* columnist and former editor (the British satirical journal *Private Eye* calls him "Lord Snooty"), could, not long ago, comfortably write in the *Spec*: "Although I shall be as pleased as anyone by spring when it comes, I regret more and more that we don't have longer and colder winters. Weather is at its best when it transforms, and that is what frost and snow do beautifully. One of the things I dislike about Tony Blair is that he makes a point of never wearing an overcoat."

It is the magazine of Graham Greene and Kingsley Amis and father and son Waugh, Evelyn and Auberon. Of Eaton, Harrow, and Westminster, and of not just Oxford and Cambridge, but the same shared tutors at Oxford and Cambridge.

And if, in Tony Blair's United Kingdom of New Labour, this high Tory world has never been so ephemeral, or ridiculous, the *Spectator* itself has never been so successful. ("This notion that because you own a 1997 Porsche Carrera you are somehow elevated in your social standing and social worth, is a deeply regrettable feature of our times and perhaps one reason why the *Spectator*'s circulation is so high," wrote Liddle in the *Spec*, this past year.) It's reached a circulation of 66,000—up from 11,000 a generation ago (the equivalent in U.S. terms would be at least five times as great)—and profits of $3 million (such "a massive faux pas" moving into profit, says the magazine's political editor Peter Oborne). Nor, arguably, has it ever been so lively, arch, waspish, funny, anarchic, envied, influential— the "last oasis of cavalier individualism," wrote Matthew Norman, the media diarist in the *Independent*, recently.

The 175th Anniversary festivities were meant to celebrate the success of the magazine and of its editor Boris Johnson, the forty-year-old, famously baby-blond, Bertie Wooster–ish Tory MP and charmer of British media. But it was also meant to put the media light on the magazine's publisher, the forty-three-year-old American Kimberly Fortier, a fashionable, boundlessly energetic force of promotional nature. The 175th Anniversary was hers—she'd grabbed it. It was a golden PR opportunity, for herself as well as for the magazine—with both Boris and her interviewed and profiled widely.

Now, most Speccie parties—and there are lots of drunken, heaving Speccie parties, famous for, among other things, the hooking up ("Pressed up against Margaret Thatcher, what else do you think about," one Speccie writer told me, eyes bright, more than half seriously)—are held in the magazine's legendary, and eccentric, Georgian building on Doughty Street in Bloomsbury. But this one was held, a *Spectator* editor disapprovingly described, "amidst uncomfortable glitz," at the Intercontinental Hotel at Hyde Park. And all paid for. Fortier had snagged De Beers, the diamond seller, as the sponsor of the event. She understood that the 175-year-old political journal had one of the most high-end demographics in British media and attracted the most powerful and influential of British society to its parties—a corporate sponsor's dream.

Under her direction there would even be, for the first time in the magazine's history, a commemorative coffee-table *Spec*—a perfect-bound issue derived from the archives and filled with luxury brand advertising. She'd personally contacted all the magazine's living former editors to come in to be photographed: to Alexander Chancellor, the *Spec* editor from 1975 to 1985, and a ramshackle monument in British journalism, it seemed "*unusual* to hear from the *publisher*."

Fortier, quite unlike past *Spectator* publishers (before Fortier they were called "publishing directors"), had management swagger and ambitions beyond merely selling ads. ("*Spectator* business types don't usually swank around town," says the columnist Quentin Letts.) In fact, by using the title *publisher*—at American magazines an appellation for the chief ad salesperson—she was implying the British meaning of something close to proprietor.

Indeed, Fortier and Johnson would tussle all evening at the anniversary party about who should give the evening's main peroration—Johnson, one of the most famous and entertaining after-dinner speakers in Great Britain, finally prevailed.

She was, on every level, supremely confident and competent—"an iron-willed coquette," says one friend of hers—trying to impose order on the *Spectator*'s essential chaos ("from a management perspective, Boris is . . . unmanageable," admits one Speccie editor, though with admiration) and on the *Spectator*'s libertarian and libertine (and adolescent) eschewing of rules and regulations. (Bad behavior is a *Spectator* high art form: Jeffrey Bernard famously wrote a column for the magazine called The Low Life, which was largely about his alcoholism, which often prevented him from writing the column. In that event, a note would appear in the column's place merely stating that "Jeffrey Bernard is unwell," which later became the title of a hit West End play.)

With great management censoriousness and practicality, Fortier had even been lecturing Johnson, the married father of four, about the affair he was having with one of the magazine's writers, the pouty-faced Petronella Wyatt, and Liddle, the forty-three-year-old father of two, about the affair he had begun with the *Spectator*'s twenty-two-year-old receptionist, the comely Keira Knightley look-alike (in Liddle's estimation) Alicia Monckton. "Leave her alone, she's nice," Fortier commanded Liddle.

Now, in the nearly all-male world of the *Spectator*, where everybody could trace back generations of sexual goings-on and public-school boy lecheries, neither Johnson's nor Liddle's was all that noteworthy. And Fortier's objections were regarded as . . . American. (No small dismissal.)

If these Speccie affairs were not unique, they weren't furtive, either, which seemed especially to rankle the often-officious Fortier. They were known to almost everyone except, by some finely developed English denial mechanism, the cuckolded spouses.

Liddle's companion of eleven years, and the mother of his children, Rachel Royce, arrived at the party only to run smack into Johnson's wife, Marina Wheeler, and to feel a "sense of miserable embarrassment" because she knew Wheeler's husband was bedding the pouty Petronella, perhaps not coincidentally, one of the magazine's only women columnists. (From one of her columns: "Most women I know don't bother about orgasms at all. Nothing—not even the prospect of death—fills a man with greater horror than the suspicion that a woman has faked her orgasm. Well, sometimes we do and sometimes we don't. There is no mystery about it. It is like the weather. Sometimes it rains and sometimes it doesn't. And if it doesn't one gets a watering can and waters the flowers oneself. Do the flowers ask if the rain is faked? Certainly not. So why should men?")

Royce knew about Boris's affair through her husband, Rod, who, she was blissfully unaware, was at that moment at the party in a particularly get-a-room sort of way with receptionist Monckton. Royce would wonder later if Marina had felt a similar embarrassment toward her. ("As I now know to my cost, there are few more thankless jobs in life than being a *Spectator* wife, " she'd write.)

Anyway, it was a smashing, drunken, celebrity-filled *Spectator* evening, with, at Fortier's instigation, all the waiters dressed in blond Boris Johnson wigs.

Of course, Conrad Black, the Canadian newspaper owner who'd moved to London and reinvented himself as a British Lord—in part by buying the *Spectator*—and who was, at that moment, unbeknownst, looting his company in order to sustain the lifestyle of a *Spectator*-owning British Lord, was there. As was his wife, Barbara Amiel, another foreigner who had—without the limitations of a class-identifying British accent—risen precipitously in London society.

Everyone was there—and, in Speccie fashion, not just Tories. David Blunkett, the fifty-seven-year-old home secretary, was famous because he was in everybody's estimation a likely Labour prime minister (as Boris Johnson was a possible Tory PM), but also because he was blind from birth—a working-class lad who'd dramatically broken the bounds of class and handicap.

Blunkett was guided around the party by Fortier—an ideal guide, at this party or any other, because she always knew all the players and all the nuances of status and hierarchy—without anyone suspecting that, three months after her marriage to Condé Nast executive Stephen Quinn, in 2001, she'd begun an affair with the home secretary, and, indeed, that her two-year-old son was, quite without the knowledge of her husband, Blunkett's, and that she and Blunkett had been planning to move to Washington—where he'd become the British ambassador—and where Kimberly would take that town by storm.

Given all the journalists who saw them together as often as they were together—and given that the adulteries of prominent people are in Britain a media staple and national pastime, virtually money in the bank for British tabloids—it's odd that this one went undetected for so long.

It wasn't until the relationship ended last summer, on August 11, that the story got its kick start.

On August 14, 2004, the *News of the World*, one of the Murdoch-owned British tabloids, broke the story that the home secretary was having an affair with an unnamed married woman—with a picture of a blurry figure, Fortier, after her formal and bitter breakup with Blunkett, leaving his London house.

Only then—Fortier knew that the *Sun*, another Murdoch tabloid, would name her the very next day—did she confess the three-year affair to her sixty-year-old husband. The *Daily Mirror*, a competing tabloid, followed up with the fact—only recently revealed to Blunkett and, apparently, responsible for the split in their relationship—that Fortier was pregnant with her second child and had been since May.

Still, with both sides uncharacteristically offering no further details or corroboration—Fortier fled on vacation to the United States—the story went quiet. Except it was the irresistible gossip among virtually every media person in London—after all, this was not only the home secretary, the third most important person in British government behind the prime minister and chancellor, having this affair, but it was the *blind* home secretary, which raised it to a further level of prurience and hee-haw (love is blind) comedy.

The irresistibleness of the *Spectator* publisher's embarrassing predicament was made all the more . . . irresistible . . . by the well-known (though as yet unpublished) fact of the *Spectator* editor's increasingly ridiculous affair. Peter McKay, who writes the Ephraim Hardcastle diary column in the *Daily Mail*, had, for months, been referring to Boris's "mentoring" of his protégée Petronella. *"What do they put in the water over there?"* jokes were . . . well, irresistible. And then there was, too, the Liddle spectacle.

Liddle, forty-four, is a Fleet Street bad boy. He was the producer of the BBC's *Today* program when Andrew Gilligan made the remarks about the "sexed up" weapons report that provoked the Blair administration's war with the BBC, as well as the author of a recent novel, *Too Beautiful for You*, a sex farce ("a shag novel," he calls it). Liddle is, too, in his weekly *Spectator* column, among the best writers of opinion journalism in the English language. And his affair with the delicious receptionist had—at least for other male Fleet Streeters—something of the writers' reward about it. Why else would the paunchy, fright-hair, fag-addicted, over-forty guy get the lovely young girl, except for his prose?

This was not the way, however, that Rachel Royce, mother of his two children, and companion of eleven years—whom Liddle married three months after the 175th Anniversary party, only to leave the honeymoon early to be with the receptionist—took it. Rather, she came undone. And then pulled herself together to write an ongoing column, through the summer and autumn, in the *Daily Mail* about her husband's carryings-on with the unnamed woman she called "the slapper"—a slapper, in British sexual hierarchy, seems to be slightly higher than a slut—complete with details of discovered Viagra and private detectives and her own, new, better-performing lover, which became a great, media-class entertainment. Boris Johnson, in the sporting spirit of the scandal, suggested to Rod that he write a competing column in the *Spectator* called Discreet Silence.

Meanwhile there is Conrad Black. Black, having been found finally with his hand in the till, was, in the fall, forced to put his holdings, including the Telegraph Group, of which the *Spectator* was part, on the block. Which may help explain—a desire to be on better, if not best, behavior—why, when a *Spectator* columnist made a slur against Liverpudlians, Boris, at the behest of Tory Party leader Michael Howard, traveled to Liverpool to apologize and, for his groveling, instantly became the butt of vast media derision. "The beginning of his end, that ludicrous journey to Liverpool," said the *Mail*'s McKay.

Such derision flowed neatly into the next Sextator chapter. In early November, the mother of Boris's paramour revealed to the *Daily Mail* that her thirty-four-year-old daughter, Petronella—nickname: Petsy—with whom she lived, had for four years been waiting for Boris to make good on his promises to leave his wife. Meantime, Petsy—"Petronella left

Oxford a week after she got there because the coffee cups were filthy," jokes a friend of Petronella's, trying to describe her certain charm to me—had become pregnant by Boris twice, birth control clearly not part of the *Spectator* style, and had at least one abortion. What's more, her friends confide, Boris paid for it.

Boris, in a moment of not uncommon verbal grandiosity, dismissed all this, declaring it to be an "inverted pyramid of piffle," which promptly becomes one of the signature lines—something like a more elegant "I did not have sex with that woman"—of the scandal. In short order, Tory leader Michael Howard sacked Boris from his position in the Tory shadow cabinet (not, technically, for his affair, but for lying about the affair).

And then, mid-November, David Blunkett—spurned like Petronella Wyatt and Rachel Royce—publicly demanded a DNA test to prove if he's the father of Kimberly's first child, William, as well as the one as yet unborn. Fortier, who around this time suddenly adopted her husband's name—literally changing how she was listed on the *Spectator* masthead and effectively undermining her *Private Eye* nickname, "Tiffany Cartier"—insisted that Quinn was the father. It is, however, shortly revealed—leaked by the Blunkett camp—that, while Stephen Quinn may think the boy is his, she and Blunkett have already had the child tested and confirmed to be Blunkett's. Blunkett, it turns out, has had a long relationship with the child—he and Fortier/Quinn and William have vacationed together in Greece and France.

Fortier/Quinn retaliates. In a series of counter-leaks, it's alleged that Blunkett has committed a variety of technical abuses of his office on her behalf—he's gotten her a discount meant for MP spouses on a train; he's used a security detail to protect her; he's given her a ride in a government car; and, more damagingly because he's taken a tough line on immigration, he's "fast tracked" her nanny's visa application.

The Sextator scandal is full born.

Stephen Quinn, assuming the mantle of near sainthood that he will maintain throughout the affair—"moving in a nanosecond from the most betrayed to the most devoted," says the *Independent on Sunday*'s diarist Christopher Silvester—declares that his wife isn't "the greatest sinner this country has produced."

"You have to understand the Catholic notion of forgiveness," lectures

Quinn, an Irishman from Kilkenny raised in a foster home, who turns down a $350,000 offer to go public with his story. "I am morally accountable to Kimberly, to William, to our baby, who I hope will be okay when he is born."

Blunkett goes into court to formally pursue his paternal and custody rights—of both present and future child.

An independent panel is empowered to investigate Blunkett's possible abuses. Blair defends Blunkett, but party opposition mounts.

The Quinns' nanny sells her story to the *Daily Mail* (the Quinns have tried to get her to sign a nondisclosure, but she's refused).

Kimberly collapses and enters a hospital. Quinn warns of a miscarriage—blaming Blunkett.

On December 15, Blunkett resigns in tears saying he only wants to be a father to his children.

Within days, Simon Hoggart, another *Spectator* columnist, after first adamantly denying it, admits to also having an affair with Kimberly, whom he once characterized in a column he wrote for the *Guardian* as "winsome." "Who would have ever thought of Simon?" says a British magazine executive I know. There's a search for a fourth man: Labour peer Sandy Leitch, financier and insurance magnate, pal of Blair and Chancellor Gordon Brown, is named. An underground list grows tying Kimberly to a wide swath of Westminster and media personalities: a prominent radio announcer, a Black broadcaster, another cabinet minister, a slew of well-known journalists, among them. "It's ménage-à-pick-a-figure," says *Times* journalist Toby Moore.

The *Sun* creates a board game about who's had Kimberly.

The *Daily Star* distributes a bumper sticker: HONK IF YOU'VE BONKED BLUNKETT'S SLAPPER.

She's a Hollywood kid. Her mother, Lugene Sanders, who played Babs, the ingénue daughter on the hit show *The Life of Riley*, retired from a career as one of the most prominent actresses in fifties television to have a family—Kimberly was born in 1961. Kimberly herself played Snow White at Disneyland for pocket money. Her father, Marvin Solomon, was a businessman. In a bit of inflated fabulousness, it somehow came to be understood in London that Kimberly was a Solomon of the famous Wall Street financial firm, which clearly suggested big (and old) money and social significance—and may smooth some of the Jewish issues that always need smoothing in England—though the financial house is spelled Salomon and, in any event, the Salomons left the firm long before modern Wall Street fortunes were made.

She went to Vassar, acquiring social vivacity and minor intellectual airs (an interest in eighteenth- and nineteenth-century British novels) and entitlement to a low-paid publishing job. She went to work, in her telling, for *Cosmopolitan* editor Helen Gurley Brown—the quintessential example of someone who gets to live the life of her magazine. She was fired, Kimberly says, because she had a long chat with Truman Capote on the phone instead of passing him directly through to Brown. Here was reverse résumé inflation—I got fired for being too charming and amazing. The former *Cosmo* editor says she can't remember Kimberly at all.

She married an investment banker, Michael Fortier, posted to London to work by Morgan Stanley, freely telling friends he is gay. "Even when she is lying in her grave," he will say in an interview shortly after the scandal breaks, "she'll be thinking if there's anybody more interesting she could have lying next to her."

In that jab, high comedy passes into deep sanctimony.

"If she turned up at the opera," says Liddle, "people would have hissed."

She becomes nothing less than the United Kingdom's most scarlet woman. Bimberly: the cold, vampish, New York socialite (how exactly she qualifies as a socialite remains, in most British accounts, unexplored). She is the Kim Philby of adultery—adultery so artfully hidden that having been revealed makes the rest of her life a pathological betrayal of everything and everyone.

Her true character is laid bare—and it's ugly.

She's revealed in her flatteries and manipulations and fashionableness to be not just a sexual adventuress but, in some sense vastly worse, a . . . salesperson. Which casts her out of the world she has so successfully joined.

And, in fact, she *is* a salesperson. A hardworking, even prodigious, promoter—a closer—whose ability to charm and to seduce and to do the deal deserves a large amount of the credit for the *Spectator*'s success. She's quite the radical opposite of the *Spectator*'s feminine ideal, the submissive Sloane Ranger with the weak English chin.

Now, promoters and salespeople—who are, by profession, suck-ups and flatterers—doing the work that pays the salaries of the more virtuous folk, are generally accorded a certain willing suspension of disbelief. But if you're caught out—this is true not just of Kimberly but of her boss Conrad Black, as well as many other corporate no-good-niks—then the suspension of disbelief is revoked and everyone suddenly, in *shocked shocked* fashion, sees you for the dreadful phony you are.

She's Becky Sharp, everybody says. A giddily upwardly mobile character, a wanter, a taker, a person of artifice—in the thrall of all those luxury brands. The demonic yuppie (indeed, Becky Sharp, if you think about it, is a fine yuppie precursor).

Joanna Coles, a former Speccie staffer and Fleet Streeter who now lives in New York, recounts: "I was working on the *Guardian* at the time and people told her we would get on so she called me up and took me to Caviateria in London, a place where Middle East businessmen go for lunch. We were the only women there. And she said, 'I simply must have caviar every day.' I was gobsmacked."

She is "nothing but a networking bitch," says one Speccie writer of my acquaintance, which seemed—*oomph!*—all you had to say about someone to send them to hell, before it occurred to me that almost everyone I know is a networking bitch. (The *Spectator* itself, with its famous parties, is a kind of temple of networking bitches.)

And she's an American—which suggests, always, a potential sociopath.

And then there is the sex. It is not just that she had sex, but that she had cunning sex. Not naturally, or helplessly, as a beautiful woman might, but trickily, mendaciously, because, like Camilla Parker Bowles, she wasn't somehow deserving of it. She "looks like she could be a manager in a large British Homes Store, efficient, homely, no-fuss hair and a nice smile," wrote the columnist Yasmin Alibhai-Brown in the *Evening Standard*, with disdain and incomprehension.

"Women are not created equal," Kimberly herself wrote with bizarre foreshadowing or keen self-parody in an article called "Kitten Women" in British *Vogue* in 1997. "Some are pretty, clever and well-connected. Others are not. But there are those who know how to circumvent whatever Mother Nature has doled out and grab the floor either way. Among those is the genus 'Kitten Woman' . . . in all her fluffy, purring, girlish glory . . .

Kitten Woman has a way of making every gesture look childlike and intimate. . . . She'll straighten your collar, clasp your hand, tilt her head and
look up into your eyes."

There's near-unanimous scorn among British women columnists
("duplicitous, disloyal, and selfish," wrote Margaret Cook—whose husband, Foreign Secretary Robin Cook, left her for his secretary, and who
also has been linked to Kimberly—in the *Mail*) at Kimberly's apparent
abilities to flatter, to make a man the center of attention, to mesmerize, to
seduce—and, what's more, to seduce the more or less helpless and infirm:
Kimberly's preferred demographic is the over-fifty-five set.

The belief in England is, apparently, that American women—Wallis
Simpson, the American divorcée who nearly seventy years ago pinched
the English king, and Jennie Jerome, Churchill's American mother, who
is not uncommonly described as an "adulteress," come up way too often
in my conversations—possess unfair powers. Kimberly is "an uninhibited
woman from the New World coming to turn the Old World upside down,"
huffed the author Elizabeth Buchan in the *Mail on Sunday*.

"You see, American women are incredibly attractive to British men of
my generation," says an editor I know at the *Guardian*, trying to parse the
Kimberly attraction among so many middle-aged Fleet Street colleagues.
"This is, I think, because of the blow job. Englishmen of a certain age all
went to America for their first blow job. English girls were very late in
coming to the blow job."

It's great seduction—with world-class flattery, come-a-little-closer con-
fidences, amusing self-deprecation. (Here's Kimberly's account, provided
by *Spectator* writer Matthew Parris, of trying to use a vacuum cleaner: "I
called my mother in America. She said, 'Check if the bag's full.' I checked.
'No, no problem, Mother,' I said. 'It's completely full.' I thought it was like
a car's gas tank. I didn't realize it had to be empty.") And she gives great
gossip—a master of the "calculated indiscretion," says *Private Eye* editor
Francis Wheen.

Kimberly is, many Fleet Street men admit, begrudgingly, "good company."

The stage here, in Kimberly Solomon-Fortier-Quinn's social and professional climb, is the long lunch, the liquid lunch, the knee-touching
lunch, the magazine business lunch.

"Do you fancy her?" Alexander Chancellor asked Auberon Waugh, who was seeing Kimberly for frequent lunches, not too long before his death. "Only physically," replied the legendary columnist.

David Blunkett, the blind home secretary, does not come naturally into Kimberly's orbit—to say the very least.

The Blunkett story is a kind of apotheosis of English antipathy and coldness and institutional cruelty (English coldness being the apotheosis of all coldness). He is delivered into a state institution for the blind at the age of four. His devoted father dies from a factory fall into a vat of boiling water when David is eleven. His education is a series of nearly insurmountable hardships. It's a background that, no surprise, creates a dedicated socialist (and also a poet). He marries a schoolteacher. He has three children. The marriage is unhappy. It is a life of overwhelming struggle and, in the telling, unremitting loneliness.

It is, at the same time, a brilliant career, taking him from the English left wing to the inner leadership circle of modern, capitalistic, nonideological, third-way New Labour politics. In the yuppie world of New Labour, he is the anti-yuppie. The postindustrial heartland figure. The everyman.

Indeed, Blunkett becomes arguably the most conservative member of the Blair team. He seizes the 9/11 mantle. He holds the anti-immigration portfolio, becomes the identity-card minister.

The *Spectator* world—which refuses to take anything very seriously (if you are a Tory in Blair's Britain it is hard to be serious)—is the diametric opposite of the Blunkett world. But, like many, he's in the thrall of it (at the height of the scandal, the *Spectator* runs a devastating critique of Blunkett's policies). If you are ambitious in London—in media and in Westminster— the *Spectator* holds one of the keys to success. It's the convergent social circle. While real media is large and anonymous—the world of Channel Four and the BBC and deal making, in which no one goes fox hunting— the *Spectator* world is focused. It's pure. All its connections are direct.

"The Left," in England, says John Kampfner, an editor at the *New Statesman*, the *Spectator*'s left-wing 10,000-circ counterpart, "has always been titillated by the Right."

There are two versions of how Quinn and Blunkett meet—in each, the other is the predator.

At a *Spectator* dinner party at the Savoy (Boris's flame Petronella is also at this dinner), not long after her marriage to Quinn, Kimberly meets

Blunkett and is said to have uttered yet another signature line of the scandal: "I've always wondered what it would be like to sleep with a blind man."

Alternatively, Blunkett hears Kimberly—ever keen for her own media opportunities—on a radio show (talking about nineteenth-century novels) and is transfixed by her voice (which is, in fact, a high-pitched, somewhat annoying voice). Shortly afterward, when the *Spectator* calls him for an interview, he says he'll agree to let Boris Johnson interview him if Boris will bring Kimberly along to dinner (Petronella is also, in the telling, at this dinner).

The relationship itself, the structure of the affair, is both public and private. Everybody, including her husband, knows about her friendship with Blunkett. She tells everyone. It's a calling card—Kimberly is, not unexpectedly, a serious name-dropper. (She is also a constant narrator of the interest men have in her. There's always a stage whisper about who might be hot for her, or who's, stubbornly, not showing interest.) She becomes, at the *Spectator*, a go-to source for access to the Blair government. Likely, part of her attraction to Blunkett is the distinction it gives her at the magazine—Boris may be a Tory muckety-muck, but Kimberly has the home secretary in her Hermès purse. With her husband's full knowledge, she goes as Blunkett's date to a Buckingham Palace dinner for George W. Bush.

The private part is masked by the public part. They're together all the time and nobody gets it. They meet, according to her intimates, at least three times a week. They weekend together and vacation together (France, Greece, Italy, Spain). In part, no one suspects she's having an affair because she acts like she's having an affair with everybody. In part, no one suspects she's having an affair with Blunkett because . . . he's blind. "A blind socialist," says one of Kimberly's friends, with continuing disbelief.

The forty-three-year-old publisher and the fifty-seven-year-old politician are in love. Blunkett is, according to his biographer Stephen Pollard, "besotted." His intimates say he was absolutely convinced, had, indeed, planned out his career based on the fact that they would be together. Her intimates don't deny that she was seriously entertaining a life with Blunkett, that she was, at least for a period, planning to move to Washington with him.

She even gets rid of her dog, Lazlo, the Dandie Dinmont who for years has accompanied her to the office, because it doesn't get along with Sadie,

Blunkett's seeing-eye dog (Kimberly's abandoned dog seems to be a particularly disturbing detail for the canine-crazy English).

She's living two lives—apparently, effortlessly living two lives. It's multitasking of an extreme sort. The ultimate compartmentalization.

There's no indication to anyone that she's at all unhappy with her husband. "They had a very healthy and active sex life, throughout this whole period. After all, they're practically newlyweds," says one of her intimates.

Even her friends say that Kimberly lives a very full "fantasy life." A "substantial" fantasy life. One friend discusses this in terms of her "perfectionism." (This friend speaks of her "well turned out" house, which, among classically unkempt upper-class English homes with their proudly chipped and broken furniture, might seem like you're leading an overly expressive inner life.) Of having everything just so, of a life that you create, that you fantasize and then create—like an upscale magazine. It doesn't *not* make sense to her friends that she could conceive of a perfect, discreet, lovely life with Blunkett, and, equally, a perfect, discreet, lovely life with Quinn. She creates her own reality—or several at the same time. She's superorganized.

Then there's the biological clock. She's determined to have a child. She married Quinn only after he agreed to have his vasectomy reversed. And when she did not immediately get pregnant, they began IVF treatment—which she was undergoing when she was with Blunkett. So Blunkett was the backup plan (or one among her backup plans), or, possibly, with more calculation even, just the "sperm butler," in the description of Rachel Johnson, Boris's sister.

She wanted what she wanted.

She conceives her second child around when she and Blunkett are vacationing on Corfu with two-year-old William, in May 2004, and, apparently, not long afterward, begins to think about ending the relationship. Reality does intrude, apparently, and, weighing the options, she chooses Quinn.

In the telling, the telling from her side anyway, the real Blunkett is now revealed. He's an "obsessive, controlling, restraining, dominating character," according to her spokespeople. They say she says he says: "If I can't have you nobody can." (That chestnut.) He threatens. She becomes afraid. Her friends refer to the "ferocity of his passion." He writes crazed letters. He contacts her friends. Finally, on August 11, in front of members of his staff, she ends it.

From his view, she was the love of his fifty-seven-year-old life. They had a pact. They had a plan. To renege on that, to withdraw, what's more to deprive him of his children, is the ultimate cruelty in his cruel life.

She, or her seconds, return to say that it is not the children; that's a canard. It is, rather, and simply, his obsession with her.

The mirror-image stories presented by each side's seconds, not just with Quinn and Blunkett, but Boris and Petronella and Rod and Rachel—these divergent narratives, this *Rashomon*-ishness—comes from not just the inevitable he-said-she-said-ness, but also the general glee and carefully drawn alliances of the British media.

Everybody has his conduit—everybody has his or her media rabbi; everybody gets to tell or sell his story.

Blunkett, the Blair conservative, has cultivated a relationship with the right-wing Rupert Murdoch (indeed, Blair has cultivated his own relationship with Murdoch) and the Murdoch tabloids. The girlfriend of the CEO of the Murdoch papers, Les Hinton—whose own adultery was recently exposed, and whose marriage collapsed—works in Blunkett's office.

Among Blunkett's best friends is Paul Dacre, the editor of the *Daily Mail*. (As a point about the sexual environment in the British workplace, Dacre's editorial meetings are known as the Vagina Monologues because of his cascade of sexual slurs; you acquire some kind of special status if you've been "double-cunted" by Dacre—that is, called a cunt twice in the same sentence.)

On the other hand, the *Daily Telegraph* and the *Sunday Telegraph* are sister publications of the *Spectator*. Dominic Lawson, the *Sunday Telegraph* editor, was the *Spectator*'s former editor (as was his father, Nigel). And there is the *Spectator* itself, which has been closely narrating this whole affair. And then there's Condé Nast, home of *Tatler*, *GQ*, and *Vogue*, with its own superb media connections.

If everyone in British media is a partisan, with a vested interest in the stories of whomever they have a vested interest in, everyone is also a wicked gossip—competitive and wicked. This is, for perhaps everybody but Blunkett and the Quinns, a vast entertainment. "It really sells papers," says the *Mail*'s Peter McKay.

But back to the sex. Most sex scandals are about something larger than sex, but this one, really, is mostly about sex. It is not just that Kimberly seems to have had masses of it, but everybody in England—where Camilla Parker Bowles is often described as bawdy—seems to have an uncanny amount.

Of course they are drunk. Which explains not only why there's so much of it, but why people who seem so unattractive have so much of it—indeed it helps explain why they are unattractive. (It may be that no one in New York has had a lunchtime tryst since the martini went out.)

Then, too, there is, it seems, some special British category of sex: the shag or the bonk. Both are words invented by the British tabloids to imply sex when you can't legally exactly imply sex, creating a level of less-than-actual-sex sex. A kind of sex that, at least when inebriated, is not at all earnest or perilous or fraught or negotiated—hence, perhaps, the lack of birth control—where the stakes are, theoretically, low level or meaningless. Plus, you generally have it within your own class anyway, so what the hell.

What's more, British men, especially older British men, men of a certain class, men who, as a matter of principle and temperament, don't take anything too very seriously (Boris has elevated exactly this to a high art) are always making passes—it's almost the chivalrous thing to do. Quite a few may have been shocked to have Kimberly, the closer, accept.

In the Profumo affair, John Profumo, the minister of war, discovered to have had an affair with a sometimes call girl who was also having an affair with a Soviet diplomat, was cast out of government and forever disgraced; Stephen Ward, another protagonist in the scandal, killed himself.

The Sextator affair, on the other hand, may end without anyone, beyond the heartbreak, being too worse for wear.

While rumors have circulated that Blunkett has had a breakdown—"he's in a nut house in Bristol," I was told with the greatest authority—the truth is that he continues to occupy the home secretary's residence and is out campaigning for Labour candidates while he fights his paternity battle. (This scandal may be remembered as the first one in which the man has tried to establish, rather than run from, paternity.) If Labour is given a majority, as is expected, on May 5, most everyone believes Blunkett will be back in the cabinet.

Likewise, Boris, who is trying to salvage his marriage—for a period he was banned from his home in Islington—and is certainly playing the part of the doghouse husband (he continues to strenuously argue that "sex is something you should be able to lie about"), will likely get back in the Tory leadership. His MP seat is a safe one and he is the Tory's big name and big fundraiser. His personal failings and mishaps seem only to further endear him to the Tory faithful. And he's only forty. Petronella Wyatt, on the other hand, has had her column dropped from the *Spectator*.

Kimberly, on maternity leave, is behind the closed doors of the extra-wide, multimillion-pound-sterling town house off Park Lane in Mayfair ("more fittingly the home of a currency speculator from Dubai," said one eager gossiper I know), which she got in the settlement of her marriage to Michael Fortier. Her baby, named Lorcan—an Irish name because Stephen Quinn, who named himself the father on the birth certificate, is Irish—was born on February 2. The picture offered by friends of Kimberly is of a transformed woman—somebody who has accepted her transgressions, someone who is facing up to her fantasy world—someone whose silence (and indeed, she has said nothing since the scandal began) attests to her willingness to bear the burden of opprobrium, even to give up her presence in the spotlight (although, of course, she has never been so much in the spotlight), and to accept exile from the chattering class. But she is, too, not just sinner but victim—and David Blunkett is her nemesis, her pursuer. And Stephen Quinn is her protector.

Indeed, Quinn lashes out in fury at Blunkett again on March 5. Blunkett makes an announcement that Quinn says, with some strained logic, is none of Blunkett's business and yet another invasion of the Quinns' privacy: a DNA test has revealed that the baby, Lorcan, is not—once more to the surprise of Quinn, who'd told friends he'd been using birth control when the child was conceived—Blunkett's.

So . . . ?

The father, according to the tabloids—according to a leak provided most likely by Blunkett—is one M. J. Akbar, the head of the Asian Age newspaper group.

Meanwhile, Quinn is maintaining his bid for sainthood, saying, "I will not draw a distinction between biological and non-biological . . ."

So not impossibly, she'll pull it off—holding together marriage and family (no matter whose family). Because she continues to be a great salesperson, selling both contrition and victimhood and perhaps a sense of the great unrealness and unfairness of all this ("the press coverage here has echoes of *The Crucible*," says Quinn), or because Quinn is actually . . . in love with her.

Ironically, the thing that may be most at risk because of the scandal is the *Spectator* itself.

Along with the *Telegraph* newspapers, the magazine has been sold to the Barclay twins, mysterious brothers in the James Bond villain role, who own the Ritz in London and live together in a $100 million Gothic-style castle in the Channel Islands, who, beyond an appetite for media properties, appear not to want any attention at all—at least not the kind of attention the *Spectator* is providing. The Barclays have put Andrew Neil, a Fleet Street swashbuckler, in charge of the *Spectator*. Neil (his *Private Eye* name is Brillo, for his hair transplants), a working-class Scotsman, is in many ways an anti-*Spectator* figure. He famously rails against the snobocracy—of which the *Spectator* is ground zero. He is also himself a dedicated spotlight-hogger (after running the London *Times* for Murdoch he becomes a television presenter), and the scandal has made the *Spectator* the hottest media property in London—you can't have a better spotlight perch. Neil has outlined a plan to raise circulation and extend "the franchise"—and has told friends he doubts if Boris or Kimberly is up to this job of, in Liddle's description, "'penetrating' a 'new market.'"

Oh yes, and when I had dinner recently with Rod Liddle and Alicia Monckton, the receptionist, who is as lovely as everyone says, I noticed that as Rod and I were drinking without limit, the comely Alicia was having none of it.

"My word . . . you're pregnant, too," I said.

The couple beamed and said I was the first in the media to know.

Monster

The Last Days of
Jeffrey Epstein

OCTOBER 2020

1.

On a morning in early 2019, with spring in the air, traffic was stalled on both Fifth Avenue and Madison Avenue by half a dozen police cars idling near the Frick Museum and, across the street, the mansion home of Jeffrey Epstein.

"Did you figure out what happened, was there a bomb? Did you get caught?" Reid Weingarten, one of Epstein's lawyers, asked Ehud Barak, the former Israeli general and prime minister as he arrived at the house. Standing in the triple-high foyer of Epstein's massive home, Barak handed his coat to one of the familiar, cheerful young women in the house—ever a surprise that, considering the ongoing legal and public fury against the convicted sex offender, Epstein continued his way of life undaunted.

"I just assumed they were taking Jeffrey away," said Barak, in his heavy accent, making the obvious joke, his eyebrows rising above his glasses. "But he is still here, so? We have nothing to worry about. The secrets are safe."

"Would you like an omelet?" a houseman asked the former prime minister.

"Ehud! E-HUD!" called out Epstein, circling down the grand staircase in his sweatsuit loungewear and Palm Beach slippers. Barak was a small man, and, as Epstein often reminded him, "cuddly," but Epstein credited the former Israeli general, one of his important confidants, with special tough-guy powers. Epstein, a germaphobe, knocked elbows with his guest.

"No. No omelet. No eggs. No cheese," said Barak.

"You can have any kind," encouraged the host, shepherding his guests into the dining room, where Epstein, quite like a talk show personality, spent most of his day at the head of the table. On the menu was almost anything you might want served at any time—a random feast.

"Thank you. I have had so many omelets here. Your kindness is measured in omelets. Salmon," he said to the houseman. "A little bit. With bread. And butter. Why not? And tea. Black tea. Very strong. And do you have a little bit of that caviar? One spoonful?"

"The caviar, the good stuff," Epstein directed his houseman. "We keep it only for you," he said to Barak. "To me it's disgusting."

"Each to his own," replied gnomic Barak, shrugging, and comfortably settling in at the table, large enough to seat twenty-five.

Weingarten, who had already been here for several hours participating in a conference call with various other Epstein lawyers, was taking a dim view of Barak's nonchalance. In Epstein's house, with its men's club bonhomie, and its thorough shutting out of the humdrum world, the seventy-seven-year-old Barak seemed ready to enjoy a few hours of relaxation. The former Labor prime minister—now, once again, contemplating a run against his longtime adversary Bibi Netanyahu—was a frequent guest, almost a fixture, and loved expounding on world issues and sharing and seeking intelligence from whoever else might be at Epstein's table. Weingarten, however, was seeking to apply some urgency today to the discussion of his friend and client's predicament. This was an official summit of sorts, meant to address Epstein's ever-mounting legal and media onslaught.

But that could be difficult. For Epstein himself this was just one more review of the legal quagmire that had engulfed him since 2004, sending him to prison on a prostitution charge in 2007 for thirteen months, spawning a cottage industry in the South Florida legal community of settlements and ongoing lawsuits, and continuing now as an epic crime-and-punishment tale. "A chronic illness," Epstein believed, "it can't be cured, but it won't kill me." Epstein's response to the storm outside was just to distance himself further from it. He seldom left his home (other than to go to another of his homes); everybody came to him.

Today's meeting wasn't all that different from any other day at his Xanadu-vast bachelor's quarters on East Seventy-First Street. Every day was a revolving door of friends, acquaintances, experts, visiting international dignitaries and despots, petitioners for contributions and investments, lawyers, and other holders of vast fortunes—a network of worldly influence and interest arguably as great as any in New York—who sat at Epstein's dining-conference table, engaged in something that was part seminar, part gossip fest, part coffee klatch, part elite conspiracy.

Said Barak, seizing the conversation, "What I want to know from you all-knowing people is: Who is in charge, who is," he said, putting on an American accent over his own often impenetrable Israeli one, "calling the shots?" This was a resumption of the reliable conversation around Epstein: the ludicrousness and vagaries of Donald Trump—once among Epstein's closest friends. "Here is the question every government is asking. Trump is obviously not in charge because he is—"

"A moron," supplied Epstein about his old friend Trump. For nearly two decades Trump and Epstein had been playboy brothers in New York and Palm Beach, until, in 2004, they had quarreled about a real estate deal. "At the moment, Bill Barr is in charge," said Epstein. Barr, the new attorney general, was overseeing the Mueller report, which was shortly to be issued and to which Trump's fate seemed immediately tied. Epstein spoke, in distinct Brooklyn twang, with merriment and confidence, a dedicated ebullience—which, together with infinite and tolerant amusement of the fallibilities of the people he knew, was his outward character note. The public grilling that would shortly ensue about how any decent person could come to Epstein's house had a simple answer: for the pleasure of it. The welcome. The ease. For a few hours outside the ordinary.

"It's Donald's pattern," said Epstein, ever the explainer of his old playboy buddy, "he lets someone else be in charge, until other people realize that someone, other than him, is in charge. When that happens, you're no longer in charge."

"A certain management approach," said Barak. "But let me ask you, why do you think this Barr took this job, knowing all this?"

"The motivation was simple: money," said Epstein.

"I'm shocked," said Weingarten.

"Barr believes he'll get a big payday out of this," said Epstein. "If he keeps Donald in office, manages to hold the Justice Department together, and help the Republican Party survive Donald, he thinks this is worth big money to him. I speak from direct knowledge. Extremely direct. Trust me."

"Always describe your direct knowledge as indirect," said Barak, with his salmon and caviar now in front of him.

"I have impeccable indirect knowledge," said Epstein.

"How do you say 'Fuck you' on Wall Street?" said Barak, less concerned by his non sequitur than with his punch line: ". . . 'trust me.'"

"I thought that's how you say it in Israel," said Epstein, now dialing the phone. "Steve has a cold and stayed in D.C.," Epstein explained about Steve Bannon, who had been expected.

Bannon was a new friend. They had been introduced in December 2017.

"You were the only person I was afraid of during the campaign," said Bannon, laughing, when they met, meaning he believed Epstein knew dangerous secrets about Trump.

"As well you should have been," replied Epstein.

Since then the two men—partly out of a shared incredulity about Donald Trump—had deeply bonded, ever reviewing the day's events together. Or competing with each other to predict tomorrow's news. Bannon was often astonished by what Epstein knew.

"Steve, Ehud and Reid are here."

"Gents—"

"Steve," said Barak, "how do you say 'Fuck you' on Wall Street?"

"'Trust me.' The same way you say it in Israel."

"Hmm."

"That's my boy," said Epstein.

"Hmm," said Ehud, who had once overseen Israel's vaunted intelligence operation, eyeing the room for cameras.

"Ehud, sometimes everybody just knows the answers," said Epstein.

"Humph."

"Reid," said Epstein, suddenly, and reluctantly, businesslike, "can you give an overview?"

Weingarten was among a small circle of the most sought-after criminal defense lawyers in the country. But, if there yet existed a showman-style trial lawyer in the model of F. Lee Bailey, Johnnie Cochran, Gerry Spence, and Melvin Belli—"flamboyant" was once the term of art—Weingarten wasn't one. After two generations of law-and-order politics, and the government's conviction rate at well over 90 percent, Weingarten carried a heavy weight for his clients, his eyes thick and deep, his shoulders sagging. It was a protective fatalism.

"Yeah." He put his hand on the table. Then he took a deep breath, running his other hand back through his hair. "Okay. The situation is bad. Bad. Heart attack bad. I think it's the fight of your life."

"But how bad is it, really?" said Epstein.

However existential, it was hard to square the stakes with the circumstances here in one of the most sumptuous residences in Manhattan, with its procession of the best lawyers and most powerful and influential men in the land. Since his release from his jail sentence in 2009, Epstein had rehabilitated his life, not least of all by putting it into a bubble. He lived inside this house, almost never leaving it except to travel by private plane to his archipelago of other luxe residences in Paris, Palm Beach, and on several personal Caribbean islands and a vast ranch in New Mexico. He did not interact, except through lawyers, with the outer world. And he had so many lawyers that their reports were often an indistinct babble. That world might hate him with unrelieved ferocity. But here, at home, in his many homes, his life was wholly charmed.

"I think," said Weingarten, trying to stay on point—digression was the meal most frequently served at Epstein's table—"it's in five different pieces. There's a judge in Florida, Judge Marra, who is determined to hurt Jeffrey." The conversation today would go back and forth between including Epstein and talking about him, regardless of his presence, in the third person. "He has prosecutors around the world who might look to prosecute him again. I think there is a Hill piece here—the calls for his head from both sides of the aisle don't give us much cover. And then there's what's happening in civil court—hurtful things. And not least of all there is a public relations piece here. Every time I turn on the television and look for the Celtics score I see that my boy is a monster. Everybody's favorite monster. The devil. Pedophile. Sex trafficker. Keeping little girls in the basement. Trump friend—"

"That would be the worst," said Epstein.

"And there is no rejoinder. Ninety percent of what everyone is saying is horseshit. But there is no rejoinder. The *New York Times* has taken a sex scandal, the fact that Jeffrey has whatever tastes he has, and made it into a human rights tragedy—I am not a naïf, but I have never seen . . ."

In absolute juxtaposition to the view in the outside world, the view among Epstein's wide circle of loyal, devoted, and largely unquestioning friends was that Epstein was guilty only of venial sins, that he had more than paid for them with his plea to a prostitution charge in 2008, serving thirteen months in a Palm Beach jail, and that ever since, and with increasing zeal, he was being pursued by plaintiffs and their lawyers, all with a clear financial interest, and a media that, feeding off unchallenged and self-serving allegations, had found a handy personification of evil.

True, no one knew what had happened in his massage rooms between Epstein and the scores or even hundreds of young women. But the Epstein they know, however compartmentalized—no one could be sure they knew the Epstein someone else knew—was at incomprehensible odds with the media portrait and the testimony of young women, all seeking financial settlements, and none ever subject to cross-examination.

It was, for these power players, a power play. The cultural turn had given women, particularly young women, vast new media power. This then was being leveraged by other forces. David Boies, the nation's most prominent litigator—and, in the legal and business community, quite among the most unpopular—had represented both the country's most famous abuser, Harvey Weinstein, and Silicon's Valley most famous fraudster, Theranos CEO Elizabeth Holmes. Now, in some through-the-looking-glass reversal and effort at his own self-repair, he had aligned himself both with #MeToo politics and with a brigade of Florida contingency lawyers to represent Epstein victims. Epstein's lawyers believed that Boies, a famous influence peddler, had become a significant voice urging the Justice Department to reopen the Epstein case—a lever to use in his settlement efforts. Then, too, Epstein's circle saw their friend as a Trump proxy. Through Epstein—regardless of his own antipathy for the president—anti-Trump partisans and media had damaged Trump labor secretary Alexander Acosta, who, a decade before as a federal prosecutor, had handled the Epstein plea deal. Indeed, the federal investigation of Epstein that began in 2004 had, Epstein-ers theorized, been part of a Republican effort to ensnare Bill Clinton, to whom Epstein had, indiscreetly, linked his name and supplied his plane. Epstein then had been a Clinton proxy.

Epstein's powerful circle saw him, an astute student of power and a collector of powerful friends, as, somehow, particularly unsuited to this power game. Too much the free spirit, too much the helpless bad boy, too heedless to properly protect himself. And they saw the outside world as a place increasingly hostile not just to Epstein, the easy fall guy, but to themselves as well.

Weingarten had met Epstein not long after his first conviction. The terms of Epstein's 2008 deal with the federal government—now regarded by many as outrageously lenient—were, to Weingarten, outside any legal bargain that he had ever seen before. Among the terms: Epstein's plea required him to pay the legal fees of those the government named as his victims, and not to contest their claims, nor to contest the bona fides of the victims themselves. Hence, the pile-on, which had cost Epstein tens of millions in settlements and created a clear financial reason for the continuing pursuit.

"Here is a man absent any—forget sympathy, forget skepticism, forget presumption of innocence—absent any humanity."

"Yeah, we get it," said Epstein. "Hitler."

"Literally, it goes on, day after day, with no effort on anyone's part, and not on our part, either, to look at the record, to question anybody's motivations—"

"So where is the comms piece in this?" asked Bannon over the phone. "Who is handling it? Who's on point? Are these your people, Reid?"

"Well—okay—in fact there really hasn't been anything in place because largely the view has been let's not call more attention to this or antagonize the judges this has been before, and not wanting to be seen attacking the victims, and so we haven't—"

"Let me get this straight," said Bannon. "I think I understand this, but it strains credulity—there's nothing in place? There hasn't been anything in place? No communications team? What was the response from Jeffrey's side to the Florida story? Who engaged?"

In November 2018, the *Miami Herald* had published a multipart story recounting the earlier charges against Epstein, with further, devastating accounts from the victims, and directly impugning Acosta's motivations in the plea deal. If every successive story about Epstein over the years had once more revived what might seem to have been a fading issue, in the new climate, and now directly tying figures in the Trump administration to Epstein, the *Miami Herald* story gave it rocket boosters.

"We didn't engage," said Epstein.

"Did we even know about it?" asked Weingarten.

"No. Roy Black's office may have gotten a call, but we didn't respond," said Epstein. Black was another world-class criminal attorney who had been among the dream team that Epstein had assembled in his first case—a team whose warring egos Weingarten believed had a lot to do with the case's peculiar and ever-unresolved outcome.

"I'm part of the problem here, I have to say." Weingarten pulled on his face. "We just have felt, and maybe this was wrong—okay, wrong—that any effort to defend Jeffrey publicly stirs the pot and makes it more likely than not that people are going to come out of the woodwork."

"This is crazy," said Bannon.

"Well, yeah. True, it's ninety percent bullshit, everything out there. But the problem is with what isn't bullshit—people choke and I choke a little, too. He"—Epstein, at the head of the table, listened with detached interest—"leads the league in number of acts of prostitution." In some accounts, Epstein had had as many as three girls a day come to his Palm Beach home to give him a topless massage with happy ending—going price $200. "Okay, fine. But in the history of man, prostitution has either been not a criminal act or a misdemeanor—even if it's a thousand times."

"Prostitution it seems is no longer called prostitution," said Barak. "It is something else. Much worse." Indeed, the crime had shifted. Where the case was about Epstein soliciting, that is paying, girls, some underage, for sexual acts, now it was about Epstein using his wealth to exploit vulnerable children.

"We are on the absolute other side of every cultural issue that has currency right now," said Weingarten.

"Reid and Steve, what kind of cover do we get from Kraft?" asked Epstein.

A month before, New England Patriots owner and Trump friend and supporter Robert Kraft had been arrested in a Palm Beach massage parlor. Behind the scenes, in another chance power nexus, Epstein had been advising Kraft, as had, Epstein knew, Trump himself.

"Bob gets dinner out, I get take-in," said Epstein with the flippancy that often exasperated the people trying to help defend him. "But otherwise there is no difference. I think there's an opportunity to use Kraft as a way to talk about what prostitution is—that it is what it is."

"You have the obvious point," said Weingarten, "that the Kraft girls are prostitutes because they are Korean and take $200. Which is apparently different when you're white and take $200 from Jeffrey Epstein, then you're innocent and vulnerable. What I've always thought—and maybe this is just insane—that somebody who isn't crazy, who writes for the *Atlantic* or the *New Yorker* . . . I mean wouldn't they give their whatever to sit down with him. Some intelligent person has got to be able to understand this . . ."

The traditional legal might that Epstein had assembled—more than seventy-five lawyers had circled through the team over the last ten years—seemed perpetually befuddled by how to deal with a righteous and weaponized media.

"Is there a friendly journalist?" asked Barak, seeming to imply that one might somewhere be found on the payroll.

"Nobody can do it. Nobody is going to be permitted to write this story now. A judicious look at Jeffrey Epstein is not publishable," said Bannon, who seemed deeply impatient with the naïveté of the group.

"To me," said Barak, "I believe that every raising of your profile in the public arena works against you and not for you. So you have to do the minimum necessary to protect you and not the maximum that could be done to expose you." With some sideline irony, Epstein was otherwise concerned that Barak's move into the Israeli prime minister's race might expose their friendship and, as well, the financial support that Epstein had been providing the former prime minister.

"He probably can't be hated any more," said Bannon. "We've flatlined on this. He can't get deader. While the chances of reviving him are remote, what's the alternative?"

"Okay, so what about something like *60 Minutes* or *Gayle King*?" said Weingarten.

"Worked very well for R. Kelly," said Bannon, about King's recent interview with the singer accused of sex abuse—a disaster for Kelly.

"I would have said no way, but now . . . Jeffrey just going. Laying everything out. It would be tough but—just to humanize him," Weingarten continued.

"Would you want to do that?" asked a skeptical Barak of Epstein, seeming to suggest that humanizing was a kind of weakness.

"I don't want to do it. But I would."

"It would take a month of hard work to get ready," said Weingarten.

"A year," said Bannon.

"What if we started with surrogates?" asked Epstein, brightly.

"What is that?" asked Barak.

"Advocates who speak for you. Would *60 Minutes* take a surrogate?" asked Weingarten.

"Would *60 Minutes* take a surrogate? Dude, come on," said Bannon, with disbelief.

"Well, Rachel Maddow, then," said Weingarten, grasping.

"Okay," said Bannon. "You're the Jeffrey surrogate sitting with Rachel Maddow and she's going to say how many girls were there, were there ten, were there a hundred, a thousand. Now you're on national television, what do you say? 'I'm confident it's less than a thousand.' Was it?" said Bannon, turning to Epstein.

"Yes, less."

"Actually, *here* is the first question," said Bannon. "What's the age of the youngest girl?"

"That would be good," said Epstein, "because the answer to that question is that there was one girl who was fourteen years old and she told the police she lied about her age. She told everyone she was eighteen because she was afraid she would never be allowed into the house and never be invited back. That's the only one."

"That's the only one who is under the age of eighteen?"

"No, the youngest one . . ."

Bannon snorted loudly over the phone. "All right, okay. So get to the issue, bang. He's been branded a pedophile—while in fact these are not underage or barely underage. I'd rather have that discussion about what is a pedophile than for people just to assume he is one. To the extent that anybody was underage, it was slightly underage and they lied about it. None of them were acting under duress—there were no drugs, no coercion. And there was no trafficking—you were a consumer of sexual services and not a provider. Does the fourteen-year-old look close to eighteen or to fourteen?"

"Twenty-seven," said Epstein.

"Really?"

"These girls, including the fourteen-year-old, worked in strip clubs, massage parlors, they had tattoos. Tattoos and piercings—which, in Florida, require you to be eighteen."

"That's helpful. But you're besmirching the victims. The line here is between having to respect the victims and having to show that they are bat-shit crazy or coldly in it for the money. Question: Are there any of these girls, girls who were over eighteen at the time, who would be willing to come forward and defend you . . . to give context, reasonable context, to what happened?"

"That could be a good idea," said Weingarten. "I'm betting that for a lot of these girls the best thing they did in their day was to visit Jeffrey—compared to what they were doing in their miserable lives . . . but you can't actually say that . . ."

"No, please," said Bannon.

The divide between the sixty-six-year-old Epstein's largely over-sixty pals, lawyers, and uber-connections, and the new language of cultural equipoise and class and race sensitivity, grew, as if by the hour, ever vaster. The right-wing Steve Bannon was, in Epstein's house, the voice of cultural understanding.

"In fact, let me take it the other way," said a concerned Bannon. "How comfortable are we, how confident that there isn't a new girl out there who could come forward and be an incredible victim? Just asking. We're good here? You're absolutely confident? A credible girl won't show up? That's the kill shot if she does."

"I'm not worried about new girls coming forward, I'm worried about fake girls. It's the fake ones who know how to construct these stories, that you had to tell your roommate, that you need celebrity names."

From a media point of view, Epstein's most damaging accuser was Virginia Roberts, a former Mar-a-Lago locker-room attendant, who had in the *Daily Mail* and in subsequent depositions described herself as a sex slave during her multiyear employment by Epstein, a sex slave made available to Epstein's friends, the likes of Alan Dershowitz and Britain's Prince Andrew. Both men had categorically and aggressively denied these allegations. The otherwise ever-unconcerned Epstein could not control his exasperation as he frequently recited the provable falsehoods of Roberts's story—including the presence of Al and Tipper Gore, whom Epstein claimed never to have met, on his plane.

"What about a woman surrogate—a woman who can make the case?" asked Epstein. It could sometimes seem as though Epstein's inside world was just rising from a deep cultural slumber. "A serious woman."

One of Epstein's close friends was a woman and a lawyer with a significant profile—but he was trying to protect her from public exposure to him.

The discussion again seemed to drift off in the ethereal bubble of Epstein's house, far, far removed from the present reality—aristocrats in the French Revolution—with the assumption that there were, somehow, somewhere, surrogates and public supporters available to him. Indeed, the long list of Epstein's male lawyers had quickly dwindled to a rare few who might now publicly make his case.

Several other high-profile women litigators were named as potential hires, most discounted as unlikely, even for a big pay day, to step forward, and one, who might have done it, for being a drunk.

"What litigator isn't?" said Barak.

"Well, I'm not," said Weingarten. "I smoke a lot of pot. But I'm not a drunk."

"Good," said Barak. "I'm thinking about investing in a cannabis company."

"I'll invest with you," said Weingarten.

"Put all your money in it," said an enthusiastic Epstein. "It's the best thing to do. It's going to be wild. It hasn't even begun yet. This is the beginning. There's every different layer of things. There's production. Distribution. Regulation."

"It goes everywhere. Into beverages, even into dog food," said Barak.

"Dog food is gigantic . . . calms your dog down," said Epstein. "But the science here is significant, too. Because pot is being genetically modified to deliver this variety of responses."

"Never inhaled, never exhaled. Never haled," said Barak.

"My two favorite investments," said Epstein, pleased to turn from his legal troubles, "are cannabis and also new augmented reality. This is spookier than anything I've ever seen. You can now take a photograph and turn it into a 3D shape, and then put in some artificial intelligence so it can have a conversation . . . so where does this lead . . . you put on your glasses and see your father and mother sitting there shimmering . . . and ask your father a question and he responds it's time for you to be serious about life . . . you want to talk to the dead . . . here you are . . ."

"Guys," called Bannon. "If you're down this road, I'm going to sign off."

"Hold on," said Epstein. "What about *60 Minutes*?"

"What about *60 Minutes*?"

"If it's going to take a year to prepare, we better get started."

It was hard to tell if Epstein might truly be focusing on the precariousness of his situation or if he just liked to spend time with Bannon.

"You want to start? You want to go on camera?"

"I don't know. I've never been on camera before."

"If you're game, dude. Maybe you'll be great. Could be a game changer."

"I could be the new Trump. Let's see how much of a genius you really are."

2.

Two weeks later, as Bannon's video crew was setting up in Epstein's baronial study—more than forty feet long with double-high ceilings—Bannon found himself arguing with another of Epstein's lawyers.

"Really, tell me, are you crazy?" asked the incredulous lawyer. "We can't have him recorded."

"Nobody knows that we're recording him. He doesn't actually know. We may not be. If he's asked, he can say he doesn't know."

"You think that's a good answer?"

"I think it's the best bad answer that I have."

"What the *fuck* are you talking about?"

"What the fuck am I talking about? You know where we are. Metastasizing. We all know this. This is life support. We may not have more than one shot to slow this down. I have no idea if we can. But at any point he might find himself in front of a camera. This is just the most basic media training we can offer."

And yet, again, the imperturbability of Epstein's house, and the authority of the people around him, and the silent staff with its 24/7 menu, dulled even the intellectual appreciation of his peril. If Epstein was up against it, it yet seemed that he had time and opportunity to tweak a way out—and that finding a way would be an amusing brain tease for all those helping him.

"I'm not opposed to media training, I just don't want a videotape out there."

"He's got to sit there and watch the tape all the time, that's how you learn. This is like preparing for a deposition, except this is preparing for the court of public opinion."

"That's my point, he never had to prepare for a deposition because he just takes the fifth. Now you're setting him up to answer questions he can't answer. And, certainly, if he answers them they're not going to rehabilitate him. 'She was only sixteen, but full of tattoos. So sixteen, but not like a good person who's sixteen.'"

"Really," continued Bannon, "there has got to be a way to answer that in an acceptable way. I don't know what the answer is, but you have got to figure out the basic positioning—which should have been done fifteen years ago. We're trying to show remorse or whatever we're trying to show. However we get there, we've got to get this to the point on *Gayle King* so that the big reveal is that he's not a monster . . . he's human, ashamed, mortified . . ."

Epstein rolled his eyes and made the gesture of the noose above his head.

"You see," said Bannon, rolling his eyes, too, "media training. Emergency media training."

"Who's going to play me on *Saturday Night Live*?" asked Epstein.

"There's a process here of getting him on camera and of having him study it like you study NFL films—like Tom Brady."

"And you think he can actually do this, even studying?"

"I'm here by the way guys . . . grandpa's up in the attic . . . he's still here . . ." said a shrugging Epstein.

"Do you really think he can do this?"

"It's beyond that. He has to do it. He has to bare his chest—"

"Not sure you want that." The lawyer laughed.

"He has to show the world he's not a monster—that's a process. Listen, we weren't going to do tough stuff today anyway. This is easy, background stuff, his story, who he is, background questions. Nothing incriminating."

"No girls? No case? No sex?"

"No girls. No case. No sex."

"I mean it."

"We can talk about Steve's sex life," said Epstein.

"That would be quick," said Bannon.

"I have no problem with that," said the lawyer.

* * *

"Is that light necessary, right in my face," said Epstein, sitting in the simple straight-backed chair that had been exchanged for the throne affair that Epstein had favored. The ground rules were that they would go straight through without stopping, with a remorseless Bannon hitting as hard as he could.

"Interrogation lights," said Bannon. "And, by the way, count on it, you will be fucked with. I was on *Anderson Cooper* the other night. It was pitch-black. I was standing outside. I couldn't even see the camera. If you're not looking directly in the camera in one of these shots, you look like a retard. I'm saying where's the camera and they wouldn't even tell me. That's pay dirt for them, the retard look. They'll fuck with you in a second. Do you have to wear your glasses? I think you look better without your glasses."

"I think he looks more intellectual with them," said the camera guy. "Disarming."

"I think he looks more like a dirty old man."

"Ready . . ."

"Okay. This is game time. You're Tom Brady. All you're going to do is watch yourself and just get better."

* * *

SB: Jeffrey, thanks for joining us here . . . um . . . what is a hedge fund manager?

JE: Are you asking me this question because you think I'm a hedge fund manager? I'd much rather be called a pedophile than a hedge fund manager.

SB: You've never been a hedge fund manager?

JE: Never.

SB: You've been called the international man of mystery, the talented Mr.

Epstein . . . but nobody can put their finger on how you actually make a living. How do you make a living?

JE: I give people advice on what to do with their money.

SB: Who are your clients?

JE: I don't talk about my clients.

SB: I assume extremely wealthy individuals? When you say you give them advice? On investments? On—"

JE: Taxes. Security. Philanthropy. Estate planning.

SB: So . . . everything. Yacht buying?

JE: At the level of wealth we're talking about, yachts are usually built to specifications. But let me explain. At a certain level of wealth, probably above $200 million, but let's say above $1 billion, you are going to encounter a range of issues never before encountered by human beings. In short, you can't spend your money, you can't give it to your children, you can't give it to charity. Instead of money solving all manner of problems, it creates all manner of problems.

SB: Hmmm. You realize how that sounds. Do you work for Third World dictators? Do you know where this money that you manage comes from? Was it taken by corrupt means or worse?

JE: The scale of money that I'm dealing with is usually such that—

SB: You have clients in sub-Saharan Africa—

JE: I have clients in varied parts of the world.

SB: The Persian Gulf? Do you represent the Gulf Emirates? The Saudis? The Qataris? Everybody? Emirs? Sheikhs? Princes? The particular prince that took the reporter, the columnist from the *Washington Post*, Khashoggi, and butchered him, you represent people like that?

JE: I don't discuss my clients.

SB You're laughing. Do you think it's funny what happened to Khashoggi?

JE: It's horrible. But I'm not political.

SB: Is that why dictators and despots come to you, because you're not political? Because you'll look the other way? Actually, why do they come to you? Again, it is the big question. Who are you? Where do you come from? Why would people trust you? You don't even have a college degree. Somehow, you've been able to accomplish things in life without seeming to need to do the things everyone has to do. You don't have a college degree but you were a teacher of math and physics at one of the top private schools in the country. So how did someone with no college degree end up becoming a teacher in an elite private school, and how did a high school math teacher end up as a top money manager? All before you were twenty-five.

JE: In part I was lucky.

SB: Lucky? Many people say you were in the right place at the right time because you went out of the way to put yourself there, that you have insinuated yourself by exploiting social—

JE: I don't socialize.

SB: No? Everything I read says there's a nonstop flying orgy wherever you go.

JE: I really don't socialize.

SB: You hanging out with guys like Clinton, Trump, Ron Burkle, Prince Andrew, at all the top nightclubs in the world, with all these beautiful women—all this is because you don't socialize? I'm not supposed to believe my lying eyes?

JE: What you read is in fact inaccurate.

SB: A thousand pictures of you at the hottest nightspots? With the most beautiful women, with the most powerful people of the moment.

JE: One picture, not showing what you think it shows, reprinted a thousand times. You should not believe them.

SB: I should not believe them?

JE: They do not exist.

SB: They don't exist?

JE: I know there is an echo in this room, but they do not exist.

SB: So you're saying—

JE: I don't party. I have never partied. I had a Yom Kippur dinner here twelve years ago. And three science conferences.

SB: So all those stories are false?

JE: Yes.

SB: If they were false, why didn't you say so? Ask for a correction?

JE: I don't respond to the tabloids.

SB: Why?

JE: It doesn't affect my life.

SB: It didn't affect your reputation as a money manager?

JE: No.

SB: At all?

JE: No.

SB: So clients weren't put off by someone who appeared to be a playboy?

JE: No.

SB: You're not a playboy?

JE: I am a playboy.

SB: How can you be a playboy and not be social?

JE: I didn't say I was a hermit. I don't go out. I meet people in different ways. I go to specialized professional gatherings—

SB: Is that a euphemism?

JE: —where I meet people who I find interesting. Or interesting people seek me out and come to my home.

SB: Are these men or women?

JE: Both. But if the question is do I like women, the answer is yes.

SB: How old were the girls you taught at the Dalton School? Middle school?

JE: No, seventeen or eighteen.

SB: Are you sure?

JE: I always asked to see IDs.

SB: Any problems at Dalton?

JE: Zero.

SB: You enjoy teaching math?

JE: Yes. Most people are afraid of mathematics. As most people are afraid of money. As most people are afraid of numbers. Girls more than boys.

SB: Girls are afraid of math? Young men were not afraid of math?

JE: This is not a revelation. If you go back and look at standardized tests, there is a dramatic discrepancy between male and female performance.

SB: Why is that?

JE: Fear, in part.

SB: So how did you dispel this fear?

JE: I made things friendly.

SB: You would focus on the females versus the males.

JE: Yes. To the extent that I had something more to give them.

SB: What?

JE: As I said, a friendlier view of the math world.

SB: You understand how that might sound creepy.

JE: That I don't know. It doesn't sound creepy to me now, and I don't think it seemed creepy to anyone then. I also tutored young Black men. I volunteered for an organization that did this.

SB: Why?

JE: Because I thought they had many of the same issues. They were handicapped in their abilities to deal with math.

SB: Genetically?

JE: Educationally.

SB: Is there a relationship?

JE: Between genetics and education? That's complicated.

SB: But you think there is a connection.

JE: Yes. There are many different variables that affect how we learn.

SB: Because of their lower intelligence, are you saying?

JE: I didn't say lower. I said different.

SB: They can play basketball, but they can't do math.

JE: No, they can do great mathematics, they just have to be playing basketball at the same time. Seriously, when Blacks learn . . . one of the nice things about basketball is that they are moving around. Blacks learn really well when they are moving around. And in American schools you tell Blacks to sit in their chairs.

SB: Seriously? *Seriously*? Okay . . . overnight you go from teaching girls high school math to a partner in one of the leading houses on Wall Street. You do understand that this is difficult to understand, no less believe? You were the youngest partner in Bear Stearns history, yes?

JE: Yes.

SB: The youngest partner in history of the firm, and, correct me if I'm wrong, most of the other partners are from Ivy League backgrounds, many with advance finance and business degrees?

JE: Yes.

SB: How does this work?

JE: In the same way that people picked stocks on the basis of reputation, investment banks hired on the basis of reputation, what schools you went to, who you knew. But in the same way that shifted for buying stocks as a function of numbers, hiring changed to focus on people who understood numbers. I met a parent at Dalton who knew that I was or had heard that I was a talented math person and he asked if I had ever thought about working on Wall Street.

SB: A girl student or boy student?

JE: Girl.

SB: A seventeen-year-old coed was moved enough by you to tell her parents about what a math genius you were?

JE: In some manner, yes.

SB: So what did the girl's father do for you?

JE: He said he had a friend who worked on Wall Street and would I like to go see him.

SB: And?

JE: And this person called me and this turned out to be the senior partner at Bear Stearns.

SB: Is that—?

JE: Ace Greenberg, yes.

SB: So one of the most famous people on Wall Street takes it upon himself to call up a high school math teacher?

JE: Yes. Because I was a math teacher. At that moment in time, recognizing that even though Wall Street was about money, it wasn't, up until then, about math, certainly not complicated math. Simple arithmetic would have been adequate for a superior Wall Street career. But now this suddenly changed. The new Wall Street wasn't going to be about relationships with clients, or blue-chip companies, or who you knew in the social world, it was just going to be about your ability to see numbers in a three-dimensional sense.

SB: So how does a guy who comes walking out of an uptown private school into a Wall Street trading floor get people to trust him enough to do millions of dollars in transactions—

JE: Billions. Because Wall Street has always had a language, it used to be the Racket Club and the River Club and Fishers Island and now it was math, which is what I could speak.

SB: How did it feel to be suddenly making—how much did you make at Dalton?

JE: Eight thousand dollars a year.

SB: And now you're making six figures?

JE: More.

SB: Seven figures. How did that feel?

JE: In fact, money didn't interest me.

SB: Money didn't interest you? You have houses across the globe, jets, art, women? Money doesn't interest you?

JE: No.

SB: How can that possibly be? Your whole life is dedicated to the accumulation of wealth—and, I might add, the depravity that it affords. If it doesn't mean anything to you, why don't you give it away?

JE: Putting aside that I do give a lot of it away, you're conflating how I live with how I feel about money. I have no interest in money for money's sake, I am not here counting my money. I am in fact often using money in a counterproductive sense, not maximizing its value but limiting its value in the way I use it to give me the life I want to lead.

SB: Jets and parties and—

JE: As I said, I don't go to parties and jets are a means.

SB: A means?

JE: A means of getting more out of life, of shortening the time between what you're getting.

SB: Tell me, what does a mathematician see in Bill Clinton, Donald Trump, Mick Jagger, and—Princess Diana? You went out with Princess Diana?

JE: I escorted her on occasion.

SB: Are you like the math nerd that just wants to hang out with the cool guys? You're the captain of the math team who actually wants to hang out with the captain of the football team?

JE: Mathematics, higher mathematics, is about thinking differently. Often men and women who achieve some distinction are people who think differently. That's what I like.

SB: So you're saying money buys you a high caliber of friends?

JE: I'm saying money can be a currency of ideas.

SB: And babes?

JE: Of a conducive life, however you define it.

SB: Conducive to?

JE: Higher levels of thought and productivity.

CAMERAMAN: Need a break.

* * *

"Oh my god," said Bannon. "You've fallen into the worst trap you can fall into. You are actually answering the questions. You're thinking you're being funny or ironic, but everything that you think is wry and clever they are going to cut to make you look unfeeling, cruel, weird, grotesque. We'll cut this to show you how bad you can truly be made to look—"

Epstein exhaled heavily and for a moment, just for a moment, seemed to feel the weight of all this.

"You see that bird at the window"—a tawny little creature, whose head swiveled in some approximation of curiosity and interest—"that's the same bird that comes the first week of April every year. It's the craziest thing. This morning I heard the bird knocking, I thought right on time."

"NEVER, NEVER answer the question," said Bannon, running his hand through his hair. "They are going to come in here, they are going to shoot two or three hours of tape, and they are going to use six minutes. You're going on, blah blah blah, but they are going to be looking for those precise moments when you happen to say what most conforms to the view they have of you. They are not here to learn who you are, they are here to get you to illustrate who they think you are. And they do not think you are a prince."

"And African Americans, not Blacks," said the cameraman.

"But having said that," said Bannon, "you were good."

"Otherwise, Mrs. Lincoln," said Epstein, "how was the show?"

"Seriously—you're engaging, you're not threatening, you're natural, you're friendly, you don't look at all creepy, you're a sympathetic figure, and this is what seventy-five percent of the battle is, I'm totally impressed. We just have to cut the content down," said Bannon.

"Anything you say, anything, about African Americans and women they will use to discredit you," said the cameraman.

"Destroy you," said Bannon.

"You give me the rules, I can follow rules."

"Says the man who is here today precisely for not following the rules."

"I can follow the little rules."

"But what we know is that you're not a stiff, seventy-five percent of the battle, more maybe. Your answers suck, but we can identify ninety-five percent of the questions, so we can get this right."

"Give me twenty minutes," said Epstein. "What do you guys want, omelets, club sandwiches, Monte Cristo, sushi, shrimp cocktail, anything, I'll send somebody up . . ."

"Man," said Bannon to the cameraman, as Epstein left, "different script he's a star."

"Kind of amazing. Natural. Artless," said the cameraman.

"I almost think he could pull this off. You want to get to know him. Just the words that are a complete fucking disaster. The problem is, he's honest. And he wants to be honest. He wants people to understand who he really is. Every answer raises more questions."

"At the same time, it all sounds pretty fishy," said the cameraman.

"Come on, dude. This is a stinking fish." Bannon laughed heartily. "God, it's all such bullshit. Nothing makes any sense in this story. Which is what makes it so fucking compelling."

The men sat in the gilded room, reflecting, satisfied in some unexpected way.

"Fuck it," said Bannon when the houseman appeared. "I'll have the Monte Cristo."

* * *

SB: What do you think of the old adage that behind every great fortune is a great crime?

JE: I don't think it has to necessarily be a great crime.

SB: What does that mean?

JE: The accumulation of money is often, even invariably, contentious. Many fortunes involve disputes which one side will regard as unfair.

SB: Okay, if you are saying there is a less-than-crooked status, then there is also probably a more-than-just-crooked status. You, for instance, represent figures near to or involved with the political leadership of the Persian Gulf. These people have in addition to looting the wealth of their countries, these people have tortured and murdered people. Let me submit that essentially your business is the management of ill-gotten gains.

JE: Money, at the level we are talking about, has an independent life. In some sense nobody, no one person, controls it. It's part of the world's capital. It has to be managed. It has to be deployed. And by the way, it's going to keep growing. You can't stop it from growing. Even assuming one person or one group of people may have taken it from another, the money itself does what it would do no matter who has the most control of it. Yes, perhaps some more or less unworthy person might get a large yacht out of it, but principally this money is part of the world's capital flow.

SB: I'm not even sure I know what that means.

JE: It means money is infrastructure. No matter who uses that infrastructure, saints or sinners, we need it to work. We need governors, and contractors, and bond issuers to see that it keeps working. And it is the management of that capital that has resulted in the greatest epoch of social justice, literacy, the free flow of information, and, just in the last generation, the raising of a billion people in China out of poverty and into a middle class.

SB: You believe that?

JE: It's incontrovertible.

SB: What seems incontrovertible is that you have no moral or ethical standard.

JE: I try to advise people on how to use their wealth in positive ways, positive ways for themselves, positive ways for their families, positive ways for their communities. To grow their wealth so there is more of it to do more positive things, to structure it so it doesn't become a negative factor to their offspring and to their offspring—great wealth can be a debilitating circumstance—and to give it away in the most productive capacity. And remember, in the end, all wealth has to be given away. You can't keep it.

SB: Why can't you keep it?

JE: Because what would you do with it? You can't spend it. That's humanly and economically impossible. You can invest it, just producing more of it. And investing it just becomes a way for someone else to use it. And in the end you're just going to shift the burden to future generations, who will have to give it away.

SB: So you're just a philanthropist?

JE: I am one of the people involved in the philanthropic economy, one of the largest and fastest-growing parts of the world economy.

SB: How many houses do you have?

JE: I don't know.

SB: You don't know?

JE: It's easier than you think. I have large properties and they each have many houses. I have a ranch that's twenty square miles, for instance. And I put money into homes, real estate, that I don't use.

SB: This house we're in must have cost forty million dollars.

JE: Twenty million dollars.

SB: Has to be worth one hundred million dollars today.

JE: Two hundred and fifty million dollars.

SB: And how did you pay for this house?

JE: I made mini-me dolls and sold them on the street.

SB: Are you the world's greatest money launderer?

JE: My business—

SB: Isn't that your business, hiding money for Third World dictators? What you actually do is launder money for the worst people in the world.

JE: What is money laundering?

SB: Money laundering is to take money that can't get into the world's formal banking and investment system—you take money from oligarchs, or guys in the Persian Gulf, or Yemen, or Africa. You take their money, which can't get into the system because it's ill-gotten gains, and, however you do it, you get into the system so now they've got it in Switzerland or the United States or in real estate or art or maybe this house that you live in. Is this house actually owned by you or owned by one of your "clients"? Is this house owned by some dictator in sub-Saharan Africa?

JE: I own the house, and anything I do is transparent. Everything I do is audited by one of the big five accounting firms.

SB: The same firms that did the auditing for the companies and banks that caused the 2008 financial crisis. You don't think that everyone believes you can outflank any accounting firm?

JE: That's probably true. I probably can.

SB: Not probably true, it is true. That's your talent. That's your business.

JE: My business is giving people decent advice on what they should do with their money.

CAMERAMAN: That's it.

* * *

"Dude," said Bannon, "I don't know who the fuck you are"—he slapped the table—"but this is a great story."

"And we haven't even gotten to the girls," said Epstein.

"The story is unbelievable even without the main event—actually you've distracted from the main event."

"I understand the story is crazy," said Epstein, happily abstracting himself from the tale.

"The arc is the arc of our time. The money, the class overthrow, the excess—the freedom, the sex," continued Bannon. "The entitlement, the rich, the rape of every decent value," Bannon added operatically, "getting everything you want because you wanted it, Clinton, the tech people, we didn't even get to you and the fucking tech, and everything fucking else until MeToo. My god. And Trump!"

"I told you, crazy," said Epstein, admiringly.

"And all this other shit," said Bannon, pointing to Epstein's framed picture gallery of friends—Epstein with the pope, three presidents, Castro, Bill Gates, various members of the royal family, Noam Chomsky, the Dalai Lama, Woody Allen, and the Crown Prince of Saudi Arabia.

"Do you know why he's laughing?" Epstein pointed to the picture of the Crown Prince.

"Because he just cut up Khashoggi?" said Bannon.

"No, because I just told him I smuggled girls into the kingdom dressed as airline stewardesses—the penalty for which is—" Epstein brought an imaginary saber down.

"When can we keep going?"

"I'm leaving for Paris tonight. I'll let you know."

3.

Epstein greeted the entourage arriving in early May at his apartment in Paris's 16th arrondissement on Avenue Foch like something out of a musical comedy—a dramatic, joyful entrance into the grand stone foyer. "My salvation!" he said, nearly on one foot as he rushed into the room, his hands in a wide embrace.

One effect of Epstein's decision to live his life without attention to the outside world, ignoring, since his release from prison, all the processes of public recompense and rehabilitation—indeed, living as quite an insult to it—was that, by the spring of 2019, he found himself so publicly vilified and demonized that he was unable to find a U.S. PR firm to finally try to help him publicly defend himself. There could hardly be a more ominous indication of his predicament than that some of the most vaunted crisis managers, those specialists in ruined reputations, had refused his business. He was way too ruined.

His supporters had now identified a London-based firm, known for representing dictators and despots, willing to come to Paris for a discussion.

Epstein's Parisian life was meant to somehow align himself with a European style—a libertine way of life, if you will, free of American moral shackles. But it was hard to find someone less European. He spoke no languages other than English (Brooklyn English); he was impatient with Parisian pretense and food; his Paris apartment was 21,000 square feet, a nineteenth-century patrician lodging, but wholly renovated to maximum American temperature controls and plumbing standards. Reid Weingarten had once stayed in the Paris apartment and then tagged along with Epstein to visit another property Epstein was considering buying—one of the largest residences in Paris, next door to the Rodin Museum. Epstein's primary concern, appalling the Parisian agents and lawyers gathered to represent the potential sale, was whether he could install a pool on the historic property.

Epstein was in Paris usually a week out of every three or four with his Avenue Foch home as the center of his Gulf region activities. Confounding almost everyone with any knowledge of the region, Epstein seemed to function as an ex officio NGO, entertaining seemingly all sides in all Gulf State disputes—the Saudis and the UAE, the Qataris, the Yemenis.

His cynical but cheerful analysis was that, in the end, in the Gulf there was no real issue other than money, making it, hiding it, protecting it, making more of it. In his telling, all these disparate figures came to see him precisely because of his ignominy. "One virtue of disgrace," he explained, "is that I'm shunned by establishment institutions. Therefore people can be reasonably sure I'm not in the pocket of a government, bank, or any other firm or institution with its own interests."

His was expounding on this view and the nature of his Paris life for the benefit of the British PR team as he showed them into one of the grand receiving rooms. Upholstered settees or chesterfields were set around a long, low table. In the corner, occupying considerable space, but, yet, proportional to the size of the room, there was a stuffed, actual, baby elephant—that is, the proverbial elephant in the room.

As in New York, there was the house staff and then, additionally, the coterie of young women—assistants, organizers, curators.

There instantly appeared a rainbow variety of vegetable and fish maki and hand rolls.

For the benefit of his guests, Epstein was now on to his latest view of how Trump would act—what, pressed to the limit, his old friend might do.

"He is never going to allow himself to be hung out to dry or to be defeated. That's an absolute. I have always known this. But I have finally figured out the fail-safe move, the point behind which no one can go because the world ends. The president of the United States has the unilateral power to declassify anything. He can disclose anything to anyone. All information is his to do with as he pleases. He literally controls the secrets," said Epstein with rising excitement. "This is a man who is aroused by nothing so much as a loophole. For a while I thought it would be his pardon power—he would merely say for the good of the country, I'm pardoning everyone. And he still might. But now I think the secrets are more powerful, because they are a kind of doomsday threat. Back off or cut me a deal or assure me immunity for my family and wealth or I'll—I'll tell the *Daily Mail* we have two agents in the offices next to Putin. Or here are the files on Bill Clinton . . . or . . . enough to . . ."

He seemed delighted by his formulation, as delighted as if he had had such power for himself. It clearly satisfied him, too, that he had, at last, matched what he knew about the president's character with the president's powers.

The British PR myrmidons—a senior myrmidon and two junior myrmidons—murmured appreciatively.

Epstein's cell phone rang. "Call me back in an hour," he said and hung up. He laughed and shook his head. "That's a man from the Middle East. Not just the Middle East, Yemen. *Yemen!* He wants my advice on money. I refused to give it to him. Just let me come talk to you, he pleaded. I said no—this is not someone . . . So he just arrived here and we had to tell him, no, go away. This was three years ago. Then, a few months later, there is a knock on the upstairs door here. And it's him. I said how did you get in—this building has great security. He said, I bought an apartment in the building so now you have to see me. He's never moved in, the apartment is empty. But now I can't escape him."

The PR man, florid and baby faced, sighed, apparently sympathetic to the problem.

Epstein put a piece of a maki roll into his mouth like a bonbon, crossed his legs, and summarized: "I'm rich, I'm a guy, and the girl issue—if you need to be angry at somebody, I fit the bill. Even broader, if your view of the world is that it is controlled by insidious secret forces, that the elites are screwing you and anyone else they want to, that even pussy is a conspiracy and Ponzi scheme."

"The Madoff of pussy," said the PR man, respectfully, likewise plopping a maki bite into his mouth. "May I make an observation," said the PR man, with pregnant pause and putting his fingertips together.

"Please."

"You are caught in the middle of a tabloid story. That's a situation that has been painful to many people before. But there is a further twist now, because there are fewer and fewer tabloids. In the past, your story would have been barely touched by the respectable press. Your story would have existed in a world wherein respectable people, even if they found it necessary to shun you, would have also understood that you were a tabloid victim—the product of tabloid exaggeration and glee. There but for the grace of God . . . But now, the respectable press, not least of all the *New York Times*, itself desperately trying to survive, and now pursuing, as tabloids have always done, single-copy sales in the form of online clicks, have grabbed the tabloid stories, but turned them into earnest issues. Your"— the PR man gestured to indicate the full sweep of Epstein's loucheness—"now becomes a seminal morality tale. That's the basis on which the *New York Times* justifies writing about it."

"That's smart," said Epstein.

"It is part of a larger mix-up of course with the president, the quintessential tabloid figure, now having to be a subject of deep and nuanced consideration. The *New York Times* finds itself out of its depth covering the shallowest issues. In this instance, to your great cost. Let me ask perhaps an unfair question."

"There are no unfair questions."

"Have you had bad advice, or did you fail in the past to take good advice?"

"Both."

The PR man's eyebrows rose dramatically. "I am not sure I've ever seen such a one-sided, entirely negative, absolutely despicable—"

"And depraved—"

"And depraved public portrait of a human being, outside of the leadership of the Third Reich. Tell me why you decided to take the original deal you took and not fight it? I understand the desire to put it behind you . . . but . . ."

"Okay . . . the original charges were in Florida, in Palm Beach. Suddenly I'm under investigation, the police outside my house—I thought they were offering extra security, that my contributions to the various police funds were paying off."

"Do you know why they started to investigate?"

"I believe I do, yes. Another involved story."

Epstein's criminal origin story involved, he believed, his breakup with Donald Trump. Epstein had bid on a Palm Beach mansion and taken his friend Trump to advise him on how to move the swimming pool. Days later, Trump jumped in and bid on the house himself. Epstein understood that the always cash-strapped Trump was likely fronting for a buyer who needed anonymity and Epstein threatened to reveal as much in a lawsuit. At that point Epstein's legal troubles began. Hence, he concluded, Trump, ever cultivating the Palm Beach police, and, as a frequent visitor to Epstein's house, well aware of his friend's proclivities, turned him in.

"I was charged with girls coming to my house, local strippers and massage parlor girls. Soliciting prostitutes. I had never been in any kind of trouble before. So I called my friend Alan Dershowitz—"

"The most famous lawyer in America," said the PR man for the benefit of his junior associates.

"And he says, 'Shocking, appalling, I'll take care of it, don't worry.' And he gets on a plane, comes to Palm Beach, and shits all over the Palm Beach police department. So instead of pleading guilty to a variety of misdemeanor charges with small fines I'm suddenly before a grand jury and now it transpires that one of the girls is two weeks shy of her eighteenth birthday—"

"I thought there were other younger ones."

"Later. We're in the land of fake IDs. You have girls who not only lied to me about their ages, they lied to the police. Which is why the police had a difficult case—the witnesses are liars. Anyway, the grand jury suddenly comes up with an indictment that involves three third-degree misdemeanors with the possibility of three months of jail time. Dershowitz goes crazy and we hire Roy Black, a major Florida trial lawyer—"

"Famous. William Kennedy Smith, the Kennedy-nephew rape case," explained the PR man.

"Yes. Major overkill, in hindsight."

"It would seem."

"At this point, because of infighting in the Sheriff's Department, or possibly other nefarious interference, there's a complaint to the Justice Department. This is to the Bush DOJ. Ashcroft is the attorney general and the allegation is that there's a sex case in Palm Beach that might involve Bill Clinton. At that point, in what little press I had had, it was all connected to my friendship with Bill. So . . . the feds are now involved. And they are reinterviewing the girls, and it's now the FBI, and the girls are threatened with . . . god knows if they lie. So now you have a bunch of girls who are younger than eighteen."

"As young as?"

"The youngest is fourteen. But you have a variety of sixteen- and seventeen-year-olds. But the federal government, having gotten itself involved, suddenly found itself stuck on how to move this quintessentially local crime, prostitution, to a federal level," said Epstein, the practiced narrator of his own legal travails. "By the way, they couldn't find a girl who would link Clinton to any of this. But now they have an open investigation. There's been press coverage. They need to save face. So . . . they try an interstate commerce claim because my assistant in New York used the telephone to make appointments with the girls in Palm Beach. But this is weak. The chance this gets bounced is at least fifty-fifty in a DOJ that likes its win rate at ninety-five percent. But because of my airplanes they are suddenly threatening to make me out as a sex trafficker, an incredibly vague, bad-guy catchall. Under this statute, you can, because you are a trafficker—a kind of mafioso by any other name—reasonably be denied bail. So suddenly the feds had their pitch: we will keep you in jail for a year before your trial, unless you go back to the state of Florida and let them put you in jail for eighteen months. So I could go to jail in Florida for eighteen months, or the feds would keep me in jail for a year to face a fifty-fifty chance in a trial which could put me in jail for forty-five years. That was my choice."

The junior members of the PR team took careful notes. The purpose here for the PR team was of course not to judge Epstein's crimes but to weigh, and ultimately improve on, his story about the crime.

"But since then, you decided not to tell your story in this way—or in any way?"

"You have to understand, I have never really cared about the public. I don't make my money from the public. I'm not someone who depends on votes or selling a product, or, even, keeping my job. My life is fine."

"Except if an angry mob storms your walls."

"Exactly. And the natives are restless. It's an accretion—my story pops up, dies down, pops up again. Every time it pops up it grows another head."

"Mmmm," said the PR man, who seemed as interested in the food.

"My problem is not with men, but with their wives—"

"Mothers and daughters and feminist journalists on the Upper East Side of Manhattan storming your walls."

"The more immediate problem is that the wives say to their husband, 'You can't go to Jeffrey's house' . . . so if you're a senior partner at a law firm," he trailed off, then added, "Everybody comes to my house."

"Why? Can I ask?"

"People find it valuable. But now they can only come before it gets light, so breakfast has to start at like four-thirty. Or they come after dark. You see the problem. I get no sleep."

"Mmmm."

"Of course, there's a group of people asking, 'Why do world leaders show up at that big house? It can't be economic advice because he never graduated from college. It can't be because of his financial expertise because there are lots of smarter people on Wall Street. So the only reason guys would have for going to his house must be something sinister . . . or girl related . . .'"

"From a business perspective, are you managing your own money? Are you helping other people?"

"I manage my own money and give advice to others."

"Is there a business transaction attached to that or is it friendly advice?"

"Both. Anybody who is the least bit funky, I take no money from them, but that doesn't mean I might not give them advice."

"Mmmm. And have you noticed a drop-off in people seeking your advice?"

"Well, for instance, in the paper last week someone put out a list of charities that I give money to, anonymously. You might think people would say 'decent guy,' but instead I'm doing something illicit in the dead of night, secretly giving money away, for shame. They called each charity and said, 'How do you feel taking money from a sex criminal?'"

"Indeed," said the PR man. "We happen to have several clients who are part of a giving community, generous donors with, let's say, a kind of 1970s style. They would get together, kicking up an enormous amount of money for good causes, and then have an orgy in a hotel suite afterward." He offered an understanding gesture.

Sneaking a look at his watch, the PR man began to draw the meeting to its point, clearing his voice. "Within the context of understanding your goals, which I think involves several more conversations"—that is, likely, conversations on the billing clock—"we would look to create a one-year plan and timeline as well as a five-year view. I think I have a better idea of that outline now." He looked to his colleagues, who murmured their assent. "But the immediate task, I believe, is to try to return to a baseline.

You are at present a man without a defense, explanation, rationale, or personal story."

Epstein seemed like a man listening to the outline of a complicated medical treatment program.

"To recover that, I think in the immediate turn, we concentrate wholly on process."

"Which is?"

"I think—thirty to sixty days, we build a book. Here is our narrative, absolutely consistent, factual, on the merits, easily accessible on every question and on every allegation. For this, of course, we will need an extensive download from all of your lawyers. But the point is nothing goes unanswered. Press calls are supplied with a comprehensive dump of information. Press is made to deal with every point. If they don't, then there are follow-up letters demanding to know why. You have to create a situation of responsibility to the facts. Right now you have a situation which is so complex, anybody can represent it to mean anything. You have to engage on each point, make each issue a negotiation. This is all block and tackle."

"Sounds right."

"We'd be running a war room, with an ample staff. There's nothing that we don't respond to. Within four to six months we'd hope to be generating stories that go from Dr. Evil to here are the issues in a complicated legal proceeding. We have to give people the opportunity to see that there are many questions here."

"What about—should I be out there?"

"*You?*" The British PR man seemed momentarily startled. "Not quite yet. Ultimately. But groundwork has to be laid. We will get to that. One more question."

"Yes?"

"Your relationship with the president. Is he a threat or an advantage?"

"He doesn't have the conscious ability to be either."

"Is he afraid of you?"

"He doesn't have the sense to acknowledge fear."

"Okay, a wild card."

The PR man now pointedly looked at his watch. "What we will do is return to you in the next seventy-two hours with a fleshed-out proposal and a structure for how we might work together."

"I would look forward to that. This is encouraging. I appreciate it."

"My pleasure. Our pleasure. Totally fascinating." The PR man took a final maki before rising. "And I genuinely believe that the needle can be moved here. Really."

Epstein agilely avoided a germ-prone handshake.

The proposal for comprehensive communications services, which Epstein received from the British firm a few days later, included a retainer of $3 million a month. For the moment, Epstein tabled his decision to go forward.

4.

Epstein returned briefly to New York in early June and then turned around and headed back to Paris for an unspecified duration. A friend asked Epstein how much time he was giving to thinking about his travails. Epstein said that, on most days, he didn't think about them for more than twenty minutes. For his entire life, he said, he had been unbothered by what other people thought. That was why, he said, he was not a podiatrist in Brooklyn, because he had happily followed his appetites and ambitions. It was no different now. He lived the life he had dreamed about. He could afford the price. What more could he ask?

But why not just stay in Paris? He was being encouraged by friends to stay out of the United States until the situation became clearer. The immediate peril was that the Florida court would vacate his 2008 plea agreement. That in itself presented a further unclear situation. It was far from certain that the court *could* overturn an existing agreement between the Justice Department and a private citizen, and that, even if it did, it would do anything more than open the way for a suit against the DOJ by Epstein's victims. This would be the DOJ's problem. It didn't change Epstein's status—well, not necessarily.

Still, why not stay in Paris? If, *if,* everything went south, his lawyers judged it highly doubtful that, in a case for which Epstein had already served state time, France would extradite him to face a seemingly politically motivated federal charge. What's more, Epstein was on the verge of pulling the trigger on the purchase of a vast property in Morocco—which had no extradition treaty with the United States.

A few weeks before, in New York, he had had an explicit discussion about this.

"Why don't you just get out?" asked a friend of high standing and public respect.

"Because you can't," said Epstein, clearly having considered this. "The famous or the infamous can't hide. Unless you have an entirely cooperative host government—Edward Snowden in Moscow—you'll be hunted and snatched. Hit over the head, bundled into a car, loaded onto a private plane. If you've got money, and you can only even try to run if you have vast sums, your literal body becomes a currency. You're a bounty. Every rich Jew becomes Eichmann."

"Where don't we have extradition treaties?" asked the friend.

"Mostly shithole countries. Places hardly better than jail. Chad. The Congo. Niger. Rwanda. Serbia. Djibouti. And no matter the treaty, these are exactly the kinds of places that would sell you out."

Curiously, of course, these were exactly some of the places where Epstein had enthusiastic business relationships.

In early July, quite on a whim, he decided to return to New York the next day. That evening, a European diplomat, one of the most eminent in the world, in Paris for a few days, called Epstein. They had been friends for many years, with Epstein helping the diplomat through several health crises. The diplomat was surprised that Epstein, partial to never leaving his house, was willing to come out to a restaurant. But Epstein seemed, the diplomat judged, in a particular carefree mood. The diplomat questioned Epstein closely about his plans, openly wondering about the wisdom of Epstein's New York trip. At one point, the diplomat became concerned that they were being eavesdropped on and perhaps shadowed.

"Intrigue is your business," said Epstein, unconcerned.

The next morning, Saturday, seven hours before his arrest, yet a bon vivant of unknown riches, careless, confident, untroubled, his Bentley idling outside ready to take him to the airstrip for private planes at Orly, Epstein, with gossipy zeal, called a friend in New York. The noose, he said, was about to seriously tighten. Not for him—at that moment, there was still no threat that he knew of, anywhere around him—but for the president. Deutsche Bank—the bank that had consistently stood behind both him and Trump—would, Epstein was confident, be forced to divulge its long history with the crooked president. After that it would be sixty days, tops ninety days, before the president was well and truly cooked. Epstein had more details to share. How about stopping by for breakfast tomorrow in New York? On the way to Orly, he called another friend—a high-ranking partner at a vaunted New York law firm—to share what he was hearing from Deutsche Bank and to schedule breakfast for Monday.

And there was another Trump aspect he seemed to be rushing back to the United States for—if only to gossip about. The journalist E. Jean Carroll had, in the past weeks, described in a new book and in an article in *New York* magazine how in the mid-nineties Trump had raped her in a dressing room in the department store Bergdorf Goodman. Epstein told one of his callers that he had seen Trump shortly after this happened and Trump had regaled him with the torrid details. Trump's move now, Epstein theorized, would be to deflect from this story by revivifying the rape charges against Bill Clinton. He was eager to discuss this with Bannon.

On board the flight home was his girlfriend of seven years, a young woman from Belarus whom he had put through dental school, and two assistants, blond and tall, as he preferred—"The law firm of Comely & Comely," as one friend yet felt free to joke.

Epstein spent most of the trip sending e-mails to friends he wanted to see during the few days he planned to spend in New York and to his New York assistant who would complete the scheduling. He especially wanted to get in another video session with Bannon. He'd been studying himself and sending the footage to movie friends for their critiques.

Thirty minutes out from Teterboro, a small airport in New Jersey that specializes in private aviation, the pilots were asked to confirm Epstein's presence on the flight.

A suddenly alarmed Epstein directed his pilots not to proceed further and tried to get someone from his litigation team on the phone. Considering options, Epstein wondered if he could have the plane turn around and head back out of U.S. jurisdiction.

Most certainly not, he was advised.

He was counseled not to assume the worst. Although, knowing nothing was far from a good sign. Epstein himself had carefully cultivated his DOJ sources, precisely to keep abreast of any changes in its thinking. Weingarten, a former prosecutor and a close friend of the former attorney general Eric Holder, had deep DOJ sources, too.

As they fastened seat belts for landing, Epstein advised his girlfriend to turn around and go back to Europe as soon as possible.

Late in the afternoon—a muggy Saturday afternoon—FBI agents, accompanied by prosecutors from the Southern District of New York in the public corruption unit, served the arrest warrant as Epstein came down the stairs from his plane and took him into custody.

What Epstein felt, as he was driven, in handcuffs, into Manhattan to the MCC—Metropolitan Correctional Center, one of the vilest jails in the federal system—was, most immediately, annoyance at himself for missing the signs. He rethreaded the last six months of legal maneuvering without it making sense.

At just about the time of Epstein's arrest, another group of FBI agents arrived with search warrants at Epstein's East Seventy-First Street home. As members of the house staff tried to get one of the Epstein lawyers on the phone to advise them what to do, the FBI entered with a battering ram. The team removed all computers and other electronic devices and used a small explosive charge to open the house safe. Prosecutors publicly announced that they had found nude pictures of women who might appear to be underage, a thirty-year-old passport from Saudi Arabia with a phony name and Epstein's picture, along with cash and diamonds. The FBI did not list in its findings a set of pictures that Epstein sometimes removed from the safe to show friends: a dozen or so snapshots from shortly before their quarrel in 2004 of Donald Trump at Epstein's Palm Beach home posing with a variety of young women in various stages of undress—some topless—sitting on his lap, touching his hair, laughing and pointing at a suggestive stain on the front of the future president's pants.

Of the two playboy friends who had ridden each other's airplanes and shared a lifestyle in New York and Palm Beach, as well, on occasion, as sharing various girlfriends, one of them was in the White House while the other was headed to one of America's darkest prison cells.

5.

Epstein's vertiginous fall might seem Romanov-like, or French Revolution–style. But yet he was confident that, if the street mob was against him, the law was on his side.

Weingarten, too, while raging against the perfidy of prosecutors and the stark politics that were at play, saw the law as, ultimately, a straightforward get-out-of-jail card. The indictment was not to be unsealed until Monday morning, but prosecutors in the Southern District took Weingarten through the particulars. Epstein was being charged with sex trafficking— the same charge that the Justice Department had agreed not to prosecute him for if he pleaded guilty to the state prostitution charge twelve years before. The government was now unilaterally disregarding that deal, and, so many years later, commencing that exact same prosecution. The deal in Florida isn't binding in New York, the SDNY prosecutors now averred, with a level of disingenuousness astounding to Weingarten. The Justice Department had never, to Weingarten's knowledge, made a deal in one jurisdiction and countermanded it in another. Who, then, in that event, would ever make a deal with the DOJ? It couldn't stand.

The immediate problem, however, was that, under the sex trafficking statutes, in one of the few instances in the U.S. criminal code, there was an exception to the basic constitutional requirements of bail and due process—there was a presumption *against* bail. The sex trafficking laws were meant to ensnare and hold the new era of borderless criminals, sex crime lords, who, like drug crime lords, had unlimited resources and an international playing field often beyond extradition treaties. They also included as traffickers anyone who profited off of sex with a minor—that was where Epstein fell, albeit it seemed quite a leap to justify how he might have profited. This meant that Weingarten and the rest of the Epstein team had little more than twenty-four hours to come up with a fail-safe bail proposal to overcome the presumption of flight.

Weingarten, as much Epstein's friend as his lawyer, suddenly realized that he had never done the kind of proctology-level exam of Epstein that he would have done on most other clients. But now, in order to convincingly impede his flight, the court would need to know that Epstein's resources were firmly constrained. Not just his planes grounded, passport impounded, guards posted, and ankle bracelet in place, but his fortune put effectively under lock and key. The true nature of Epstein's finances was known only to the compartmentalized Epstein himself. And if he had $500 million in evident assets—the number that was hurriedly settled on—it was not unreasonable to assume that Epstein, the international man of mystery, with a fortune of unclear provenance, had at least that amount again hidden somewhere else. By Monday morning all that could be submitted to the court was a cursory one-page overview of the $500 million.

Epstein had been brought up through the underground tunnel that connected the MCC to the Federal Courthouse. Rather than touch the soiled bedding, Epstein, the germaphobe, had, without sleep, stood and paced for the past two days in his cell. A bit after noon, a marshal in a TV sort of garb—T-shirt, nylon jacket announcing U.S. MARSHAL, baseball cap—came in through a side door and stood legs apart, hands crossed, in front of a side door. Ten or fifteen minutes later, Epstein seemed to be pushed out, a child at a first recital, and, for a second, hesitated. Then he slowly shuffled forward, head down. His blue prison shift was wrinkled and soiled, a brown streak down the left side. He was unshaven, his gray hair wild. It seemed surprising he had the strength to pull out his own chair at the defense table. The faces of people within days or weeks of death can often seem aghast and uncomprehending, their eyes already seeing another world. Epstein looked as bad.

Weingarten, understanding that the one-pager outlining the $500 million was hardly going to suffice—even if they were willing to sacrifice it all, they needed to somehow show there wasn't another $500 million hidden about—asked for a continuance on the bail hearing. Another week.

* * *

Epstein, the sixty-six-year-old man, whose lap of luxury was as over-cossetted and splendid as any, was yet regarded as someone who could do the time. He was, after all, an ex-con. He regarded himself as someone who could do the time.

A prison story he liked to tell was about the visit he received in his Florida jail from a prison rabbi, who strongly suggested he opt for the kosher meals, prepared by a Jewish charity that employed an outside caterer—the food was handled under strict rabbinical supervision. If possible, the rabbi added, a contribution would of course help. A grateful Epstein had immediately authorized a gift of $50,000. And in short order, he had his daily kosher meal—a slice of white bread and slice of American cheese.

Once, at a dinner party at his Paris home, one guest was the former head of the Port of Djibouti—whose strategic nexus in the Horn of Africa made it a fabled center of corruption—who had also spent time in jail. Together the two men, with adventurers' bravura, assured the others at the table that real-world prison, as opposed to Hollywood prison, was as manageable for the savvy as anything else.

Indeed, an aspect of the fury against him now was that he had seemed to manage his prison time in Florida with quite some facility. Midway through his sentence there he had secured rare daytime release privileges. Then, when he was finally released, he held a party at his Palm Beach house for his prison guards.

"Hello?" said Bannon, happily trying to explain Epstein's Houdini character to a friend. "Hello? Of course he's an intelligence asset. We just don't know whose."

* * *

If Epstein's press had seemed as bad as it could be, in truth, up until his new arrest, he was yet someone of specialized mendacity, a little-known figure in a scandal blurring into #MeToo and anti-Trump lanes.

Bannon had wanted to do some polling, believing that most of the country had never heard of Epstein—and that this would be where to start to rehabilitate him, with people who didn't know who he was in the first place. Indeed, with people who found Trump appealing.

But in the hours after his new arrest, Epstein became, quite literally overnight, an international household name. The devil had been captured. The worldwide media was shocked, aroused, fascinated, fevered, absolute in its assertions. Epstein was a pedophile; he was also a pimp and sex trafficker, supplying his powerful circle with underage girls; and, doubling down, he was a blackmailer, leveraging the unspeakable secrets, of which he undoubtedly had secretly recorded evidence, of the rich and powerful.

Six days after his arrest, a *New York Times* editorial, formalizing guilt by association, declared, "At this point, anyone who has shaken hands with Mr. Epstein in recent decades should be scrutinized."

With the prosecutor and victims' lawyers briefing on the courtroom steps, Epstein's lawyers now moved to hire the $3-million-a-month British PR firm to develop and manage a last-ditch media effort. But the firm said that there was little it believed it could do at this point.

Epstein had drawn federal judge Richard Berman. Among district court judges, Berman was regarded as one of the most sensitive to media influence and most concerned with his own press. When the bail hearing reconvened Judge Berman came with a sheaf of recent articles that he read into the record. He also opened the court to statements from any women who claimed to be an Epstein victim, even if they were not part of the government's case against him. Then, in the name of the victims' dedicated efforts to bring him to trial, Judge Berman denied bail, meaning Epstein would stay in jail for at least another three weeks until his appeal to the second circuit.

* * *

Maneuvering to stay out of the prison population, Epstein was buying enough of his lawyers' time to keep him in the lawyers' room at the MCC from morning until evening. When his lawyers had no more time to spare, they in turn hired lawyers who had babysat El Chapo, the Mexican drug lord and, before Epstein, the most famous MCC prisoner. Paying thousands of dollars an hour, Epstein mulled his situation.

There were two likely scenarios, Epstein believed. The White House, through the Justice Department, was looking to press a longtime Republican obsession, and Trump ace-in-the-hole, and get Epstein to flip and reveal the sex secrets of Bill Clinton—Trump, if he was obsessed with Clinton, which he was, was also obsessed with what Epstein knew about Clinton and, likely, especially in the days after the E. Jean Carroll rape story, badgering whoever could be badgered to squeeze him. Or, in the other scenario, the Southern District of New York, which, according to many reports, was hot on Trump's tail, had moved through its public corruption unit—with its focus on bribery of public officials, it could avoid having its investigations approved by Washington—to arrest Epstein and pressure him to flip on Trump. That is, SDNY had slipped Epstein's arrest past Trump's attorney general and watchdog Bill Barr—who, indeed, oddly recused himself after the arrest and then hurriedly (at Trump's urgings, Bannon was sure) unrecused himself.

There were many likely holes in these theories. What's more, they did not account for the more obvious likelihood that Epstein was just one more fallen sexual villain, his time up. No matter, in Epstein's view—shared by Weingarten—that did not mean there wasn't, even in this climate, a deal to be made.

Here was the question: How much was he at the very center of the power struggles of the day, a figure to be reckoned with at the highest levels of government, versus, how much had he been utterly rejected by respectable society, eager now to rid itself of his presence and memory?

The latter reality seemed to be winning.

Indeed, it could be that even if the government wanted to make a deal with him, he was too universally reviled to make a deal with.

In a blow that some later speculated turned out to be fatal, his closest friend and confidante, Dr. Eva Andersson-Dubin turned on him. A model, former Ms. Sweden, and Epstein girlfriend in the late 1980s, Epstein had put her through medical school and introduced her to her husband, Glenn Dubin, a hedge fund billionaire. They spent holidays together, and Epstein doted on their children. The Dubins now downplayed the details of their association with Epstein, expressed regret at ever having known him, and denied that they had given Epstein the honorific of godfather to their three children.

Ehud Barak, who had joined the prime minister's race in Israel and whose association with Epstein immediately became a campaign issue, declared, "Like many respectable people in the U.S., in retrospect, I would have preferred never to have made contact with him."

And Bannon, too, seemed suspiciously unavailable.

The list of those who had eagerly accepted his friendship but who now rejected and reviled him grew every day.

On July 23, Epstein appeared to try to commit suicide. His lawyers believed he had cooked up the scheme with his cellmate, who, for a fee, was helping steer him to somewhat better prison accommodations.

After this, he began a frantic effort to rewrite his will.

He named a trust as his single beneficiary, a move shielding his ultimate heirs and creating a further barrier to litigants and their lawyers.

This was not necessarily so much a desperation move as it was a characteristic one. For almost every one of his friends he would sooner or later urge them to see their financial lives in highly personal fashion. In part, this was the root of his relationship with wealthy men, to help them see their wealth as a living, emoting, vital part of themselves. Your fortune reflected your life. Your life reflected your fortune. Own it. The fact that he was updating his affairs was not necessarily a sign that he was thinking of ending his affairs.

He believed he had nine lives, at least.

And yet, coolly, he might have judged himself to have played them to the end. Hence, a suicide not of despair but of finality and accomplishment.

But, more immediately, the news was in fact fairly good.

In an all-hands-on meeting with his lawyers on Friday, August 5, he was told that his bail appeal would be filed with the Second Circuit on Monday. The expectation was that the Second Circuit would reverse the district court, or, failing that, return the case to Judge Berman with instructions that he could not take evidence from news accounts or base Epstein's flight risk and danger to the community on circumstances more than a decade old.

What's more, his lawyers believed that, beyond high conspiracy, they had identified a low conspiracy to explain the government's strange and hurried actions. In this, the Florida judge, Judge Marra, was about to throw out the DOJ's 2007 non-prosecution agreement (NPA). This would have been deeply embarrassing to the DOJ; as well, it was unlikely that the DOJ would have been able to prosecute Epstein again. It would be the DOJ, not Epstein, hung out to dry. Hence, the fallback: have another jurisdiction prosecute him under the guise of new issues; that would remove any need for Judge Marra to actually throw out the NPA and directly challenge the DOJ. But to accomplish the switch to New York, it appeared that secret grand jury testimony was, improperly, sent to the SDNY prosecutors—just the kind of technicality that might hopelessly taint the prosecution.

That day, Epstein, still the player, sent a note through his lawyers to Bannon noting that, as now appeared to be true, China's strategy in the trade war was to use its negotiating position to manipulate its currency downward. Just the point that Epstein had repeatedly made!

Sometime before morning, either in an almost unimaginable act of violence against himself, such that he would have had to repeatedly slam himself against a sheet tied around his neck until he crushed his Adam's apple, or by a hand or hands unknown as guards overseeing the most infamous prisoner in federal custody conveniently slept, Epstein was dead.

6.

For two weeks, the Office of the Chief Medical Examiner of the City of New York was unable to confirm the cause of death after an autopsy, finding suspicious circumstances, until, without apparent new evidence, it suddenly confirmed suicide. Videotapes outside Epstein's cell, which would have captured anyone entering it, went missing. "That fucking jail is a hundred yards from the courthouse and fifty yards from the U.S. Attorney's office and the very idea that something could have happened, and it gets harder and harder to think it didn't, just turns me upside down," said a grieving Weingarten.

A longtime friend of Epstein's, the investigative journalist Edward Jay Epstein (no relation), much of whose career has been focused on disputed deaths, noted that not only was his suicide implausible, with its lack of means and with the extra attention on a high-profile prisoner, but that, equally, so was his murder, requiring the complicity of the FBI and virtually every prosecutor in the Southern District. It was like, he said, Roberto Calvi, the 1970s Vatican banker caught in a financial scandal and found hanging from the Blackfriars Bridge in London—there was no way he could have strung himself from the bridge and yet no way, without boats and hoists, anyone else could have hung him there, either.

A few hours before his death, Epstein had relayed through his lawyers a note of reassurance to a friend: "Pretty crazy. But still just hanging around—no pun intended."

Acknowledgments

Many of the pieces in this book first appeared in either *New York*, *Vanity Fair*, *British GQ*, or the *Hollywood Reporter*, magazines where, at various points between 1998 and 2018, I wrote a regular column. Under the broad umbrella of writing about the media, each of these magazines allowed me to write mostly about anything I wanted to. If there is a better job than that, I don't know it. This book is the product of that privilege and the thanks of a lifetime is due those who gave it to me.

Simon Dumenco recruited me at *New York* and shepherded most of my words there. Much of this book came out of that collaboration. More recently, he helped select from twenty years' work and millions of stray words the pieces in this book and to turn it from a collection to a tale. *New York* was a place of unflagging support and lasting friendships. Caroline Miller, *New York*'s editor in chief, saved me often and defended me always—hers is a permanent voice in my head and counsel I continue to seek. The late John Homans was an ever-available idea machine and our long friendship even with its frequent spats continued to be a vital resource years after we had formally stopped working together.

When I moved on from the easy politics at *New York* to the Kremlin politics at *Vanity Fair*, Doug Stumpf navigated my column through that elaborate and complicated court each month.

As a busman's holiday, in 2010 I took on a column in London at *British GQ*, vastly different from its American cousin, and, in my view, one of the last of the great high-low, surprise-entertain-inform-me, this-is-how-we-live monthlies. In a world where I could only thank my lucky stars for the freedom and space that magazines provided me, *British GQ*'s editor Dylan Jones, impresario, cheerleader, man-about-town, and ever-in-the know, gave me more of both.

In what will likely be one of the last great feats of magazine publishing, Janice Min transformed a moribund trade magazine, the *Hollywood Reporter*, into the most important publication in the entertainment business and a vital read for anyone interested in media and culture. She took me along for a bit of the ride. Gossipy, sagacious, tolerant, inventive, and always ready to make some trouble, she is exactly what you want in a magazine editor.

There are, too, various new pieces here seeing print for the first time. This includes the portrait of Rudy Giuliani's extraordinary last act, originally written and recorded for Audible, and, as well, pieces on Jared Kushner, Steve Bannon, Tucker Carlson, Ronan Farrow, Harvey Weinstein, and Jeffrey Epstein. My thanks to the Audible team and to the sources who helped me on the new material.

At Henry Holt, Sarah Crichton immediately got where I wanted to go with this book and sharpened every part of it. This is the fourth book I've published with Holt in fewer than four years. To say the least, it's been a productive association and I am grateful to everyone there: Don Weisberg, Amy Einhorn, Sarah Crichton, Pat Eisemann, Maggie Richards, Marian Brown, and Natalia Ruiz.

Andrew Wylie, Jeffrey Posternak, and James Pullen at the Wylie Agency have supplied the wise counsel and negotiated the high fees without which none of this would be possible.

This is the fifth of my books for which Eric Rayman has done the legal reading. I can only hope he will do all the others to come.

I am indebted to all the subjects and sources who have wittingly or unwittingly, anonymously or forthrightly, contributed to this book.

About the Author

Michael Wolff is the author of three books about the Trump White House, *Fire and Fury*, *Siege*, and *Landslide*. His six other books include his biography of Rupert Murdoch, *The Man Who Owns the News*, and his memoir of the early internet years, *Burn Rate*. He has been a regular columnist for *New York* magazine, *Vanity Fair*, *British GQ*, the *Hollywood Reporter*, and the *Guardian*. The winner of two National Magazine Awards, he lives in New York City with his family.